Against the Conventional Wisdom

AGAINST THE CONVENTIONAL WISDOM

A Primer for Current Economic Controversies and Proposals

Douglas Dowd

WestviewPress

A Division of HarperCollins*Publishers*

*For Paul M. Sweezy, who has meant so much
to so many of us for so many years*

Copyright © 1997 by Westview Press, A Division of HarperCollins Publishers, Inc.

Published in 1997 in the United States of America by Westview Press, 5500 Central Avenue, Boulder, Colorado 80301-2877, and in the United Kingdom by Westview Press, 12 Hid's Copse Road, Cumnor Hill, Oxford OX2 9JJ

Library of Congress Cataloging-in-Publication Data
Dowd, Douglas Fitzgerald, 1919–
  Against the conventional wisdom : a primer for current economic controversies and proposals / Douglas Dowd.
    p.   cm.
  Includes bibliographical references (p.   ) and index.
  ISBN 0-8133-2795-4 (hc.)—ISBN 0-8133-2796-2 (pbk.)
    1. United States—Economic policy—1981–1993.   2. United States—Economic policy—1993–   3. Free enterprise—United States.
  4. Radical economics.   I. Title.
  HC106.8.D68   1997
  338.973—dc21   97-11797
                                                                                 CIP

The paper used in this publication meets the requirements of the American National Standard for Permanence of Paper for Printed Library Materials Z39.48-1984.

10   9   8   7   6   5   4   3   2   1

Contents

v

Preface and Acknowledgments

The continuous rightward drift of socioeconomic policies in the United States has appalled a goodly share of our people. That drift has been facilitated by an onslaught of supporting arguments almost totalitarian in their force and scope. Moreover, those enabling ideas are as meretricious as the policies they seek to justify are odious. The consequence, nevertheless, is that the opposition has been rendered scattered, muted, feckless.

The unifying core of this stampeding political economy is its born-again deification of "the free market." Acceptance of that position makes it difficult to undo the economic policies already savaging our society and to oppose still others under consideration. It is clearly essential to analyze and to rebut the conservative-to-hard-right economic arguments propping up these trends in thought and public policy. It is vital to show that what has become common sense for so many is not *good* sense—economically or socially— now or later, is neither necessary nor desirable, and will deepen existing troubles, not resolve them.

This book seeks to explain and expand upon the foregoing assertions and, if it does so successfully, to revive the confidence and energies of those who would reverse the present course. That course, more likely than not, will take us to disasters worse than those already afflicting us and others.

The first three chapters explore the reasoning and the realities of the free market ideology as it originally developed and now functions. Succeeding chapters treat in more detail the human, social, and natural consequences over time of "rule by the market" and in that light examine recently adopted proposals of Congress and the White House as well as some being discussed.

There are alternatives to current tendencies that are simultaneously desirable, necessary, and realistic. The book will conclude with a brief discussion of some of those alternatives, with broad suggestions for meeting our needs and achieving our potentials in more hopeful ways.

The numerous notes are meant to document and to elaborate upon various ideas put forth in the text; they are also meant to be a guide to further reading. A belief in democracy has always carried with it the implicit and accompanying requirement of an informed public. The necessary information and understanding can be found in a multiplicity of ways; indispensable among them is reading—and reading, and reading, and reading. That need rises as the habit of reading declines; this book hopes to be a small contribution toward an opposite tendency.

Finally, and with much pleasure, I wish to express my thanks to those who in various ways played an important role in bringing this work into existence. First, to the students in my three classes in the San Francisco Bay Area (Berkeley, Petaluma, and San Francisco). The classes have been conducted on and off for more than twenty years; they take place in bookstores, not universities, involve no exchange of money or grades, and their students range in age from twenty to eighty; normally we meet about ten times for two hours a session. The recent class that led to this book was called "Getting Our Heads Screwed on Straight on Current Economic Controversies"—a title considered unseemly in the publishing world. I enjoyed and learned much from teaching that class.

Once that writing had become a first draft, Barbara Ellington, who had ushered a previous book of mine to publication, persuaded Westview Press to accept it. And then, much to my gratification, Marian Safran, the copy editor of that earlier book, worked on this one. Readers can never know how much is owed to the copy editor, for they rarely if ever see the manuscript whose breaches of grammar, style, and clarity have been dealt with—in this case, handily and gracefully. Overseeing the project from start to finish, Melanie Stafford was an astute facilitator, for which I thank her.

And I offer a special thanks to my good friend Howard Zinn, who helped much and in various ways. Then, as always, and always more, I thank Anna, for what she has meant to this book and to my life.

Douglas Dowd

1

Myths and Realities of the Free Market

Markets are useful guides for certain purposes. But as economist Samuel Bowles has warned, "Markets not only allocate resources and distribute income, they also shape our culture, foster or thwart desirable forms of human development, and support a well defined structure of power. Markets are as much political and cultural institutions as they are economic."[1]

The marketability of *everything*—the aim of free market guru Milton Friedman and his numerous followers—means the commodification of everything. Commodification has been and will remain lethal for a goodly number of vital economic and social processes, the very processes that do so much to determine the quality of our existence, those that involve health, education, and the preservation of natural resources. The need is great to disentangle what is valuable from what is harmful in the operation of free markets, to extract what can be a useful guide to economic policy from what has now become an indiscriminate endorsement of the market.

"Listen to the Market"

The spuriousness of today's free market dogma is quickly exposed if, in response to the command to listen to the market, one asks *"which* market?" Only rarely is there a hint of what would almost always be the accurate answer: the financial market—and there is more than one. Even if that is made clear, however, scarcely ever is it also acknowledged that the financial sector is dominated, not by the servicing of productive investment that has provided its reputability, but by speculation in securities and in the foreign exchange market (the latter exceeding $2.6 *trillion* per *day*).[2] And one would have to follow such matters closely indeed to know that those who do the speculating are mostly in their late twenties (Nicholas Leeson was just twenty-eight when he brought Baring Brothers down), and that their daily exertions resemble fraternity high jinks considerably more than the staid behavior once thought typical of bond traders: today Nintendo, tomorrow derivatives games (in which it is estimated more than $40 *trillion* are involved).

All that is a far cry from what Adam Smith (1723–1790) had in mind in his *An Inquiry into the Nature and Causes of the Wealth of Nations* (1776), the newly canonized bible of free market capitalism. Smith's aim was to break the hold of concentrated and corrupt power over the British economy—power held by the monarchy (the "mad" George III and his decadent court) in conjunction with the most powerful merchants and industrialists of the time.

The power those business groups possessed had been granted to them by the Crown—in a "patent of monopoly"—to their mutual enrichment. Such monopolies were granted to the members of giant trading companies (e.g., the East India Company) and, among others, to industrialists, giving them the sole right to produce a commodity (e.g., the Batteries Royal for arms or, for that matter, Johnny Walker for whiskey). Those arrangements, which Smith called "the mercantile system," were initiated in the sixteenth century as a response to the weaknesses of traders and producers in the early modern era. They needed state protection and support to survive and flourish, and the Crown needed economic strength in an epoch of almost permanent war among the budding nation-states.

Smith had many aims; central to all of them was his recognition of the burgeoning of the new technology. For well over a century before the publication of the *Wealth of Nations*, the productive forces that would underlie modern industry had been emerging, but their application to production was suppressed by the entrenched beneficiaries of the old system.

By Smith's time, when Britain's private sector and its state were poised at the very edge of economic and military triumph, the fused relationships between the private and state power centers had come to mean always-deeper corruption, always more lost opportunities for what otherwise could become a dynamic industrialization process. Although his current devotees ignore it, Smith trusted neither the means nor the ends of businessmen—"an order of men," he observed, "whose interest is never exactly the same with that of the public, who have generally an interest to deceive and even to oppress the public, and who accordingly have, upon many occasions, both deceived and oppressed it."[3]

Smith *did* trust a free market—free of social, political, and business power or control—made and kept free by "the invisible hand" of market competition. He believed that such competition could come to be and would "transform individual selfishness into social well-being"—*if and only if* all sellers were small, no single company were big enough alone or with others to control *any* portion of the market. In other words, the market would determine the sellers' fates, not, as with the twentieth-century supercorporations, vice versa.

Smith died in 1790, a quarter of a century before the founding of the first enterprise to realize his technological hopes—an English cotton textile factory. In subsequent decades something like his free market ideal developed in that industry, with large numbers of competitive small producers and sellers. However, the profits of those enterprises depended upon the exploitation of powerless textile workers (including very young children), who worked twelve-to-fourteen-hour days, received bare subsistence wages, and led sickly and short lives. Smith's analysis, like those of the classical economists who followed—and like Marx—accepted the "labor theory of value," which took harsh working conditions and subsistence wages as given.

The Wealth of Nations, the fount of today's "economic wisdom," may be seen as a set of arguments that in Smith's time was reasonable, although seriously flawed by omissions—more understandable for one who wrote before rather than after the amply documented social outrages and human damages of industrialization. The harsh realities of nineteenth-century industrial capitalism notwithstanding, Smith's analysis hardened into ideology—in Britain and later in the United States (but not in other leading countries). As always, the costs of those "errors of omission" were borne by the powerless, whether in the industrializing or in the colonized countries. Those costs not only rose but also became socially explosive. The nineteenth century ended with a plague of wars over colonial interests, and the twentieth began with the most disastrous war in history—until that time.

Then, bent and battered almost beyond recognition by the economic and political convulsions—wars, depression, revolutions, and counterrevolutions—of the first half of this century, the philosophy and practices of "free market enterprise" were shunted into the shadows. For most of the period after World War II the leading capitalist nations were characterized by some degree of social democracy (as in Western Europe) or by the "welfare-warfare state," as in the United States.

But as the 1970s ended, both the ideology and the policies of the market were resuscitated—first in Margaret Thatcher's Britain, then in Ronald Reagan's United States. By now, free marketry, powered by the governments of the United States, Germany, and Great Britain and by their leading corporations, central banks, and the global financial institutions they dominate, has become an epidemic throughout the world. One should note, however, that free markets do not in fact exist if the business world can help it: With one arm business elbows out public controls; with the other it develops private controls—alone or, all else failing, in concert with rivals. Nevertheless, the market ideologues blithely use Smith's language, even though they cannot legitimately employ his analysis.

Smith's reasoning and policies had their moment in history, in Britain, a long "moment" of nascent industrialization, when it was the *only* industrializing power. The ideas, after substantial controversy, were *not* adopted in the United States until after the Civil War, and then only very selectively: "free" labor markets, on the one hand; a subsidized railroad system and protective tariffs, on the other.

Thomas Jefferson was the prime supporter of Smith and market capitalism in the United States, but the processes of industrialization in the first half of the nineteenth century were those of the "mercantilist" Alexander Hamilton. It is revealing that when the German interest in industrialization took hold, their Friedrich List came to the United States to study the Hamiltonian system, and his works served as the German model.

The small firms idealized by Smith (and the free world trade later idealized by David Ricardo) were just fine for the *first* nation to industrialize, but not so fine for the others. By the end of the nineteenth century, industrial capitalism was characterized by giant corporations or cartels (groups of relatively small companies united to control their markets) in the United States, Germany, and Japan, the countries destined to be the twentieth century's industrial titans. Smith's leading ideas had become obsolete before the turn of the century; his eighteenth-century political economy was no more serviceable by 1900 than would have been the transportation system of dirt roads and barge canals of 1776.

When Smith's arguments are made these days, they are driven by ideological passions and greed. Those who cite Smith are not aiming to usher in a new system, as he did, but trying to make the most from one wheezing with age, unable to function profitably without increasing the already great concentration of economic and political power and the harshness of a highly unequal distribution of income and wealth. To argue that public policy now can or should be based on the assumption of free markets is to combine a disdain for economic realities with ingenuousness and, in some cases, intellectual dishonesty. The result cannot help but be what Veblen called "a trained inability" to understand the social process.[4]

The recent ceaseless intonation of the rhetoric of free marketry has shouldered aside the richer vocabulary of a century of economic studies. That vocabulary (and associated analyses) stressed the data of a century of economic life, especially those related to the mores of business and their consequences, confirming the main tendencies toward the concentration of economic power. Virtually nothing has been heard about that concentration in recent years, years in which it has reached horrendous heights.

Call for George Orwell, from whom we learned that the truism "words can never hurt us" is not true. If uttered endlessly from on high and if translated into public policy, words can hurt us, as indeed they now do. They can increase existent social cruelty and tear further the damaged social fabric of the nation.

The markets Smith had in mind in the eighteenth century were those of production and trade, not finance. What connections, if any, might they have with what we are supposed to "listen to" today? And do such connections strengthen or undercut the analyses of those who now push us to the right?

Nowadays, almost all commodities (and many services) are produced and controlled by mammoth transnational corporations (TNCs)—300 of which control about a quarter of the entire world's productive assets.[5] A substantial number of TNCs are simultaneously production and financial companies— for both defensive and offensive reasons: Operating over the globe means moving large amounts of diverse currencies, which translates into speculation. The latter is not only essential to avoid losses but also a means of making gains from the constant fluctuation of currency values.

Moreover, like their nineteenth-century predecessors (though much greater both in scope and power), the TNCs seek out the cheapest possible labor and roam the earth to find it—leaving in their wake the devastated occupational structures of their own countries (and no perceptible improvement in the lives of the workers of the poor countries). And, financial commentators report with satisfaction, there is no end in sight to the processes of "restructuring, downsizing, and outsourcing."

The power and profits of the TNCs are much enhanced by their connections with the state, of course. Their great size, however, an outgrowth of large-scale production, was usually established *before* the basic political link rather than, as in Smith's time, after. Size is the main source of their financial power, pays their thousands of lobbyists, and facilitates increased strength and influence. Rhetoric aside, none of that has much to do with a "free market."

The point implicit in the foregoing should be made explicit now: Smith's concern was with *production*, and he believed that the unleashing of technological possibilities would bring about—in what he assumed must remain a harsh world for most—the best of all *possible* worlds. That is the origin of what today is called "trickle down" economics and the slogan "It's each for himself and God for all."

Today's economies, through both domestic and global power structures, are dominated increasingly by their *financial*, not their production, sectors. That can also be seen in the relative economic gains and political power of the financial world. Since the 1970s, incomes classified as unearned (interest, profits, and rents) have doubled as a percentage of all incomes.[6]

Among other mysteries that the dominance of finance helps one to understand is the unsettling and frequent coincidence in the financial news noting that this or that corporation is either taking over or being taken over and "downsizing": At the same time as jobs fall, the corporation's security prices rise, and the deal makers rake in millions.[7] Long chains of reasoning are employed to assure us that such changes will ultimately benefit one and all. Up to now, however, the benefits have been confined to those few whose "work" is speculation and takeovers: the most successful competitors in what has become a "winner take all" economy.

Viewing the 1920s ancestor of this process, John Maynard Keynes called it "a gambling casino . . . , a congeries of possessors and pursuers." But the speculators of the 1920s were goldfish lazing in a garden pond when compared with the feeding frenzy in today's shark and barracuda tanks: One of the most ravenous of them, Ivan Boesky, when asked to give a commencement address at the University of California in 1986, entitled it "Greed Is Good."

In Smith's day that "order of men" inclined to "deceive and oppress" could at their worst hold back economic progress; the economic ruthlessness permitted and encouraged to run amok today has no such modest effect. It is nothing less than a recipe for economic and social catastrophe, made inevitable if current political tendencies are allowed to continue.

It has become common knowledge in recent years that since the early 1970s the real income of four-fifths of U.S. families has declined about 25 percent, except for those with two or more wage earners (who manage only to stay even). That is bad enough, especially as the decline steepens, but the most recent data show something else: When the figures from 1989 to 1995 alone are examined, "the unbalanced income growth of the 1980s . . . caused the bottom 95 percent [!] of the population to lose income share to the upper 5 percent" (and within that 5 percent, the bottom lost share to the top 1 percent). In those same processes, of great importance, the *quality* of jobs (in terms of work satisfaction and benefits) hurtled downward always more precipitously.[9]

"Ill Fares the Land"

Ill fares the land, to hastening ills a prey,
Where wealth accumulates, and men decay.

Thus begins the epic poem "The Deserted Village," by Oliver Goldsmith (1728–1774). Writing in 1770 (when the acutely observant Adam Smith, had he been less mesmerized by technology, could have noted the manner in which the "free market" for land was operating), Goldsmith was referring to the raging processes in England that were converting the land into a commodity—"the enclosure movement"—driving the people off their "livings" and casting them into utter desperation, an inferno of misery.

By the middle of the next century, Dickens would be the scribe (in, for example, *Hard Times*) for the disastrous costs of the free market for factory labor. Children, men, and women worked in the "dark satanic mills" (or the coal mines or in the sinkholes called "workhouses"), with killing wages, hours, and "safety" conditions.

As seems to happen with predictable regularity when new social horrors appear, the advocates of soaring industrial capitalism soon found a supportive voice, Jeremy Bentham (1748–1832). Bentham created the social philosophy of Utilitarianism, which he liked to call the "science of moral arithmetic."

That arithmetic centered on his presumption that all would calculate the pleasures and pains yielded by any action (purchase or sale, saving or spending, work or leisure, and so on). Given that Bentham was also the gentleman who—noting the use of four-year-old children (working fourteen hours a day, on average) in the cotton textile mills to tie up the spindles' threads with their small fingers—wrote that the new industrial technology had shown that "infant man, a drug at present so much worse than worthless, may be endowed with an indubitable and universal value,"[10] it was an easy next step for his disciples to reckon the pleasures of the rich and powerful while neglecting the pains of the poor and the weak.

Well might a *moral* arithmetic also neglect, at least as much as the pains of the textile children, those of the children (or small women) in the coal mines who had to pull on their knees what we might call "kiddie carts" of coal, allowing narrower and therefore cheaper tunnels. The pain—or "disutility"—of doing that, in the Benthamite utility theory, which came to be a major element of modern economics, was assumed (against all good sense) to be voluntary. The costs paid by the children and the adults may be found in governmental "reports" of the time, as today's equivalents (in "sweatshops," for example) may be found in private and governmental reports.

The free market for labor was a disaster for a good half of the British population for at least a century after Smith's magnum opus, and the land fared no better: By 1880 or so, four-fifths of the cultivable land of Britain was owned by fewer than 3,000 families—the land that once had been the freeholds of England's "bold peasantry." That "once proud yeomanry" suffered joblessness and despair for half a century; in the next half they had to settle for what has been termed wage slavery: The long run was going to be very long indeed.[11]

And now that long run has come for many, stayed a while, and is leaving. Here and now, our society is being devastated in a new way, by what *Business Week* (already in March 1983) called "the hollowing out" of industrial production and the disappearance of good jobs. The change has provided great wealth to a relative handful in the corporate world. Here and now, with different scenery, "wealth accumulates and men decay."

A set of economic explanations is required to understand why such processes—dramatically reversing the real but limited progress made after World War II—have already gone very far and seem likely to go much further in the current "race to the bottom." Because we live in a politically democratic society, however, no economic explanations by themselves can tell us why virtually an entire population has only weakly resisted, passively allowed, or actively supported its own economic undoing. Let us take a moment to explore why that is so.

U.S. Democracy, Ltd.

We live in the most capitalist of all societies. Naturally, then, only an embattled minority has resisted what was earlier called the commodification of everything. Nonetheless, this minority has won many a battle since the 1930s, limited in scope and durability though they may have been: battles to hold down and cushion unemployment and poverty; to diminish repression and discrimination of all sorts; to render work conditions safer; to provide health care, pensions, paid vacations, and better housing and education for many—though by no means all; to protect our health and our environment from ecological recklessness; to enhance economic stability.

Though seldom seen as such by those of us in that embattled minority, such battles were part of a larger war. The issue was to identify the areas of daily existence that had to be exempted from the "law of supply and demand" and protected from the market, areas requiring sociopolitical interventions. If the areas of human, economic, social, and environmental fragility had not been exempted, the costs would have become intolerable— as in many ways they long have been.

Over a period of about forty years some of that territory was won, but never secured. Apart from a political moment now and then, we lacked solidarity; we functioned too much as individualistic groups. At our best we were tactically astute. But we always lacked a strategy, there not being a unified movement that could develop and sustain a strategy. That lack was an explicable outcome of U.S. history, and virtually unique in the industrial capitalist world.

Since the 1960s, in part prompted by our successes, the economically powerful and politically reactionary have steadily built an imposing political force. They are supported by groups with diverse social, political, and economic agendas; many of the members of those groups are beneficiaries of the very achievements now under siege.[12] The movement to the right has already chipped away at many of our gains; now relentlessly it tries to return our socioeconomy to the free market ideology and practices of a century ago, with all their brutality and social foolhardiness.

Giant companies already dominated the industrial economy in the 1920s, but they were small and weak and naive when compared with the super TNCs of the present. The latter now dominate not just industry but also the services (including finance, advertising, and health care) and agriculture. More to the point, their concentrated economic power is enhanced by their ability through the media (also tightly owned and controlled) to "manage minds" for both commercial and political purposes; and the generous sums they pay lobbyists to initiate and prevent legislation are of course tax deductible.

The whys and wherefores of today's savage politics must be understood if we are to reverse it and begin to move toward a sane and decent society. Whatever else that requires, we need to know who and what made those politics possible. The "who" was those possessing economic and political power, cheerfully abetted by the media and the academy, the "what," a deteriorating economy. Let us look further at what has happened since the 1970s, a transformation from a seemingly permanent bounteous economy to "stagflation"—a milder version of the economic "prosperity decade" of the 1920s that first faded and then fell into the dislocations and confusions of the 1930s.

The Failures of Success

The contrasts between the quarter century leading up to 1945 and that following it were extraordinary. During the first twenty-five years there were economic, political, social, and military upheavals and destruction unlike any comparable period in history; the years 1945 to 1970 were marked by spreading and deepening economic well-being, political and social stability, and—without forgetting the cold war, Korea, or Vietnam—a period of relative peace in the leading industrial countries, similar to the "century of peace," 1815–1915. Like that century, the latter period was peaceful between the major powers while (and in part because of that peace) violent between them and the colonized world.

Those who lived through the terrible earlier period, in Europe or the United States, had anticipated economic hard times when World War II ended; political probabilities were unpredictable almost everywhere. Surprisingly instead, a new world system was put into place—largely created and dominated by the United States. The new system meant the "reindustrialization" of the economies of Europe and Asia (especially Germany and Japan); what is more, it came to depend upon ubiquitous and swift modernization, an extraordinary transformation of both technology and business organization. It also depended upon the emergence of the social democracies in Europe and the "welfare-warfare state" here. But there were, of course, other effects.

The economic buoyancy that was taken for granted from the mid-1950s into the early 1970s was unprecedented—whether measured quantitatively or qualitatively, by rates or kinds of change, by absolute or relative numbers of beneficiaries, or by its duration. A reading of the histories of other periods of easy domination (by the Dutch in the seventeenth century or the British in the nineteenth, for example) should have warned one and all that Easy Street, U.S.A., would at some point also come to an end and do so also as a consequence of *its* achievements. Most vital of the many such incongruities was the growth and spread of productive capacities, which for many years meant expanding markets—until they inexorably came also to mean the duplicative excess capacities that jeopardized profits in all sectors: industry, agriculture, services.

The positive aspects of the era's economic achievements meant something else: a population (both businesses and consumers) that had previously taken uncertainty and intermittent hard times for granted began to relax: to save less or not at all, to spend freely, to become casual about their accumulating debts, to act "as though there were no tomorrow."

When, therefore, the economic troubles of the 1970s began to emerge—soft markets plus rising unemployment plus rising prices plus rising interest rates: "stagflation"—instead of seeing any of this as a time of trouble once more come around, too many began to look for scapegoats, ranging from the poor (a racist code word from the 1960s on) to the liberals to the unions to the government to whatever was vulnerable. And the result, its seeds dropped in the 1960s and its sudden flowering in the 1970s, was what Garry Wills called "the politics of resentment."[13] Such a politics becomes one of irrational fears and hates, sharply slanted toward the Right. What relatively powerless people resented was the leveling off or decline of their incomes (even with more than one job per family), along with rising Social Security taxes.

This was very different indeed from the resentments of the economically powerful and of the rich, who, seeing their high corporate and personal incomes nibbled away at—never more than that—by rules and regulations and unions and income taxes, longed for the "good old days" when what they saw as burdens were far lesser or nonexistent. The rich and powerful did not understand that those burdens were the flip side of business benefits in the same period: expanding purchasing power led to expanding markets; "high" income taxes (lower by far than in the other leading countries) financed expenditures (for the military, for roads, for construction, for welfare, and so on) on goods and services, at great return to the sellers and service providers.

Moreover, unions and left-of-center political groups, the principal sources of pressure for "the great society," were declining in strength; and university economics departments (universities were never the robust centers of leftist political activism they were caricatured as being) emerged as enthusiastic cheerleaders of monetarism and free marketry. To cap it all off, the Young Americans for Freedom who seemed paranoid and laughable in the 1950s and 1960s would be elected to Congress in the 1990s—and guess who's laughing now?

Nor was the cause of social decency helped by the media (see Chapter 2). Quite apart from the media's propensity to offer trash and violence as entertainment, those responsible for information, few of whom ever display social insight or courage, broke some kind of record in the Reagan years and were mute as corruption and sleaze became the politics of the country. Characterizing Reagan as the "Teflon president" was not necessary: Little stuck to him because so little was thrown at him.[14]

From the late 1970s to the present, then, the combination of frustrated consumerism and job fears on the one hand and greed and power on the other energized and financed the lurching politics now driving the United States to the right. And worse was on the way.

Institutionalized Fraud, Legislated Embezzlement

It is a commonplace that the key element for understanding is the asking of good questions, and that the best questions lead to more questions. Different disciplines of course have different sorts of questions. In the realm of economic policies, the most useful question regarding proposals has two parts: Who benefits? Who pays? Some decades ago, economists asked those questions. Nowadays?

Good question. Nowadays, the profession would find such questions too mundane, as well as (if economists can feel shame) embarrassing; the profession's longtime attraction to abstract reasoning has placed it in a lofty sphere. Economists' questions are as abstract as their answers: ruminations about power or need are absent (you cannot find the word *need* in economic theory today, although you can in Smith).

It's all in the numbers; or rather, it's all in the algebraic symbols. The reasoning is done by positing, by assertion, by placing the answer one wants in the premises one establishes—as in any logical system. But the economy (or the socioeconomy) is not just any logical system; it is not a logical system at all. It is, if anything, a biological system, evolving organically in a process of dynamic interaction—interaction between those matters abstracted from in economic theory.

There is, however, one part of the economy that comes reasonably close to the models of economists: financial markets. Everything is numbers there, and the numbers can be put into equations with little difficulty. Unlike an economy, the limits of the speculator's focus normally are the very short-term, to instantaneity—not the least of the reasons why global financial markets are now open and operating twenty-four hours a day.

When the people who work in that sector tell us that the market's response to a given economic change is the best—indeed the only trustworthy—response, they are being perfectly honest, as they see things. The things they see, however, are the gains or losses of speculators, gains and losses that can be huge and sudden, spectacular, exciting, like Nintendo, Star Wars, you know.[15]

The "economics" behind the policies being hawked in Congress and its cohorts these days is all sideshow, artifice, a cover story, despite the probability that in that clamorous crowd there are true believers. The paths trod today were laid out long ago by people whose focus was on business and whose aim rarely went beyond their profits and power. Economics makes it possible for those lusts to be dignified as a search for universal well-being.

Milton Friedman has been the analytical inspiration of this shift to the right; its most widely read and effective apostle has been George Gilder, whose books and essays portray businessmen—his principal readers—as "conscious philanthropists," vying with each other in generous giving, in emulation of the potlatch feasts of the tribes of the Northwest United States. Among those guffawing at such a notion must be at least a few businessmen; the rest of us can read it and weep.[16]

In every case of the main regressive policies already or soon to be in place—balanced budgets, taxes, the end of welfare entitlements, health care, the North American Free Trade Association (NAFTA), and all the rest—the congressional advocates have portrayed themselves as the true supporters of the "middle class" family and ("in the long run") of the poor—but never, no never, of the rich; not of corporations, but of workers; not of giant insurance companies, but of the weak and the ill; and so on.

This stage is but the latest in what began to take hold about twenty years ago, the most rapid and profound *upward* redistribution of income in our—probably any—country's history.[17] What has become a tidal wave today follows upon the earthquakes of the Reagan years; the first underground rumblings sounded even earlier, however, when Carter was president—when, in a Congress with Democrats in charge, "tax reforms" that would benefit the rich and hurt everyone else were passed (vetoed by Carter, but veto overridden by Congress), when military expenditures began a new rise, and when social expenditures took their first fall.

The earthquake hit first as Reagan mounted the throne, with his first "tax reform," massive military expenditures, and heavy pressures downward on social expenditures. It added up to a tripling of the public debt, from $1 trillion to over $3 trillion (with another trillion added in the George Bush years and still another since 1992), an extraordinary feathering of the nests of the very rich, whose overall taxes went way down while those of the bottom 80 percent went up (because of large increases in Social Security taxes and small decreases in their income taxes) and an acceleration of the decline in social expenditures for those on the bottom.

It is amazing that Reagan, the politician whose campaigns from Sacramento, California, to Washington, D.C., always stressed balancing the budget, is only rarely seen as the man who presided over the most unbalanced budgets in either California's or the nation's history and quite simply got away with it: "The butler did it! The butler did it!" he might well have said.

In some sense, that is true, if by the "butler" one means Congress: Throughout his presidency, Reagan faced a Democratic Congress; those protectors of "the common man" never even came close to taking on the massive thefts carried out by the Robin Hood for the Rich. To take on Reagan would not have been easy, of course; however, as almost all of the legislators were both makers and beneficiaries of unjust laws, it was unlikely. After all, congressional salaries alone—not to mention their generous health care and pensions—place them in the top strata of income: Why not reduce the tax load at the top, just a *little*? And the corruption thickens.

The congressional accomplices of this vast fraud are on both sides of the aisle and of course know the sources of their wining and dining and of the largest part of their campaign contributions—and of threats of less as well as promises of more. In a time-worn pattern, they—not all, surely, but a majority—speak in a soothing voice while their hands move swiftly to a vile purpose. By legislating what would under normal circumstances be seen as theft, they are perpetrating a fraud in order to secure their own positions and enhance the profits and power of the rich and the powerful. All that done "democratically"—supported by a bit more than half of the bit less than half of eligible voters that vote, allowed by the rest—except for the fragmented groups that have stood against it.

The free market economy Smith argued for was meant to reduce governmental influence in the economy to a minimum. For him that meant ample expenditures to keep the peace at home and to fend off hostile nations—although as an anticolonialist, his preference was to keep the fights if any very close to home. Other than that, Smith acknowledged the need for some assistance for road building and for public education.

As we now turn in Chapter 2 to the controversies over taxing and spending and budget balancing, it should be remembered that if there is any *principled* basis at all for the cutters and balancers, it too is to be found in Smith; however, the zealots wish education to be private ("vouchers" for the poor notwithstanding). They have shown no inclination to cut back on highways, prisons, or the military-industrial complexes.

In Chapter 3 the focus will return to the "free market," this time for the global economy, and again, with theoretical roots deep in the past. Their author, the most important follower of Smith, was the English stockbroker David Ricardo (1772–1823), who extended Smith's arguments to the foreign trade arena. His arguments remain the basis for international economics today; even more, his mode of analysis—highly abstract, fully dependent upon deductive reasoning—came to dominate *all* economic analysis by the latter half of the nineteenth century.

Smith and Ricardo were the founding fathers of what is called classical political economy. Their leading arguments and the latter's method of highly abstract analysis led to what by the end of the nineteenth century had become "neoclassical economics," the hard core of economic theory that supports today's guiding ideology.[18]

It is vital to note that the main uses to which Smith's and Ricardo's thought have been put defy (or ignore) the key assumptions made in their works, which is like ignoring the assumption of friction in Newton's law of gravity. As noted earlier, for Smith the self-serving intentions of private business would be transformed into public good by the forces of market competition—in turn assumed to be effective only to the degree that all producers were (relative to their industry's production) small, and thus that all firms were powerless to control or shape the market for their goods. That assumption had become substantially invalid before the end of the nineteenth century; as this century ends, the supercorporations, their behavior and their power, have rendered Smith's saving assumption absurd. Market rivalry exists, of course; but any economist has to know that market rivalry and market competition lead to sharply opposing economic—and political and social—consequences.

As for Ricardo, his justification for the beneficence of global free trade was based squarely on the assumption that capital (the factories and associated technology) was *immobile*. But if there is any outstanding characteristic of capital today, it is its extraordinary *mobility:* Take that away and there could *be* no TNCs. And again as will be discussed later, it is precisely the TNCs that are the principal force behind "free trade" today—a force whose economic strength is much enhanced by its ability to shape political decisions—and vice versa.[19]

2

Fiscal Policy

Where Confusion Is King, Chaos Awaits

The word *fiscal* comes from *fisc,* Latin for "treasury." The U.S. Treasury is the instrument of U.S. fiscal policies—it banks the taxes and writes the checks. The architects of the policies are Congress and the president; the realm of fiscal policies is the spending and taxing by the federal government. When more is spent than is taxed in a given year, the difference is a deficit, which increases the national debt by the same amount. The deficit must be financed by selling U.S. bonds and notes. When the government's annual budget is balanced, there is neither deficit nor surplus, and the national debt is unchanged. A surplus—more taxes than spending—reduces the debt.

Beginning in November 1995 and repeated twice in the first weeks of 1996, many government offices were closed because "there was no money left" in the Treasury to pay wages and salaries. The Republican-controlled Congress, seeking to pressure President Clinton into accepting the GOP budget, had not authorized the continuing appropriations necessary to pay wages and salaries (excepting, it should be added, those of Congress and the military and a few others), by refusing to raise the limit on the debt (then $4.9 trillion)—a permission granted routinely in the Reagan and Bush administrations (when the debt rose from $1 trillion to over $4 trillion).

Around April Fools' Day 1996, the GOP gave in, having realized that each additional day of deadlock was increasing its, not Clinton's, unpopularity. The debt limit (that is, the Treasury's borrowing authority) rose another half trillion, and the U.S. Government could once more pay its bills.

As "balance the budget" mania was increasing, Clinton had become a convert; by early 1995, Clinton had agreed that the budget *had* to be balanced. Setting aside the "how," the noisiest issue dividing Congress and the president was when—by the GOP's arbitrary year 2002 or Clinton's equally arbitrary 2005? Although until 1995 Clinton had not proposed balancing the budget ever, as the year wore on, he was haggling only over which year. Late in 1995 he too embraced 2002 as necessary.

As most Democrats and many Republicans know, the important issue is the components of expenditures and the identity of the taxpayers, not whether the annual budget is in balance. The current dispute has its origins in Reagan's 1981 budget, where the strategy was to lower taxes significantly for the rich while raising military expenditures (hereafter: milex) to new highs: a 10 percent increase in real milex after 1982, yielding an outlay $160 billion higher by 1989.

One of the predictable results was horrendous and record-breaking deficits—and thus the strengthening of pressures and a further rationale for lowering expenditures in the realms of welfare, education, and health care. Another result, sought by Reagan's inner circle, was the stunning upward redistribution of income: Comparing the late 1970s with the late 1980s, there was a 10.5 percent income drop for the poorest 10 percent in income and a 24.4 jump for the richest 10 percent—along with an amazing 74.2 percent for the already quite rich top 1 percent. Wealth—that is, what is held in financial assets—is the main source of income for those at the top, and high incomes allow for increasing wealth. Thus it is no surprise that in those same years financial net worth also took an upward leap: By 1989, the top 1 percent of families as ranked by financial wealth owned 48.1 percent of the total and the next 9 percent had 16.2 percent, which left just 35.6 percent to the other 90 percent of families—and gave new meaning to the expression, "Them that has, gits."

The framework allowing such changes was both financial and political: (1) As the deficits and the debt rose, the *amount* of interest payments to service the debt doubled (now in the area of $250 billion annually), the largest share of which goes to the top 10 percent of the population who own the banks and the bonds, and of course interest *rates* also rose—a contributing factor in the "deindustrialization of America"; and (2) the reforms that began in the 1930s and escalated in the 1960s—largely at the initiative of the Democrats— were made vulnerable.[1]

President Clinton allowed and even encouraged all this to occur without calling attention to the realities of the struggle, seemingly calculating only what was useful for his reelection. In this way, as so often before, Clinton showed himself to be a very sharp politician—but not a very good president.

By the time these words are read, the issues are likely to have been resolved through compromises causing much damage to those least able to afford it. Though Clinton emerged politically victorious in the 1996 election, the move back toward the pre–World War II socioeconomy also accelerated.

Fanatic though some congressional participants may be about balanced budgets, the balancing of the budget *ever* is not the issue. As Robert Eisner (one of the most sensible of the leading economists) pointed out, "The real question about government deficits should be: What would be the effect on the economy of the drastic deficit reduction necessary to get 'balance'?"[2]

As with so much else in the realm of economic affairs, contemporary discussions of fiscal policies are presented in almost purely quantitative terms. That tendency alone renders the achievement of desirable fiscal policies most difficult. Add the assumption that comparisons with individual households' incomes and expenditures are a valid basis for decisions about governmental budgeting is customary; and we are guided by a compass taking us in wrong directions.

Such obtuseness and its accompanying social dangers move into the realm of absurdity when—as is also customary—it is assumed that the financially astute household "balances its budget"—that it spends no more in a given month than its monthly income. No debt? (that is, no house, no car, no TV, no vacation, no education for the kids?). That condition was on its way out for the average U.S. household before the ashes had cooled from World War *I;* and of course, rarely, if ever, would it apply to those whose public stance it is.

Would it be wiser then to use businesses as our basis? Even less so: No business *ever* exists without a constant balance of short- and long-term debt, and the larger the business, the larger the debt—the interest payment on which is mostly tax deductible. Commercial and investment bankers have been servicing those needs over a long stretch of time; now they're lending to everyone, all the time, all over the world. Yet bankers—when they're not trying to get companies and individuals to borrow more—are among those who clamor for "balanced budgets."

Household debt (exclusive of mortgages) in 1996 stood at 19.5 percent of disposable (that is, after-tax) income, and "the market" worries that it is not increasing rapidly enough. The aggregates of household and business debt exceed the national debt. On those occasions when the rise in consumer debt falters or declines, the financial news routinely registers concern.

So who's fooling whom? How can we explain the conflict between economic realities and political positions? We can point to two factors, ideology and cynicism. The ideologists take little or no account of reality—even the reality of their own household or business. And the hardheaded cynics know very well that all this is a fig leaf to cover something better left unseen: policies to benefit those at the top, whatever the cost to all others. There are many aspects of fiscal policy to be explored. We begin with the national debt, the deficits and unbalanced budgets from which it has arisen, and the current state of virtual unanimity that we *must* do something both unnecessary and socially dangerous.

Debt, Anyone?

First, it should be noted that if debts and deficits were a real problem, the United States would be the nation with the least worries, for ours is the lowest budget deficit relative to gross domestic product (GDP) of all the major industrial nations. Next, the federal deficit for fiscal 1996, $109 billion, was the smallest since 1981—less than 2 percent of GDP, down from 4.9 percent when Bush left office. In Carter's final year, the figure was 1.7 percent; it began to rise steadily under Reagan. Finally (and neither the GOP nor, inexplicably, the Democrats mention this), if it were not for the servicing of the debt run up in the Reagan and Bush years, the budget would now be balanced.[3]

Be that as it may, whether debt (or a rising debt) is a problem—for a household, a business, a government—depends upon whether it is associated with and/or contributes to a rising (personal, business, governmental) income, the context in which it occurs, the nature and reasons for its size, and its relationship with other relevant measures. Some of what has just been noted have had quantitative, some qualitative, references; over time the latter are likely to be more telling than the former, and to determine whether the acquisition of debt will have positive or negative consequences.

In that connection, it is more than an aside to remark that those who complain the most about the *size* of the national debt have shown the least concern about *how* and for *what* it has risen. Since 1946, the largest single category of expenditure has been the military: about $9 trillion (in 1992 dollars)—and that excludes the $3.9 trillion spent on nuclear weapons that was a secret until late 1995 (to be discussed in Chapter 9). Congressmen Newt Gingrich, John Kasich, Bill Archer, and Dick Armey (house speaker, Budget chair, Ways and Means chair, and majority leader, respectively), leaders of the fight for a balanced budget for fiscal 1996, never once raised a voice against high military expenditures; indeed they sought successfully to *increase* those expenditures 5 percent beyond the Pentagon request. Their budget also called for tax decreases for the top brackets almost equal to the military budget, but that troubled them not at all.

Thus, the Reagan strategy continues with a different tactic: Set a limit on overall (but not military) expenditures and seek a huge tax cut for the rich; then, once more, cuts in social expenditures become irresistible, in fact, welcome. Revered conservative thinker Friedrich von Hayek (Milton Friedman's mentor) commented in 1995 that Reagan's vast deficits served nicely as a long-term tool for dismantling the welfare state.[4] The balanced budget mantra serves the same purpose today.

Among the many important consequences of debt accumulation by the federal government, perhaps the most vital is that altering the relationship between taxes and spending is the single most effective means for slowing down or speeding up the overall economy in the face of inflation or recession. That is the principal tool of "countercyclical fiscal policy" following upon the macroeconomic analyses of John Maynard Keynes.

When Reagan supporters mistakenly point to the 1980s as the longest economic expansion in U.S. history (in fact that occurred in the 1960s), they neglect to mention that it was also in the 1980s that Reagan's deficits added more to the national debt than the total accumulated in all of our prior history. Those supporters never acknowledge that the sheer size of the deficits assured continuous expansion and perhaps can never grasp that the *content* of the expenditures, along with other economic depredations (myriad takeovers, financialization of the economy, restructuring, S&L scams), meant that the economy was being "hollowed out." Just how perturbed Reagan was by all that could be gleaned when he declared, as he was signing the Garn–St. Germain Act (1982), which legitimated the S&L embezzlements, "All in all, I think we've hit the jackpot!"[5]

Apart from other deeper considerations, one would like to know whom he had in mind when he said "we." Clarification of the balanced budgets, expenditures, taxes, and deficits is aided when—as suggested earlier—we ask: Who benefits? Who pays? Then we should trace out the paths to those consequences.

Winners and Losers in the Biggest Game in Town

My intention in emphasizing qualitative considerations for assessing fiscal questions was to divert attention away from the *level* of expenditures or taxes and much more to their *composition*. Sheer numbers are never irrelevant, but they are seldom sufficiently instructive in this area. First, let us look at expenditures: The three biggest areas of federal expenditures (hereafter, fedex) are defense, interest on the debt, and social spending.

Defense Spending

It is useful to begin the discussion of defense spending by changing the term *defense* to *military*, the former serving as a useful spin to deflect attention. The euphemism dates back to 1947, when the Department of War (its name since the nation's beginning) was renamed the Department of Defense.

Milex are regularly cited as amounting to around 6 percent of GDP and 20–25 percent of fedex. Just as there is a large difference between the number of jobless and the official number of unemployed—the definition of which, like that of milex, is made by the government—so there is between expenditures classified as "defense" and the amount used for past, present, and future military purposes. Whatever party occupied the White House, there has always been sufficient political reason to understate joblessness and the relative importance of milex.[6]

Taking into account other fedex serving military purposes, the military share exceeds 50 percent of fedex—instead of the much lower official figure. The larger percentage is arrived at by including what the government does not: interest on the public debt attributable to past, present, and future wars, actual or expected; some realistic share of expenditures on space, energy (nuclear weapons research, for example), foreign affairs, veterans care and benefits, and, among other matters, some share of the secret budget of the Central Intelligence Agency (CIA).

Next: Although it is true that milex in the past half century or so have had numerous positive meanings for the economy (including technology, jobs, legitimate profits), it is also true that they have been the most wasteful of all governmental expenditures and—in a very crowded contest—among the richest fields for corruption. That waste is quite apart from high-tech weapons and planes and subs and so on that have been rendered obsolete before their completion and the temptations posed by "cost-plus" contracts.

Interest on the Public Debt

About half the interest owed on the public debt stems from military affairs, and as noted above, the interest paid directly or indirectly to private parties goes to those in the top layers of income and wealth. Consequently, a rising debt and rising interest payments on it create additional sources of an upward redistribution of income (everyone pays taxes, but those who get the interest pay less than their share). Rising debt and interest payments also have a deflationary impact on the overall economy (because the rich *spend* a lower percentage of their income than the rest of us). Put more exactly, every dollar of tax-financed interest payments results in a net transfer of 9 to 16 cents from all of us to the richest 10 percent, with most of that going to the top 1 percent.[7]

It is relevant in this regard to note that bankers like high interest rates, whereas those who wish to stimulate the economy know that lower interest rates are appropriate. Interest rates of the United States in the past two decades have been the highest in the industrialized world.

Social Spending

The biggest social spending item is Social Security and its health care counterpart, Medicare. The former was enacted in the New Deal of Franklin D. Roosevelt (FDR), the latter (along with Medicaid, medical care for the poor), in the Great Society of Lyndon B. Johnson (LBJ). Social Security provided pensions for people over sixty-five, assistance for the disabled, and Aid to Families with Dependent Children (AFDC). It is financed by payroll taxes on workers and employers, which go into the Social Security Trust Fund; from there the checks flow to the beneficiaries. The difference between the collections and the outpayments is a substantial surplus (now about $75 billion a year). But the current wisdom is that Social Security taxes have to go up and benefits down or "your children—or you—will get nothing when you are eligible." Sounds like another one of those incongruities, but it's not: It's another political/ideological argument dressed in economic clothing, the latest effort to privatize the old age and disability and eliminate the welfare provisions of the Social Security Act.

Social Security and its variations will be examined more fully in Chapter 6. Here we look at only two matters that connect directly with deficits and the debt. First, Social Security does not properly belong in the budget, not at all. It is financed entirely by the contributions to it, now called payroll taxes, but originally called payroll deductions, which is not just a game of words. The change came when President Johnson, trying to disguise the costs of the Vietnam war, had Social Security officially made part of the budget (in name only, however; nothing else changed). That meant that the total government "expenditures" rose by the amount of Social Security benefit payments and thus the ratio of milex to fedex was automatically sharply reduced. For example, if milex had been $200 billion and total fedex, $600 billion, when $200 billion of Social Security payments were added to total fedex, then milex fell from one-third to one-fourth of the total. (In the modern era, almost every administration has done something like this, such as changing the definition of unemployment, poverty, or the labor force: Both the inclination and the power to do so go with the position.)

Second, the surplus in the Social Security Trust Fund is regularly borrowed from (and called "off budget" when it is). When the government does this—$50 billion plus annually—its official figure for the deficit is reduced by that amount. Senator Moynihan called this "robbery"; the late Senator Heinz thought "embezzlement" was a more accurate term. The government must pay back what it borrows from the fund. In order to pay it back, it has to get it from the taxpayer, some time later—such as when the fund is no longer running a surplus. So that's what they mean when they say that Social Security is going to run out of money? That is in fact what is meant: It will run out of money because the government has borrowed from it, for no other reason. Then the Treasury will have to sell bonds to repay the trust fund, and we will have to pay taxes to finance the bonds. Every president and both parties in Congress have been implicated in this deception that has been going on for many years.

The winners and losers on the expenditure side will be considered in later chapters; now we look at the winners and losers on the tax side. As socioeconomic policy has steadily moved to the right, the winners have gained from changes in both taxes and expenditures; the losers, at least 80 percent of the population, but especially the bottom 20 percent, have lost from both kinds of changes. As we'll soon see, the winners seem never to have won enough. When they can't increase their bottom line with income, they can do so by getting their taxes reduced; normally, those who can do either, do both.

Taxes

When he was running for the presidency in 1912, Woodrow Wilson remarked that "when the State becomes important, it becomes important to control the State." It began to become *very* important in his years in office, as did the realization that among the most important activities of the state was its newly developing need to tax.

The income taxes that were put in place during World War I soon became a target of those in the top brackets, a target that was hit in the bulls-eye. Between 1923 and 1929, incomes and tax reductions were related as follows: $5,000 or less a year, 1 percent reduction; $10,000, 3 percent; $25,000, 4 percent; $100,000, 10 percent; $500,000, 27 percent; $1,000,000 or more, 31 percent. The 1920s were also a period of stagnant or falling before-tax incomes for all but 8 percent of the wage-earning population, whereas profits averaged a 65 percent rise. Fair's fair.[8]

There is a striking similarity between the 1920s and recent decades with respect to the upward redistribution of income and downward tendency of income taxes. What has happened in the decades between the end of World War II and the beginning of the 1994–1996 Congress was aptly summarized by Kevin Phillips in 1993:

> A succinct, one-paragraph history of federal taxation of the ordinary U.S. family since World War II, if penned by angry progressives [Phillips, of course, is a conservative], might read this way: During these years, the top income tax rate on the richest Americans fell from 91 percent to 31 percent while the burden on the average household soared because of bracket creep [inflation], FICA [payroll tax] increases and the eroding value of family exemptions. Back in 1948 a family of four earning the median income would have owed little or no federal income tax while paying a mere 1 percent of its income to social security. By 1955 that same family would have been laying out 9 percent for social security and income tax together, and by 1990 a median-income family faced a combined federal tax rate of almost 25 percent, or, by some calculations, from 26 to 29 percent.[9]

Phillips went on to note the radically altered sources of federal taxes by category, from the 1950s to the 1980s: personal income tax, from 42 down to 38 percent; corporate income taxes, from 27 down to 7.7 percent; payroll taxes, from 11.5 up to 29.2 percent. He added that if the family exemption of 1948 ($600 per family member) had kept its proportion to income, in 1993 it would have been $7,781 instead of, as it was, $2,050.

Another important and widely neglected note on tax deals: Whenever taxes on the rich and powerful have been passed (usually in wartime), a swarm of amendments and other laws that allow exemptions to those who have paid the lobbyists (or supported politicians) who arrange those exemptions has followed quickly. Because over time the federal government's expenditures have always risen—in all industrial nations—the tax *exemptions* have become "tax *expenditures*": If government expenditures stay the same (or rise) and various interests are exempted from paying a particular set of taxes, it is just as though expenditures have risen even more—from the point of view of those whose exemptions are unchanged (or lowered). A tax exemption for some is an increase in taxes for all other taxpayers.

These tax expenditures rise continually. From around $20 billion in the 1950s, they were estimated as being in the $200+ billion range by the 1980s and are now seen as in excess of $300 billion annually. Most spectacular of the recent developments in this respect are the tax expenditures associated with leveraged buyouts (LBOs). When USX (formerly U.S. Steel Company) buys out Marathon Oil and borrows billions to do so, the interest on that loan (usually high, because the LBO players issue "junk bonds" for that purpose) is tax deductible, and the taxpayer pays for the deal.

The House budget bill of 1996 proposed to reduce income taxes by $270 billion by 2002, a good 90 percent of which would apply to those with incomes over $200,000 year. Clinton said a big "No!" at first, then said a smaller one: He'd go for about $200 billion.

But there is more to come in some future Congress: The "flat tax," for which a movement is steadily developing on both sides of the House and Senate and if the poll cited by the *Wall Street Journal*[10] is to be believed, by a majority of the public. The flat tax provides that *all* other federal taxes and tax deductions be abolished and that the government's revenue depend entirely on an income tax rate that is the same for all. (And as Representative Archer has so accurately put it, "That'll be the end of the progressive income tax!") The proponents of the flat tax generally say the rate should be "around 17 percent," but supporters who have looked at the probable amount that would have to be collected (to balance the budget, of course) put it somewhere over 20 percent.

Unless you're pretty well off, you are not paying anything like 20 percent in income taxes; if you're the median family (average income in 1995 = $40,611),[11] you pay closer to 5–6 percent; and you don't have deductions to forgo anyway (fewer than 25 percent do), except for the interest on your mortgage. Most flat tax-ers would allow that deduction, as well as one for charitable contributions, to continue.[12]

Those with incomes over $200,000 annually pay about 39 percent of their taxable income in all federal taxes; the flat tax would give them a 50 percent reduction. (There would be *no* capital gains tax, *no* estate tax, *no* corporate income tax; the main beneficiaries of their disappearance lie almost entirely in the top 5–10 percent.)

Well, you may think, 20 percent, and that's that, might not be too bad (even though it is more than you are now paying), with no infuriating form to fill out. You would, of course, go on making your Social Security contribution, which, now called a payroll tax, would have its name changed back—you can bet on it—to payroll *deduction*. That is, unless Social Security is abolished in favor of private insurance schemes, where you invest your own monthly "deductions" in securities. In a feature essay in the *New York Times* on this matter, it was estimated that those earning $30,000–100,000 a year who seek "social security" through their own savings would have to save $1–3 million over their working lives—this in a society whose people have learned to borrow more and more and save less and less.[13]

But the real kicker is this: As noted above, all this discussion concerns *federal* taxes. The states have the need and the right to decide on their own tax structures and levels. Almost all their taxes except for income taxes are "indirect"—consumption or user taxes and, as such, regressive (the lower your income, the higher the percentage you are paying).

The recent budgetary shift of federal grants-in-aid (particularly for AFDC) to block grants will mean at least two changes: damage to the social fabric and increased sales taxes. If your family income is under $50,000 a year, you are already paying more in payroll and indirect taxes than in federal plus state income taxes.

Therein lies the dirty secret of the flat tax—whose simplicity appeals to the gullibility of John Q. Public on economic matters. That ex-governor Jerry Brown was the first since World War II to propose the flat tax (when he sought the presidency in 1992) gives us some insight into why he was called Governor Moonbeam. These matters lead to the question of how we have *become* so gullible; that requires looking at what might otherwise seem to be an aside: the roll of polls and of the media.

Listen to the Polls?

There was a time when for the making of important decisions a goat was killed and its entrails examined for guidance. Today there breathe few politicians indeed who do not depend, instead, on the ever-increasing number and frequency of polls: a less grisly way of proceeding, but not necessarily an improvement. When the politicians are highly placed enough, they can hire their own pollsters. More often than not, the polls are merely reporting the state of opinion; but there is also much shaping of the opinions reported.

Clearly, opinions are shaped by the media—print, electronic, information, entertainment—not just in what the media say and do, but in what they do *not* say and do; in how they say and do; and with respect to what and when and why they say and do. The media are paid to serve their clients in the business and the political world; they are also serving their own business interests: After all, the media, in and of themselves, are among the biggest of all businesses.

Here we can only skim the surface of the matters involved, sufficiently, it is hoped, to show how dangerous the shaping processes of modern "communications" have become to our social health. Only two aspects of that process will be examined.

First, historically, capitalist societies have found it necessary and desirable, sooner or later, to function within the framework of *political* (but not economic and social) democracy—Britain sooner, South Korea later, for example. The reasons are complicated. Capitalist societies are characterized by structures of substantial inequality of income, wealth, and power. That being so, as industrial capitalism has been linked with political democracy, the maintenance of economic and political stability (here's where the media come in) has depended on "winning the hearts and minds of the people," to use the phrase that was so important in the Vietnam war. The alternative—tried in Nazi Germany and Fascist Italy, for example—is coercive capitalism. That proved very costly even before military defeat, not only to ordinary people, but also to business.

The necessary, if not sufficient, conditions for noncoerced acquiescence and support in advanced industrial societies are (1) that real incomes be reasonably high for a reasonably high percentage of the electorate, and (2) that as industrialism matures, mass purchasing power will rise to help absorb the extraordinary productivity of modern industry. It may be noted that both these conditions seem on their way to being forgotten by companies that "downsize" their workforces—who, taken together, are (or were) a substantial percentage of their customers. But it is both natural and—in some sense—essential for each company's managers to think of their own company's bottom line first and hope for the best for the economy as a whole.

Patterns of income and other inequalities can be ignored at the top or middle while the economy is expanding more or less briskly; one doesn't pay much attention to one's *share* of the pie as long as the slice is filling. As with so many socioeconomic processes, however, nothing lasts forever: The seemingly endless expansion after World War II slackened in the 1970s, even as the "consumerism" that is vital to contemporary capitalism became increasingly voracious—as indeed it had to, to feed expansion (or slow a contraction).

Since the economic softness began, those in power have increasingly found means of keeping their own incomes high (or pushing them higher) by suppressing those of the strata beneath them—80–90 percent of the population in the United States. As noted earlier, it was this set of developments that provided the backdrop for the economic follies of the Reagan years, which continue, if in somewhat different guise.

The Reagan cure almost killed the patient: tripling of the national debt, moving the United States from being the world's largest creditor to its largest debtor, financial scandals galore, the deliberate weakening of a significant economic or political role for trade unions, and a resulting social malaise that carries in it the seeds of rising social turbulence. The socioeconomic policies wrought in earlier years have by now been overturned or seem likely to be before long.

Both as consequence and cause of the condition of the U.S. political economy, the major U.S. trading partners have also been foundering in recent years: Japan has been in recession since 1991, and Germany and France have been since 1994–1995 (with 10, 12.2 [1997], and 12.5 percent unemployment, respectively, using the European mode of measurement). The "market" continues to dictate that these and most other nations drop everything—most especially their social expenditures and the real incomes for the majority—to balance their budgets, an act that, if it occurs, is more likely to deepen recessions than to counteract them.

The second aspect of the role of communications is the change in the function of the media. So essential in creating and expanding consumer demand, soon after World War II the media also became essential in the selling of ideas and politicians. Gradually, and initially in (very probably) an unconscious process, the media came to do some of its best "selling" through polls.

Success in selling both commodities and politicians depends on the creation of appealing appearances. When polls actually shape attitudes rather than merely reporting them, it is not "appearances" but the questions asked—and, perhaps more important, left unasked—that constitute the shaping process.

It is well-known that a question in the realm of welfare, for example, produces substantially different results from the same respondents, depending upon the wording of the question: If people are asked if they believe in welfare reform, almost all will answer yes; if asked if they support leaving the poor (especially if poor children are mentioned) with lower or no financial assistance, almost all will answer no. Part of the explanation for that sharp contrast is ignorance on the part of the respondents (who may not know what is meant by "welfare reform" even if it is more narrowly specified, such as moving to block grants to the states for AFDC), the fault of the pollster more than of the respondent. Is the "fault" conscious or not? The answer depends upon which pollster is doing the poll: Polls sponsored by political candidates or by major media are almost always consciously slanted. Be that as it may, for even neutral polls to have taken on the importance they now have is akin to evaluating the competence of students graduating from high school or university based only on their scores in true/false or multiple choice tests.

And who controls the media? Is that an important question? It would seem so. The media giants are themselves at the very heart of the concentration of economic power—with a handful of companies dominating the main flow of information and entertainment. Their political and economic interests are not demonstrably different in general from those of General Motors, EXXON, USX, or Du Pont. Their two principal sources of income are from advertising, designed and paid for by the latter, and from the major political parties and their candidates.[14]

Does this suggest a conspiracy to shape opinion and polls and politics and society? Doubtless such a conspiracy could be arranged, were it seen as necessary. It does not seem to *be* necessary. There is instead an "innocent" confluence of interests, as when tiny streams pulled by gravity ultimately form a great river. Similarly, the grand diversity of business interests, when expressed as advertisements or as news, emerge ultimately as positions consistent with the interests of the most powerful in the socioeconomy. There are, of course, differences of opinion, differences of the order of magnitude of those between the Democratic and Republican Parties, but those differences do not disturb the patterns of inequality—of income, wealth, comfort, status, security, prestige, and, most important, power.

In the next chapter the focus will be upon the always more dominating processes of the global economy, in turn always more dominated by its behemoth corporations. That examination will shed important light on how and why our government moves steadily beyond our reach and our job market spins out of our control: social harm once more aided and abetted by the free market ideology.

3

International Production, Trade, and Finance

What's Good for Great Britain

Two years after the first cotton textile factory in England began production, David Ricardo published his *Principles of Political Economy and Taxation* (1817). As a London stockbroker, Ricardo was tuned in to the waves of the future more than those of the past; his ideas, like Adam Smith's but with a different focus, were designed to foster industry. Though less well known than Smith, Ricardo's theory, his method, and his policy aims have been at least as effective and durable. Again like Smith, Ricardo's positions have taken on a new life in recent decades.

The "taxation" of Ricardo's magnum opus was that of the "Corn Laws"— tariffs (taxes) on imported grain (called "corn" in Britain). The tax favored the landed gentry, who could get a higher price (which Ricardo termed a "rent," an "unearned income") for their crops, and it harmed manufacturers, whose costs were thus artificially higher: higher grain prices meant higher bread prices. If we assume, as Ricardo (and, later, Marx) did, that workers' wages were set by their subsistence needs (and that bread was their major purchase), we see that the tariff on grain required higher wages, causing a shift of income away from factory owners to landowners. Thus industrialization was held back. Therefore, the slogans, Free Trade! Abolish the Corn Laws!

They were abolished in 1846, by which time industrialists—politically Whigs—had more political clout than the landowning Tories. Ricardo (in accord with Smith) accepted the "labor theory of value" and saw profits as well as rents as "unearned"; but profits favored industrialization, and so did he, so he didn't object to *that* form of unearned income. Marx did, of course; Using Ricardo's logic, he demonstrated that profits, like rents, were a reward to power rather than a contribution to production. That enabled Marx to argue the dependency of capitalist profits on worker exploitation.

Ricardo both figuratively and literally took Smith's perspectives into new territories where, in Ricardian form, they have become permanent settlers. Ricardo's innovations reveal the important ways in which he departed from his mentor: (1) Smith's generalizations depended upon observation and history; Ricardian theory was entirely based upon abstraction and deductive reasoning, the practice of economic (macro, micro, and trade) theorists ever since; and (2) Smith's focus was very much on the national economy and the impact of the state on the production process; Ricardo's focus was on foreign trade and its (as well as industry's) impact on national strength, which became the heart of trade theory and policy. It is the latter we now examine.

Ricardo's theory yielded a principle that at first sight seems to make a lot of sense: Each nation should specialize in the production of that in which it is *comparatively* most efficient (or least inefficient). (His most famous example: Britain might be more efficient than Portugal in producing both cloth and wine, but if more so for cloth, then specialize in producing and exporting cloth and import wine—to the advantage, he argued, of both Britain *and* Portugal.)

Further reflection and less-abstract reasoning make clear (as they did for the United States, Germany, France, Japan, and others) that this principle makes unequivocal sense *only* for the nation in the lead, and its practice would leave the structure of world power unchanged—with Britain on top militarily and economically.[1]

That was good thinking for Britain. With the "principle of comparative advantage" as the guiding theory, in a world in which Britain industrialized first, it would also be the *only* industrial society. All others would remain lodged in their preindustrial condition: The United States, for example, would go on raising rice and tobacco and cotton and selling it to the British and would import manufactures from the permanently "relatively more efficient" British. That sounded fine to the planters of the South, but considerably less so to the restive Yankees of the less fertile Northeast.

Industrialization then as now also meant military strength, so another implication of Ricardo's doctrines was that Britain would dominate the entire world, not just its economy. The United States was one of the first nations to see that;[2] indeed our Civil War was very much fought over whether the South's planter agrarianism (with Great Britain as major buyer and supplier) or the North's vigorous (and tariff-protected) industrialization would be our way. In the event, *no* nation except Britain took Ricardo's advice, except those colonies powerless to choose (such as India, where the once-strong cotton textile industry was forced into ruin by the British imposition of "free trade").

Smith was an ardent opponent of colonialism—whether in the American colonies, the Caribbean, or elsewhere. Colonialism as such did not fall within Ricardo's focus, but his policies of free trade accommodated nicely with the spread of British imperialism in the nineteenth century. Like so many of his followers today, Ricardo simply ignored the fact that free trade policies were imposed upon colonial areas—beginning with Ireland—by the threat or reality of military force. And neither Smith nor Ricardo could imagine how very much more invasive the new imperialism would be, by comparison with the colonialism of the sixteenth century; totally unimaginable for them would have been the devastating power of today's "neocolonialism."[3]

The differences between the three periods of overseas domination by Europeans and, later, by the United States and the Japanese arose from the huge changes in business organization and technology that have occurred, and their associated needs and possibilities. The colonial era was limited to sailing ships and what we would see as primitive weapons. Such weapons were nevertheless decisive in contests with people armed with even less effective weapons: spears, swords, and the like. More to the point, the spread of colonialism was generally limited to coastal areas (although, in the case of the slave trade, the slaves were often taken from the hinterland).

Industrial technology in the nineteenth century brought not only steamships and more powerful weaponry but also deeper resource needs, investments in mines, plantations, harbors, railways, and so on, carrying with them the push for political control of entire territories, not just port areas. The essential strengthening of political rule and economic penetration made for the principal difference between colonialism and imperialism and exacerbated the harmful impact of outsiders on the societies of the imperialized.

Serious and damaging though such infringements were on the autonomy of the imperialized societies, they were trivial compared to the developments of recent decades. The relationships between the major industrial powers and the weaker countries must be seen as an onslaught—against not only their resources and politics but also their cultures, their very beings. As Helena Norberg-Hodge has written: "It is a world in which every society employs the same technologies, depends on the same centrally managed economy, offers the same Western education for its children, speaks the same language, consumes the same media images, holds the same values and even thinks the same thoughts—monoculture."[4] A far cry indeed from the visions of Ricardo and Smith, who would have been startled had they lived to see the uses made of their ideas already in the nineteenth century, to say nothing of what is being made of them as our century ends.

The current world economy had its institutionalized beginnings in Bretton Woods, New Hampshire, in 1944, with the creation of the International Monetary Fund (IMF) and the World Bank and, in 1947, the General Agreement on Tariffs and Trade (GATT). Much assisted by the evolving political economy of the cold war, the United States reinvented the "integrated world economy" of the late nineteenth century. This time, the United States rather than Britain ruled over it; it was "integrated" even more tightly this time, but within processes and schemes never dreamt of—or needed—by the British. Since 1944, as economist David C. Korten points out:

> economic growth has expanded fivefold, international trade has expanded by roughly twelve times and foreign direct investment has been expanding at two to three times the rate of trade expansion. Yet, tragically, while the Bretton Woods institutions have met their goals, they have failed in their purpose of bringing prosperity to the people of the world. The earth has more poor people than ever before. There is an accelerating gap between the rich and the poor.[5]

As we have seen, that U.S.-guided world economy worked reasonably well into the 1970s, however incompatible its operations with either Smith's Old or Ricardo's New Testament.[6] But at least the years of easy U.S. dominance were designed by nationalists; nowadays the Smithian-Ricardian arguments are put forth in the *name* of the nation, but whatever favorable effects they might have are *for* the mammoth transnational corporations (TNCs) and speculators. The rest of us, as used to be said when one lost out in a child's card game, can "go fish."

What's Good for the TNCs

Like Smith, Ricardo (though himself in the financial world) was concerned in his theory with production and trade, not with finance. Like our national economy, however, the world economy has also come to be dominated by finance—if also with considerably greater complexity.

The TNCs, prompted by both the search for profits and the survival instinct, scour the world for cheap labor and natural resources, for productive investment opportunities and markets, and for the freedom to do as they please in all those respects. Moreover, because they *are* transnational, the TNCs are at any given moment able to make major gains or suffer major losses through financial as much as (or more than) through "real" activities (as touched upon earlier). They have no choice but to be involved in financial markets, including those permanently roiled by speculation.

One measure of what this has come to mean is found in the foreign exchange ("forex") market, in which the convertible currencies of all nations are bought and sold—and in which the TNCs are perforce among the very biggest players. That market caused little comment until the 1980s—by which time it was impossible not to notice it: In 1986, economic observers were startled to learn from the Bank for International Settlements that the *daily* transactions in the world forex market were $150 *billion*, only 10 percent of which was attributable to the financing of productive investment or trade. By late 1996 (as noted in Chapter 1) the amount was $2.6 *trillion* per day, an increase of such rapidity (doubling every three years) that if it were a malignancy it would be seen as metastasis. In those same years, the role of investment and trade in the daily forex market fell from the 1986 figure of around 10 to perhaps 1 percent, leaving the remaining 99 percent for speculation in one or another of its many forms.

Quite apart from the fragility and instability for the world and the national economies implied by those numbers, they also imply that both companies' and nations' decisionmaking processes are in some basic sense compromised. Decisions are made by gamblers more than by, in the approved sense of the term, "enterprisers." But the story does not end there; it continues relentlessly into the structure of economic and political power.

The classic company of the late nineteenth century had to move toward corporate giantism, be bought up, or risk being destroyed by the emerging giants; survival in today's economy in all sectors—industry, agriculture, services—means becoming a *super*corporation, typically transnational in size and scope. The millions of small companies that manage to retain their formal independence may be compared with small airplanes caught in the slipstream and downdrafts of giant jets.

In 1950, there were a few international corporations (in automobiles and oil, especially), but the concept of the TNC did not emerge until the 1960s (then called "multinationals"), and the numbers were only in the hundreds. By 1970 there were already 7,000 TNCs, which then seemed a lot; by the early 1990s there were 35,000–40,000, more than a fivefold increase.

Fierce rivalries are a natural outcome of such a development; as on the domestic front, however, such rivalries are seldom permitted to erupt into competition by the always-shrinking hard core of power. Two hundred of the largest corporations now control more than a quarter of the world's economic activity and at least 60 percent of all foreign investment—valued at $2.1 trillion—and they engage in at least one-third of all *new* foreign investment. As noted earlier, three hundred TNCs control about a quarter of the world's productive assets.[7] They are becoming what Richard Barnet and John Cavanagh have called "the world empires of the 21st century. . . . [They control] the four intersecting webs of global commercial activity on which the new world economy rests: the global cultural bazaar, the global shopping mall, the global workplace, and the global financial network."[8] That doesn't leave much for others—governments, for example—to "control."

But, as we have been told over and over again by our government, our economists, our TNCs, we must not only submit to but also enhance "globalization" for our own and other economies. Interestingly enough, Alan Blinder, shortly after he resigned his post as chairman of the U.S. Federal Reserve, disagreed in blunt terms:

Only two gains have accompanied globalization in America, he said. They are "strong export growth, and strong corporate profits," and globalization may not have caused either. . . . During the same period [since 1985] in which the U.S. economy was being downsized and globalized . . . the dollar has given up approximately half its value against the yen and the deutsche mark. This devaluation, Mr. Blinder said, "is sufficient to explain what happened."[9]

The beneficiaries of that new world have been relatively few: the top 10 to 15 percent of the world's people, at the very most. That is a lot of high-income shoppers, of course, 500–800 million of them over the globe. As purchasing power for others continues to decline, those at the top have to absorb an increasing percentage of high-powered production. "Shop till you drop," now a wisecrack, could become the main occupation of that elite group.

The other 4.5 billion people are either mired at the bottom, in sight of it, or rightly very much concerned about their prospects.[10] Their worries are not only about shopping; linked to declining average wages is the decline of decent jobs—or any jobs: Unemployment in the fifteen-member European Union averages 11 percent; if we and the Japanese measured unemployment in the European method (see Chapter 4), our rate would be at 10 percent, not the official 5+ and 3+ percent (respectively).

What the implications of these trends are for our politics, our social processes, our cultural and personal lives, cannot be predicted with any confidence; but one would have to be foolhardy indeed to view the range of probabilities without alarm. It is not only likely that, in Yeats's image, "the centre cannot hold"; soon, there could be no center *left* to hold.

The processes taking us toward that looming tragedy were identified by Nobel laureate Wole Soyinka, when he argued that "global corporations, which are eroding nations from the top (even as rising ethnic awareness, squatter settlements and refugee migrations erode them from the bottom), have no incentive whatsoever to be moral, nor do they accept responsibility for the social consequences of their activities."[11]

The seemingly ineluctable movement into these nasty conditions was facilitated by a set of business chiefs and publicists proclaiming that we were on the road to global abundance mixed with freedom—just as we were told that ideology was finished (in the 1960s) and that the long travail called "history" had ended (the end of the 1980s). To all those proclamations, the facts murmur "not yet."

What went wrong? Even posing such a question makes one an outsider, a heretic: From the point of view of those in the top levels of income, those who hold most of the wealth and power in society today, *nothing* has gone wrong. It's in the theory, after all: The market provides the most efficient and the best possible outcomes: efficiency and justice.

In subsequent chapters not only the long-awaited justice but also the vaunted efficiency will be scrutinized and found wanting. Injustice continues to spread and deepen, systemic waste (including "deliberate obsolescence") is joined now with destructive wastes, as nature's bounty is consumed with frightening rapidity. These contrasts between ideas and realities require further examination.

The Triumph of Unreason

As with the growth of corporate giantism a century or so ago, the emergence of transnational giants in the past few decades was made necessary by the dynamic interaction between a rapidly changing technology and the desire of business to muffle destructive market competition. The "transnational" quality of today's giantism arises from the extraordinary technological capacities now common in communications, transportation, and production itself (e.g., in automation and in synthetics). The megagiants had to expand and exfoliate, become much bigger and, usually, "conglomerate" (function in more than one industry and/or sector): A business that did *not* move in those directions might survive, but increasingly as a serf for one of the transnational barons (GM, for example, has 40,000 suppliers).

Concurrent with the rise of the TNCs was the rebirth in the academy and politics of free marketry as ideology, in both Smithian and Ricardian terms: Minimize government at home; do away with barriers to trade in the world. But the theme of "minimization of government," irrespective of party in power in the recent past, has accompanied the reality of enlarged government. The diminution of government spending for meeting certain social needs and possibilities has been accompanied, however, with rising fedex (in real terms), the maintenance or expansion of government to satisfy the pressures of those at the top. That translates as "corporate welfare,"[12] vast expenditures on the military and crime, and the like.

Neither Smith nor Ricardo would be pleased. Today's "free trade"— GATT and the North American Free Trade Agreement (NAFTA) and their cousins (most recently the Asian Pacific Economic Council [APEC], for the Pacific Rim nations)—are touted as opening up markets (meaning, we are led to hope, getting rid of tariffs and lowering prices for consumers everywhere). The trade pacts do have some such impact, but mainly they move TNC capital into the cheapest labor markets and unprotected natural resources of the poor countries. The TNCs are usually big enough not to need their nations' gunboats so long as there are such agreements to render national borders economically meaningless.

More than two-thirds of the world's most valued natural resources are located in the poorest countries, as is the largest part of the supply of compliant and tragically cheap labor. There is a large difference indeed between someone who works at $10 an hour or more with the most advanced equipment, and another who gets 50 cents an hour or less using the latest technology.[13] That, plus the absence of environmental controls, is sufficient to explain the TNCs' virtually unanimous support of GATT and NAFTA.

When it is demonstrated that jobs have been lost at home in consequence of transnational trade agreements, it is then argued that new customers are being created in the poorer countries and eventually new jobs will be created *here*. Perhaps—but in the decade 1983–1992, 783,000 jobs were lost in TNCs' plants in the United States, whereas those same companies increased their employees by 345,000 abroad.[14] The overwhelming weight of data pointing in that direction means little to those who make those arguments, for *their* truths are to be established in the now fabled long run.

While the processes of leveraged buyouts, restructuring, outsourcing, and downsizing go on here, as well as in Europe and Japan, real wages are essentially stagnant, and corporate profits (and average CEO incomes) rise. All that has come to mean a serious retrogression in the United States (and much of the world), a falling away from the progress wrought in earlier decades, a falling away with much falling yet to come.

In those parts of the world where the cheap labor and bountiful natural resources are found, "retrogression" is very much a euphemism. Those areas have long been subject to predators from Europe, the United States, and Japan. In a crescendo of changes over the past several centuries the "less-developed countries" have had their economies, their governments, their cultures, their societies taken over and destroyed. Along the way—whether through enslavement, mistreatment, wanton slaughter, or the loss of subsistence—the lives of untold millions have been shattered and shortened.

We must acknowledge that such ruination now accelerates. The numbers since the 1980s alone have been devastating: Already in 1986, 40,000 children *daily* (14 million per year) died from malnutrition-related causes; in 1993, 700 million suffered from famine; 2 billion were malnourished. However, as the distinguished economist-philosopher Amartya Sen put it, "Starvation is the characteristic of some people not *having* enough food to eat. It is not the characteristic of there *being* not enough food to eat."[15]

Though you wouldn't know it without digging for it, agricultural production has outstripped population growth for all of modern history, until the very present. For the past century and a half, free marketeers have assiduously overlooked not only the lack of genuinely "free" markets but also their costs.

That aloofness began with the Irish "potato famine" of 1846–1848, the terrible costs of which were then blamed on the Irish—portrayed then as "blockheaded," "stubborn," "lazy," "witless," and the like. The British were in control, and free marketry in its first heyday: Ireland (its lands owned mostly by the English) was *exporting* food (grains and meat) to England throughout the famine years, years in which at least 1 million starved and another 2 million emigrated (of a total population of 9 million). Lord Trevelyan, who supervised all this, was saddened by it; withal, he averred that the people would have been worse off with any other than "the market solution." It is hard to see how that would have been possible.[16]

So much for "labor." What about the land, the natural resources, that is, agricultural land, forests, mines, rivers, air and water "supplies"? By now, it is clear to many that a crisis of nature has long been under way, and that its running partner has been a heedless industrialization process, now exacerbated by consumerism. For a few decades now, various groups have sounded alarms. There have been successes, although usually the revised policies have only reduced, not reversed, the rate of destruction, and the spoliation goes on—if, sometimes, more slowly.

With more global trade agreements, those processes are allowed to speed up once more in both the poorer parts of the world and here. The environment is the focus of Chapter 8; suffice it to say here that the powers of corporate behemoths to have their way with "the environment" through GATT, NAFTA, and the like are presently matched by their powers in Congress to undo environmental protections here at home. Whatever else comes to mind, it makes one wonder about those in the corporate boardrooms, their publicists, and legislative friends: Do they think they live on a different planet than the rest of us? Do they have their own air supply? Are they childless?

Nevertheless, when it comes to the economic process, those with power may be forgiven their recklessness, at least up to a point: An economic "science" that might have informed them otherwise has taught that socioeconomic irresponsibility, if not quite a virtue, is far from being a sin.[17] Put differently, over the course of its development, industrialization and its two main supports and consequences—economic growth and world trade—have taken on the status of unquestionable values, and anything that might foster either or both by business (or government) is by that fact seen as valuable. How and why that happened, and what it has come to mean, requires a digression.

Means Become Ends

Economics and capitalism entered history hand in hand: There were tracts on the economy, but there was no *economics* before Adam Smith. As was briefly noted, that which arose from his and Ricardo's works, initially called political economy, ultimately came (respectively) to be called "microeconomics" and "trade theory." The focus of both was the market in which commodities (labor too treated as a commodity) were bought and sold—national for Smith, global for Ricardo. But anyone who has studied even beginning economics will think, what about "macroeconomics"?

That was born, belatedly, during the depression of the 1930s. What earlier passed for understanding in that regard (as is becoming to be so again today) had been provided by Jean-Baptiste Say (1767–1832). Say was a French disciple of Smith who argued that there cannot *be* a depression (and therefore an economics concerning it is unnecessary). He said, "Supply creates its own demand," that is, (1) every production yields incomes equal to the value of that production, (2) those incomes will either be spent on consumption or saved, and if the latter, (3) the savings will be in response to an attractive rate of interest, which (4) is itself owing to the demand for loans that will be used for real investment. Therefore, supply creates its own demand.

When ups and downs in the economy (what we would call recessions) occurred intermittently in the nineteenth century they came to be treated by an emerging "business cycle" theory. "Cycle" is the key term: It was assumed that the overall ("aggregative," "macroeconomic") movement of the economy was like that of the seasons—a change this way *yielded* the next change (spring brings summer brings autumn brings winter brings spring . . .). That was fine and dandy, until the endless winter that began in 1929, stretching on to 1933, to 1937, to eternity perhaps, had it not been for World War II.

It was Keynes who put stop to that argument. He explained that whatever might have been true for the adolescent economies of the preceding century, the mature industrial capitalist economies of this century could enter a recession that would sink into deep depression—and just stay there, "stagnating" (unless, as Keynes feared, the stagnation would be ended by capitalism's overthrow). Keynes, the leading monetary economist of the 1920s, in making that argument in his *General Theory of Employment, Interest, and Money* (1936), was refuting his own earlier theories—as well he might, Britain having suffered an average of 10 percent unemployment throughout the 1920s.

Growing out of that analysis was the widespread acceptance (until recently) that governmentally initiated tax and spending policies were the solution. A connected analytical position took hold. It was first applied vigorously and consciously in the Kennedy administration and soon became part of a widely accepted gospel: that lagging economic growth can and must be avoided by deficit-financed government spending. In the past twenty years or so, there has been a transformation of that position: Economic growth is seen as essential, but rather than by government spending, it should be financed by cuts in the taxes of those at the top. They will save, their savings will be used for real investment, and the economy will grow—especially and only in an expanding world economy.[18]

Although Keynesian analysis and policies fell (or, more accurately, were pushed) into disfavor as the 1970s ended, the support for growth and world trade did not. The forecast of how they would be achieved and their benefits distributed did change greatly, however: The formula was Smith plus Ricardo minus Keynes, in a combination distorting *all* their aims and means almost beyond recognition.

What remains are two economic means resting so much beyond dispute that they have become ends in themselves, seen as combining the essential with the desirable: (1) unremitting national economic expansion, and (2) an always more integrated and expanding world economy. There are people, of course, who dispute some of today's means to those ends (such as outsourcing or environmental recklessness)—ineffectually, as long as the aims are accepted.

But the aims as presently viewed should not be accepted, not even by that small percentage of the world's people that gains the most. In these times, the sails of both national and global economic expansion must instead be trimmed: They are harmful for most already and threaten to become a calamity for all. We must disenthrall ourselves from obeisance to growth and trade, and place our hopes on qualitative more than quantitative changes.[19]

A Heresy Whose Time Has Come

We, meaning especially but not only the United States, depend too much on domestic growth and global exports. In doing so we allow avoidable economic and social problems to take hold, both because of and despite those same two processes: we have a two-headed tiger by the tail.

We cannot deal with one without treating the other: To change the metaphor, growth and trade are and always have been the Siamese twins of the capitalist process, dynamically interdependent, the system's functional center. Let it be said that what follows will not be an argument against growth as such, but against heedless growth; will not be in favor of protectionism or economic nationalism; nor will it contend for sudden or massive reductions of world trade.

Rather, the position taken here is that at this stage of capitalist development it is—on *economic* grounds—desirable, necessary, and practical (and easier for the United States than others) to undertake a deliberate and systematic alteration of those means and ends in favor of meeting the broader needs and possibilities for social and economic development. If we do so, it will be only the latest time the capitalist framework has been significantly transformed in order to remain viable.

First we must examine the basic functional—as distinct from ideological—principles of the capitalist process. For capitalist development to flourish and to persist, there must be a vibrant interaction within and between the national and world economies.

The process has been something like a circus tightrope act: The capitalist system, when strong, has moved through time dynamically from crisis to crisis, balance achieved and lost and regained, always at higher levels of technology, organization, production, and real income—and requiring, at those higher levels, always more nonmarket interventions for both businesses and persons—to reduce, forestall, or compensate for the concomitantly rising business, economic, and social dangers of industrial capitalism.

To prosper, even to survive, capitalism (given its exploitative needs) has had to satisfy its strongest imperative: to *expand*—"vertically" through capital accumulation (net real investment) within each *national* economy and "horizontally" through increased trade and investment in a buoyant *world* economy. The need for these mutually supporting and transforming processes of expansion is primary to the *system;* the needs of each country's and of the world's people remain subordinated to the needs of capital accumulation—for better or for worse.

However, what constitutes a *sufficient* rate of economic growth and/or volume of foreign trade stands in direct proportion to some combination of the inequality of income distribution and the resource inadequacies of each nation. All capitalist societies must have a highly unequal distribution of income (and wealth and power), and all lack at least some vital resources. But there are broad and shaping differences between nations. Let us look at Japan and the United States, for example. Both have great income inequalities, but Japan is vastly poorer in natural resources than the United States. Therefore Japan *must* have high savings (and relatively low consumption) rates and *must* have higher rates of real investment and growth; also, given its resource shortages (apart from any other matter), Japan *must* import and export more as a percentage of its total production than we do. These imperatives are considerably more demanding for Japan than for the United States.

In that connection, it is pertinent to recall that in recent years the United States has frequently sought to persuade Japan to decrease the inequality of distribution of its real (if not its money) income through governmental measures (bringing about a rising "social wage" and higher consumer/GDP ratios) and thus to reduce its need for enormous and rising export surpluses. The United States should (and by comparison with nations like Japan, relatively easily could) take its own advice: By internal socioeconomic reforms that would alter structures of consumption, production, and investment while broadening domestic markets, our rate of growth of and dependence on foreign trade could be reduced (without any move toward protectionism). In doing all that—neither a modest nor an overly ambitious program—we could both lower our persistently high levels of unemployment and raise the quality of jobs, along with much else desirable; if we do *not*, the dreary, painful, and perilous "race to the bottom" will continue and, inevitably, accelerate.

The capital accumulation and the exports of each nation have in common the following: The production of neither is purchased by consumers *within* the national economy, but to the degree that "free market capitalism" holds sway, both capital accumulation and exports are required to maintain levels of profitability. Either capital accumulation or exports *can* lead to higher levels of consumption and of course have done so, but that is neither their purpose nor their functional consequence—indeed, as we have seen, today's consequences are perverse.

An important *similarity* between domestic accumulation and an export surplus is that both act to stimulate the economy's growth. An even more important *difference* is that domestic capital accumulation leads directly to increased productive capacity in new or old products and often to improved productivity, and therefore to the need to find new outlets for consumption, *and/or* exports, *and/or* further investment, *and/or*, as has been vital since World War II, to higher levels of government spending in order to cheapen and to enhance both the accumulation process and mass consumption.

Net exports, in contrast, constitute a use of existing productive capacity having no *necessary* connection with any further national economic development, except insofar as the economy becomes habitually structured to supply an export market. If this export market declines, serious national economic problems arise. This is not an insubstantial exception, considering the already harsh realities of our many shrinking and—most especially in terms of jobs—already devastated industries, the most publicized of which are autos and steel.

Also, just as investment is directed by and for the class of owners and controllers of capital, exports/imports are either for use in production—raw materials, machinery, and so on—or mostly for the consumption of the top layers of incomes in the importing nations. Thus, both capital accumulation and exports/imports are in the realm of a small fraction of the world's people. Although in some sense it has been true that "a rising tide lifts all boats," that has *not* been so in much of the past, and it becomes considerably less so in the present—when hundreds of millions don't *have* a boat—with the worst yet to come.

In both the nineteenth century and our own era, the dynamic relationships between national economic growth and world trade have assured that the system's very successes shorten its viable life span. Moreover, it seems certain that the present world economy will have an even shorter life span than its predecessor—and with no successor in sight, except one spinning toward a black hole. If that is so, it is principally due to the very stimulating effects of today's rapidly changing technologies and organization, which, because of and despite their positive impact on both growth and trade, accelerate all the processes of "peaceful"—and disruptive—economic and social change.

The decades since World War II, calm though they have often seemed on the surface (setting aside civil and international wars), have dissolved innumerable stabilizing social institutions—only rarely for the better, almost always for the worse. As the strong waves of economic expansion have subsided, the fragility of underlying social and political structures have been more clearly revealed—the latest phase of those unsettling processes that first became evident when industrialization began to take hold. The quantitative and qualitative achievements of the epoch of industrialization could not but have disrupted the economies, the politics, and the culture of the entire world; and that pace quickens.[20]

In addition to all else we might seek, then, there is the need to make the socioeconomic process less destabilizing, to protect ourselves from the storms created by incessant growth and swirling trade. The breathing space for meeting the whole range of our species' and the rest of nature's needs is already dangerously confined. It would be rash to assume that the human, physical, and social disasters of this century can be separated from and incidental to the central processes that have produced what are seen as its achievements, and reckless to ignore the often irreversible damages accompanying rapid capital accumulation and expanding world trade.

Too Much and Too Little

It is absurd as well as dangerous to continue along those paths. As a people we have come to resemble the patient who continues with medications that produce lifelessness and may even hasten death, hoping to avoid pain or arduous alternatives. It may be said flatly that contrary to the conventional view that pressing economic problems *require* us to live by the gospel just noted, the serious problems facing us are not *economic;* they are problems of power and politics and, it must be added, of morality.

An economic problem is one arising from scarcity: "Economics" is indeed defined as the "science of allocating scarce resources to unlimited wants." Quite apart from the fact that the gap between "needs" and "wants" is constantly widened by design, any business can tell you that *its* problem, if ever it is one of scarcity, is that of scarce customers, not of scarce resources.

Increasingly in this century—except for the catastrophic decades between 1914 and 1945—the economic process could have been characterized as "too much and too little"—too much of useful things that can't be sold because of too little purchasing power; too much of goods and services that supply no human (though they may meet a business) need; too little of those goods and services we need badly; too much production that is "throwaway," wasteful, and destructive; too little where quality is the standard, where conservation is the aim. As will be seen later, it has been conservatively estimated that 50 percent of U.S. production is waste. These matters will be pursued in more detail in Chapters 4 through 9; alternatives will be put forth in Chapter 10.

4

Jobs and Joblessness

The Worst Waste of All

Much has been made earlier, and will be again, of how gravely circumscribed economic understanding is. With its analyses molded in largely or entirely quantitative terms, it could scarcely be otherwise, given that guiding economic theories are abstracted not only from the social processes within which economic life abides but also from the structures and processes of economic life itself. The findings of such procedures are more likely to do harm than good when they are taken seriously—as, all too often, they are.

Those strictures apply with particular force to the complicated and dynamic world of jobs and joblessness—an area of life demeaned in its very characterization by economists as "the labor market." It is worth repeating here that what ultimately became economics took shape as industrial capitalism became plausible, with Adam Smith the first methodical voice for both. Smith's analysis was historically and socially rich in history and observation, spectacularly so when compared with the wispy filaments that now constitute economic theory.

Willy-nilly, however, Smith facilitated the process by which today's "neoclassical economics" has come to pass for erudition. He did that by insisting on the free market as the center and basis for the economic process:[1] Smith's reasoning justified the commodification of all goods and services; that led inexorably to the quantification of everything, labor, of course, included.

If economic theory won't help us to have a balanced view of what may be seen as the world of work, we must look elsewhere—in studies of economic reality by "institutional" economists, economic historians, and in (among other areas), sociology and political history. It wouldn't hurt to begin by reminding ourselves of what in our bones we already "know" about work: Like other species, ours has survived because it worked sufficiently and well enough over time to allow our reproductive instincts to take us to the present.

Unlike other species, however, we have gone beyond the simple achievement of the conditions for survival; through what Veblen called "the instinct of workmanship," we have created an infinity of work processes superseding simple hunting and gathering and the finding of sheltering caves. Over the millennia this has come to include agriculture and trade and industry, violin making and playing, weapons making and using, medicine and painting and teaching and writing and carpentry and physics and . . . Moreover, with our unique creativity, we have made of ours both the most constructive *and* the most destructive of all species.

Indeed, very much to the present point, we are the species most able to work in ways that are inspiring and also to do much, much more work (to be called "labor" in a moment) in ways that are dispiriting, soul-destroying. Only the ants (and perhaps the bees) come close to us in the latter regard, except that they do not have our capabilities to be alienated and demoralized.[2] (It does appear that lions, tigers, bears, performing seals, and other circus and zoo creatures can be "alienated"—but not by their own kind.)

It is important here to underscore the centuries-old distinction between "work" and "labor."[3] Work—but *not* labor—means that which *directly* maintains life. It is seen by those who perform it as *useful,* and the decisions concerning it—what is done, and how and why and where and to whose benefit—as the worker's decisions. Thus it clearly applies to an era of self-sufficiency rather than to the highly specialized labor processes of industrialism. And although "work" more often than not has been difficult or harsh, the worker's dignity (whether "bold peasantry" or artisan or other) is thus maintained through his or her autonomy. However, insofar as loss of control over what "laborers" do is the main source of their alienation, it is conceivable that institutional changes democratizing the economic process could effectively provide morale to those who work for wages (among others).

Labor, in a sharp set of contrasts, is performed under another's direction and control, for wages (thus only indirectly maintaining life), producing something decided upon by another, as are the means, the conditions, the purposes, as is everything. Therefore, dignity is likely to be an early casualty.

"Work" in the pure sense noted above is rare indeed in societies as industrialized and as intricately specialized as ours, in which everything is, in some sense, mediated. The most skilled of workers and artists must shop, travel by commercial means, et cetera, et cetera. And among those who perform labor for others—notably among the highly trained (for example, doctors, musicians, writers, craftspeople)—there often remain substantial areas for their decisions, and the maintenance of some or even much dignity.

The processes of modern industrialization have had the ineluctable tendency to shrink the areas of work and expand those of labor. Harry Braverman's important study of the transformation of labor (and its "de-skilling") that took hold in the late nineteenth century shows that a main aim of "scientific management" has been to develop workplaces that are "foolproof." To spend a good portion of one's life doing work that fools can do cannot but have a corrosive effect on the meaning of that life.[4]

Smith always spoke of labor as "irksome," very much a euphemism given his belief that "the difference between . . . a philosopher and a common street porter . . . seems to arise not so much from nature, as from habit, custom and education . . . ; for the first six or eight years of their existence, they were, perhaps, very much alike."[5] However, he also said "the man whose whole life is spent performing a few simple operations . . . has no occasion to exert his understanding . . . and generally becomes as stupid and ignorant as it is possible for a human creature to become."[6]

What is striking about those views (and there are many variations on them in *The Wealth of Nations*) is that Smith held them but *nevertheless* enthusiastically proposed a social transformation guaranteeing that almost all workers would become laborers "performing a few simple operations." In its subsequent evolution, economics has never swerved from seeing labor as a "disutility" for those performing it. Unlike work, which can—and for our mental health must be fulfilling—labor *is* "irksome," a "disutility," although some who must perform it might use a more colorful term.[7]

As the twentieth century ends, the landscapes of work and labor seem to darken with each day. For most, the quality of jobs deteriorates; rates of joblessness are almost everywhere on the rise.[8] That statement is really appalling, especially because the awfulness has two sides: (1) After all, what most people *now* do "for a living" usually results in low job satisfaction *and* lower incomes, along with (not the same thing) increasing bitterness and multiplying frustrations. In the same process (2) our capabilities, our creative and constructive possibilities, the often profound joys of learning to do good work and doing it (farming, carpentering, nursing, teaching, printing, and so on), both despite and because of galloping new technologies, are lost for more and more people, and (Goldsmith again) "when once destroyed, can never be supplied." Along with twentieth-century genocides, racism, and ecological damages, that dehumanization of production has been a major (if unintended) crime of our civilization, a waste of humanity, a form of living death.

Along with those human and social distortions has been the creation of "consumerism" as, in effect, an ersatz way of life for that large majority who "can't get no satisfaction" from their work lives. That the consumerism of so many can only be sustained by piling debt upon debt must also decrease whatever satisfaction their purchases might bring.

In addition to the social infantilism that consumerism feeds and ultimately depends upon, it also produces a set of economic processes that are quite simply unsustainable in ecological terms (as will be discussed in Chapter 8) or, because of consumerism's direct dependence upon always-rising consumer debt, portentous of disaster in economic terms.[9]

Now we turn to an appraisal of qualitative and quantitative deterioration among both the employed and the jobless. In the concluding chapter I will touch upon means for slowing or reversing that descent; though such means are markedly better than nothing, they leave much more that is vital to be done. Immediate reforms in the structures of production and labor/work are needed and practical, but we must also work for a society that encourages and supports the constructive and creative best in us rather than, as now, diminishing both.

Work Versus Labor; Good Versus Bad Jobs; No Jobs Versus Unemployment

Statistics on unemployment were not systematically collected until the Depression of the 1930s. Of course there was unemployment before then, and "guesstimates" concerning it were made: For example, it was estimated that in the Britain of the 1920s unemployment never fell below 10 percent; for the same period in the United States, the estimates vary between 5 and 13 percent (in the "prosperity decade").[10]

The likely inaccuracy of those figures is understandable, relating as they do to a period when the collection of such data was casual at best. For the past six or seven decades that excuse no longer applies: The resources of our Department of Labor and its Bureau of Labor Statistics have been substantial since the 1930s; the inadequacies of our unemployment data remain and worsen, if in changed form.[11] The resistance to improving those data is not a matter of stubbornness, however, but of power and politics.[12]

Not only do those in power have the authority to define and announce data, the nature and scope of the "data collection problem" are such as to forestall others from doing much more than using available government data. Whether with respect to joblessness, poverty, pollution, or whatever, a major result is that such information "accentuates the positive": It requires no conspiracy theory to observe that bad news never helps those in charge, irrespective of party affiliation.

In the United States the starting point for determining unemployment is the official definition of "the labor force" because only those who are in the labor force can *be* employed *or* unemployed: One is in the labor force *only* if one has a (full- or part-time) paid job[13] or is *known* to be seeking one. If you have long sought a job and have finally given up looking, you may be among the "hard-core" *jobless* but you are not *unemployed*. Were those who have become discouraged and stopped looking counted, the unemployment rate would rise by at least a full percentage point; if you need, seek, and have been accustomed to full-time employment but now have a job working for as little as one *hour* a week, you are employed; if you have been a skilled steelworker (with all that means in money wages and benefits) but are now a part-time temp flipping burgers at the minimum wage with *no* benefits and want and need a full-time job—all that is to be regretted, but officially you are *employed.*

Decade after decade after World War II, the average official unemployment rate has risen:

> A survey of the past half-century discloses a disturbing trend. In the 1950s the average unemployment for the decade stood at 4.5 percent. In the 1960s unemployment rose to an average of 4.8 percent. In the 1970s it rose again to 6.2 percent, and in the 1980s it increased again, averaging 7.3 percent for the decade. In the first three years of the 1990s, unemployment has averaged 6.6 percent.[14]

Until the Reagan administration, those in the armed forces were not *in* the labor force; since then they have been: in increasing the size of the labor force by definition, that also reduced the official rate of unemployment—but not the number without jobs—by definition. (Sly folks that those definers are, for a number of years after this change, the data were presented both with and without the armed forces; now there's only one figure, with the armed forces included.)

As the European Common Market moved toward becoming the European Union, it also had to standardize one thing and another, among them, the measure of unemployment. In ways that would be surprising here, European countries provide larger and longer-lasting unemployment benefits. Businesses and economists in the United States, not consulting available data, say that if unemployment benefits are enhanced, people won't even try to get work. In fact, Sweden, the country with the highest benefits and longest entitlement period, also has the shortest average time on compensation.

As noted in Chapter 3, the average official rate of unemployment in the European Union is now over 11 percent and slowly rising: Germany, the healthiest of the group, saw its rate rise from 9.3 in early 1995 to 12.2 percent in 1997; with a recession under way, that rate is unlikely to decrease. Hardest hit have been Eire and Spain, with rates wobbling around 15 and 20 percent. Were we to measure in the same fashion, our rate, instead of hovering between 5 and 6 percent, would be around 10 percent; if those with part-time but seeking full-time work were counted (they are not), the rate in 1996 would have been 12 percent.[15]

The foregoing applies only to rates of unemployment; there is much more to be said about wages and benefits. There is also more to be said about the qualitative deterioration of jobs for an already large and rising number of the workers. This requires a close look at the main current meaning of treating labor as a disposable commodity—to be bought, used a while, and thrown away.

The Downsizing of America

The "Downsizing of America" was the title of a book-length seven-day report in the *New York Times,* drawing negative comments from the worlds of both Big Government and Big Business—as well it might have, considering some of its conclusions:

1. Nearly three-quarters of all households have had a close encounter with layoffs since 1980. . . . In one-third of all households, a family member has lost a job, and nearly 40 percent more know a relative, friend or neighbor who was laid off.
2. One in 10 adults—or about 19 million people . . . acknowledged that a lost job in their household had precipitated a major crisis in their lives. . . .
3. While permanent layoffs have been symptomatic of most recessions, now they are occurring in the same large numbers even during an economic recovery that has lasted five years and even at companies that are doing well.
4. In a reversal from the early 80s, workers with at least some college education make up the majority of people whose jobs were eliminated, outnumbering those with no more than high school educations. And better-paid workers—those earning at least $50,000—account for twice the share of the lost jobs than they did in the 1980s.
5. There has been a net increase of 27 million jobs in America since 1979, enough to easily absorb all the laid-off workers plus the new people beginning careers, and the national unemployment rate is low. The sting is in the nature of the replacement work. . . . Labor Department numbers show that now only about 35 percent of laid-off full-time workers end up in equally remunerative or better-paid jobs.
6. Adjusted for inflation, the median wage is nearly 3 percent below what it was in 1979. Average household income climbed 10 percent between 1979 and 1994, but 97 percent of the gain went to the richest 20 percent.[16]

As the *NYT* study makes clear, even counting the hard-core and involuntary part-time and temporary workers would leave "unmeasured" the agony of those many millions who have a job but, by comparison with what they once had, a demeaning one—as it ignores also the "fear of falling" of those who have to wonder who's next.[17] It cannot be more than very cold comfort for those already afflicted to know that as time goes on, they are being joined by many others. The adage that misery loves company was not coined by those experiencing it.

But after all, aren't the companies doing the layoffs and downsizing just trying to keep going? In the long run, when you get right down to it, aren't they *saving* jobs? When you *do* get right down to it, the answer is a resounding NO:

☞ The American Management Association (no friend of workers), after a study in 1995, proclaimed[18] that "job cuts are no longer driven by market demand." Their data showed that over two-thirds of job cuts were due to "organizational restructuring"; that between 1988 and 1995, although association members dismissed 4 million workers, they did not do so "because demand for their products has weakened substantially." The man who supervised that study was trying to tell his bosses something when he said (earlier in the year[19]) that "what these companies have been doing since the mid-1980s is firing their customers."

☞ In addition to which, these same companies, the largest ones, utilize several times as many "supervisors" for a given workforce than other industrial nations, paying them higher wages than production workers, using "the stick strategy"—commands, threats of dismissal for presumed miscreant behavior, and the like, not the kind of atmosphere likely to produce a cooperative labor force. In comparison, the supervisors in Japan, Germany, Sweden, for example, "supervise" less and consult more. Hard to believe though it may be, supervisors in the United States begin by watching over only two to three workers. In an era of stagnant wages and falling benefits, this ever-expanding bureaucracy amounts to something worse than waste.[20]

☞ We may recall Alan Blinder's view (reported in Chapter 3) that the gains in exports and corporate profits in the decade 1985–1995 were mostly due to the devaluation of the dollar in those same years, the profits aided and abetted, of course, by the cheapening of labor.

Perhaps then the problem is that economic growth has been too slow? In 1995 the economy grew at 3.5 percent, a rate that rose in 1996, equal to the "healthy" average for the past century (excluding years of depression and war). In that same period, the stock market broke all records and corporate profits were generally strong. But did wages and benefits rise accordingly? No: After discounting for inflation, wages and salaries rose by 0.3 percent in 1995—the smallest amount on record—and business spending on health benefits *fell* by 0.1 percent. All this led Labor Secretary Robert Reich to comment that "there is something wrong with rising profits, rising productivity and a soaring stock market but employee compensation heading nowhere."[21]

It was worse than that for workers, for (as doubtless Reich knows) the *average* (arithmetic mean) for "wages and salaries" includes those of CEOs and other top incomes, which skews the number significantly upward. In 1978 the pay ratio of CEOs to average workers in the big companies was a hefty 60 to 1; by 1995 the ratio had soared to an average of 172.5 to 1 as compared to the Japanese ratio of 7 to 1.[22]

In 1994 average annual pay for all workers in companies with more than 25,000 employees was $20,000, approaching the poverty level for a family of four; for their CEOs it was $3,700,000.[23] Suppose we doubled the workers' pay, to $40,000, at best a comfort level. And suppose our CEOs had received twice instead of twelve times the ratio of their Japanese counterparts, $560,000 (that is, 14 to 1, instead of 172.5 to 1)? Would that have hurt the economy's efficiency or its purchasing power or its stability?

Examining the *median* wage (half above, half below, instead of the arithmetic average) shows workers' wages dropping by 2.3 percent for the year ending March 1995—the largest drop in the eight years the Labor Department has collected such figures. Moreover, Bradford de Long, an economic historian recently with the Treasury, said, "The drop might be the largest since the 1840s."[24] That drop came at the tail end of a fall of 6.3 percent in hourly wages, 1989–1995, for the typical male worker.

Layoffs rose rapidly from the late 1980s and continue: In 1995, layoffs rose 28 percent over those of 1994; 270,512, compared with 211,771—an amount 6 percent higher than the comparable period in 1993, the biggest job-loss year of the decade.[25] And two-thirds of those laid off, when they found another job, found one at lesser pay and benefits.[26]

Adding insult to injury, those who do lose their jobs are seldom viewed with either understanding or compassion. Marx argued that the jobless serve as "the reserve army of the unemployed," keeping wages down and workers weak. Others, more supportive of business means and ends, agree with Marx in principle if not with his stand when they view recessions as having a salutary effect on the "labor market."

In the United States the injury of unemployment is compounded, for unemployment compensation is "mingy" (that is, mean and stingy) in both amount and duration. We didn't even *have* unemployment compensation until 1935; it was provided for in the Social Security Act, gutted for families with dependent children in 1996, with more cuts on their way. In its original form it covered less than half the labor force (discriminating against women and blacks and others working in agriculture, restaurants, and as domestic servants, for example).

Why "mingy"? Originally, the coverage was limited to half the wage for a maximum of twelve weeks. (In Europe the rate goes as high as 85 percent and can last for an unlimited period.) Both amount and duration have varied since, from state to state and from time to time—rising from the 1950s into the 1970s, falling ever since. Recent congressional proposals indicate that the fall will continue, leaving only pittances in some states, nothing in others.

In addition to the overall slashing of social expenditures, the reason for the pessimism is the general diminution of federal power—that is, a "redelegation" of power to the separate states, as it was before the New Deal. The idea has a nice ring to it—decentralization, Jeffersonian democracy—but in the future it will likely mean what it meant before 1936. The separate states would *never* have provided for unemployment compensation (or other needed social reforms, in health, housing, education, women's and black voters' rights) without strong federal pressure.[27]

Since the 1930s the pressure has been applied, using both the carrots and sticks of fiscal policy. Take away the carrots and/or the sticks, and local powers and prejudices prevail—often using the customary reasoning that "if we do that, businesses will leave the state," which, as it happens, is not so. (The reasoning applies to block grants, welfare, Medicaid, and related measures, so the point will here be left at that, to be elaborated upon in Chapters 6 and 7.)

As this is written, the outlook for jobs is bleak, indeed, in all respects: availability, quality, wages, and benefits. All have been in decline, as noted; with most of the leading economies long in recession or "market softening," the deterioration of the job market is likely not only to continue (it does so in good times and bad), but also to accelerate. Along with that slide it may be expected that the power of organized labor will continue to be diminished. This process, which has been under way for several decades, and which has received considerable cooperation from politicians, is one of the reasons why it has been easy for workers to be given short shrift by business.[28]

We now take a longer look at these "qualitative" dimensions of the problems facing wage earners. That look can be kept mercifully brief because the processes have by now become all too familiar, intensified more and more by the intertwining of domestic with global processes.

The Whirling Dervishes
of the Global Economy

The earlier discussion of world trade and production noted that globalization was an outcome as much of possibilities as of needs, but needs there were and are. They began to be pressing in the 1970s as global excess capacities in almost everything became obvious. As had occurred in the emergence of the integrated world economy of the nineteenth century, new technologies combined with rising global competition to facilitate the growth of giant companies. The consequences of these developments both in the earlier and the present period have been numerous, some positive and some not.

A vital difference between the late-nineteenth- and late-twentieth-century global economies is that the former was associated with strengthening nation-states and the emergence of strong labor and socialist movements; in our time the opposite has been the case in both respects. Moreover, "big business" is much, much bigger: The giant corporations that began to form after the 1870s seem by comparison small business, as measured (in constant dollars) by assets, revenues, profits, employees, percentages of the market, and, not least in importance, their market and political power, whether to pursue their global or national aims—including the weakening of labor's powers.[29] Now let us look at some highlights showing both the absolute and relative dimensions of these mammoths (all data are for 1995):

- The Top 500 U.S. corporations had revenues of $4.7 trillion, up 9.9 percent from 1994; assets were $10.5 trillion, an increase of 9.7 percent; profits were $244 billion, up 13.4 percent; employees numbered 20 million, a rise of only 0.2 percent.
- The Top 500 global corporations (153 of which are U.S. companies) had revenues of $11.4 trillion, up 11.1 percent over 1994; assets were $32 trillion, up 4.2 percent; profits were $323 billion, up 14.7 percent; employees numbered 35 million—up only 1.8 percent.
- Companies are ranked according to revenues. No. 1 was Mitsubishi; though No. 4 in ranking, GM was No. 1 in profits (after taxes): $6.9 billion, a rise of 40 percent over 1994 and *20* times those of Mitsubishi ($346 million). Of the six Japanese companies in the Top 10 globals, only one (Toyota) had profits measured in the billions ($2.7); Ford's were $4 billion and EXXON's, $6.5 billion. Philip Morris, No. 31 globally, had profits of $5.5 billion, an increase of 15 percent, even though its revenues declined by 1.2 percent.
- For purposes of perspective, note that in 1995 the U.S. GDP was about $6 trillion. The global Top 10 (that's *ten*) had revenues (roughly equivalent to GDP) of $1.5 trillion—just about equal to Germany's GDP, half of Japan's, more than either Britain's or Italy's, a quarter of ours.
- The U.S. Top 500 collected about two-thirds of *all* business profits—the Top 10 garnering 30 percent of the 500's—and the roughly 15 *million* other businesses divided up the rest.

To hold back the tidal wave of globalization battering them, workers and unions would have had to undertake a major organizational effort while also placing strong pressures on their one-time ally, the Democratic Party, for support. The bell tolling had begun to ring as the 1970s began; it was heeded by too few in or outside of organized labor or their supporters. Those few warned that unions had to speed up organizing at home and to extend their efforts abroad, to become international in more than name. That was the only way to contend against the already pronounced strategy of corporations using their workers in one industrial nation against their workers in another. Damaging though that strategy was, it was mild compared with what took hold in the 1980s: using powerless workers in the poor countries to profit themselves and weaken the workers in the rich countries.

Perhaps a sufficient response by the unions was no longer possible; a high percentage of both union leaders and members seemed content to relax and enjoy the fruits of earlier struggles. Even worse, younger workers—whether unionized or not—had little or no knowledge of just how bitter (and necessary) the struggles had been even to *get* a union, and of unions' role in improving wages, working conditions, and benefits (in conjunction with a Democratic Party that *had* to respond to union pressures); no sense that eternal vigilance (to paraphrase) is necessary to defend social gains.

Unhappily, it must be added that all too often union leadership had become not only lazy but corrupt—playing footsie with the cold war and the bosses, cutting deals, and getting soft. (Someone remarked, after seeing a photo of the "suits" leaving a negotiating conference, how difficult it was to tell who was union and who was management. There would have been no such trouble in the 1930s.)

Thus, no meaningful effort to organize within, let alone across, national boundaries took place. The early 1970s predate the real drive toward using the cheapest labor in the world; then corporate policy was to allow, say, an auto plant in England to languish on strike while a branch in Germany took up the production slack. But business became always more bold as its union adversaries "turned the other cheek."

As the 1980s opened, continuing excess capacities were already fusing with technological and organizational changes, heating up TNC rivalries, which turned to the present mix: the cheapest labor with the most advanced technology. A process that had begun slowly in the 1970s was thus transformed into the headlong rush of recent years—a rush that business reporters expect to speed up over an indefinite period into the future. Considering what has already happened, there is a dark future ahead, and even worse if a recession occurs—which seems likely if the spending and tax cuts proposed in the United States and in Europe are even partially realized, as they surely will be.

☞ "U.S. Official Sees Risk of Deflation in Europe."[30] "Deflation" is a polite word for recession, as the article went on to make clear. The "official," Lawrence Summers (top economist in the Treasury) considers "Europe's slowdown a source of concern . . . and stressed that the priority now is maintaining recovery." But what he called a recovery cannot be "maintained," because it is already a "slowdown." The budget cuts required by the (currently faltering) Maastricht Treaty assure that the slowdown will become serious recession. What is slated for the European Union by Maastricht is almost certain for the United States, a gift from Congress; with the economy already slowing down (January 1996), the spending cuts to come will give it a hard downward shove.

The outlook for jobs is thus grim indeed. If the TNCs were busy at work downsizing and outsourcing *before* a market squeeze, what will they do *during* the squeeze? In addition to the pressures guided by opportunity, there will be those forced by need, and they will be more intense: pressures to lay off even more U.S. workers and replace them with even more desperately poor workers in Latin America, Asia, Africa, wherever; to cut back on already inadequate benefits; to push labor even further toward the wall.

We Can Do Better

"A mild recession is a normal and natural part of the capitalist economic process. The businesses that survive it usually come out stronger; the weaker ones go under—for the good of all, in the long run. Small businesses, farmers, workers, and the poor are hurt, but the hurt is usually temporary. With a recovery, the damage for all can and will be undone, in a newly expanding, stronger economy." That was the position of the economics profession a century ago and has become so once more, after some second thoughts occasioned by the depressed 1930s—thoughts (and Keynesian theory) accompanied by the development of integrated fiscal and monetary policies to contain recessions and inflations.

The government interventionism of those policies was seen as required because an advanced industrial capitalist economy left to itself can so easily go berserk—into depression or into a dangerous inflationary process. As suggested earlier, the combination of several decades without a serious depression and a steady growth in the power of business in state policymaking has revived support for "laissez-faire"—a free market economy, an economy left to itself, come what may. That position does not rest on the notion that nothing can ever go wrong with the economy; rather, it asserts that if something *does* go wrong, market forces will carry it out of the trouble: whether recession, unemployment, or other ill and that *any* governmental intervention would, now or later, make a bad situation worse.

This situation is very much the concomitant of what has come to be called the "winner take all economy"—an eerie revival of the outlook of the rich and powerful and comfortable during "the prosperity decade" of the 1920s. Unemployment was high, wages stagnant, important elements of the economy (staple agriculture, coal mining, the railroads, textiles) were in trouble, but the stock market was soaring and the rich were becoming very much richer.[31]

The horrendous depression that followed those years is unlikely to be repeated, assuming that enough has been learned about economic "prevention and cures" to slow down and halt any slide or collapse before it reaches such depths. There are already, however, far too many living desperately in this country (to say nothing about those in the poorer nations, also caught up in the swirling global economy). Although the official unemployment rate is low, the realities of unemployment and underemployment on a large and growing scale cannot be disputed—though they have been neglected.

The question then arises: Is it possible for there to be good jobs at a livable wage for all those who want such work? "Good" and "livable" are meant deliberately to suggest jobs that hold some promise for the worker, with a wage that, for a forty-hour week, keeps one out of poverty. "End welfare as we know it"? End it entirely, by ending poverty.

Much will be said of poverty and welfare in Chapter 6; here it is enough to assert that all but a very few of those now mired in poverty would enthusiastically become part of a jobs program of that sort. But wouldn't such a program be impossible? Hardly, for it has already been done once in the United States: the jobs program of the New Deal years. Nor can it be disputed that the skills and training essential for such a program would constitute a vital improvement not only in the lives of those directly affected but also in the well-being of the economy, over both the short and the long term.[32]

For anything like that to happen, it is necessary for the ways and means of our political life to change, for ordinary people to shape policies, rather than to continue to allow those at the top of the power pyramid, through bloated campaign contributions, lobbying, and the habitual steady pressure on legislation at all levels to set the direction of our socioeconomic life. Something of that sort is beginning to happen: Organized labor has begun to come back to life, reinvigorating existing unions, broadening their sweep at home and globally, and simultaneously organizing in hitherto untouched areas. At the same time, there has been a flowering of new parties, among them the Labor Party, the Green Party, the New Party. Although derided by the traditional parties and much of the electorate, their possibilities reside in the widespread unease in the country, an unease reflected in the fact that a majority of the electorate does not vote at all.

After one heart-breaking defeat after another (perhaps the worst was the agelong and lost struggle of the Caterpillar strikers), "Organized Labor Is Turning to New, Militant Leaders."[33] It will take more than that effort to save the wages, the working conditions, the benefits, the jobs of the ordinary people of our country, but without an effort of working people to increase their political power, there is little that can be achieved by others.

Organized labor in the past two generations has been in the forefront of almost every necessary and desirable social effort in this society (although some of its leadership and members have also been implicated in very much the opposite).[34] The rest of us cannot change the social process for the better without a vigorous labor movement, and labor cannot do without the rest of us. We are, after all, in the same boat. It's time we not only agree to that, but act on it.

The next chapter examines the inequalities of income and wealth exacerbated by the domestic and global doings of the U.S. economy over the past two decades or so. Political and economic changes beginning in 1947 brought with them a significant lessening of inequality; but now the degrees of inequality of income and wealth have returned, not to those of 1947, but even worse, to those of the 1920s. And there are depths below those depths likely to be plumbed.

5

Income and Wealth and Power and Poverty

The Name of the Game

Given the structures of socioeconomic power, struggles over the distribution of income and wealth are the main realm of conflicts between those who own and control capital on the one hand and the other social interests on the other. But the seemingly innocent phrase "given the structures of . . . power" must be put back in focus almost as soon as it has been taken out: *Changes* in the structures of income and wealth accompany, follow upon, and/or precede alterations in socioeconomic power structures; the three structures live in dynamic interaction with each other. Most generally, it may be said that the possession of wealth *bestows* power and *yields* rising income; the latter in turn feeds the acquisition of wealth—and more power. And round and round it goes.

Thus, the lessening of inequality of income and wealth in the 1960s both depended upon and produced alteration in the structures (and lessening of the concentration) of power. In one way or another after World War II, more "power to the people" was gained—and poverty was reduced. The increase in inequality of income and wealth in the years since the 1970s depended upon and facilitated a recapture of power at the top and a reduction of income, wealth, and power for the bottom four-fifths of families—and poverty increased.

What underlay those important changes has been barely touched upon earlier; it was embedded deeply in a complex historical process that combines politics, technology, and diverse socioeconomic developments at home and abroad. Here we limit ourselves to putting in view the changes in the distributions of income and wealth of recent decades, looking first at those patterns, then at some relationships between taxes and income shares, and conclude with an examination of the nature and extent of poverty in the United States. In sum, from 1973 to the present, there have been striking changes in all the foregoing respects, all of them bad news for a large majority of the population, all very good news indeed for those at the top of the triad of income, wealth, and power—especially the top 1–5 percent.

Them That Has, Gits

Figure 5.1 provides a quick view of what has happened to *income* distribution since 1960. Note that the 1960s was a period of income improvement for the bottom 40 percent of the population, increasing their *share* of the income pie (as national real income also grew at its highest rate); but that their betterment also ended with the 1960s. Since then it has been hard cheese for those in the bottom half, and smaller amounts of even that.

The top 5 percent had to settle for being plain wealthy until the 1980s: What had been a long flat period after 1960 for the top 5 percent, from Reagan's first year (changing the metaphor) shot into outer space while, in a connected process, the bottom 40 percent's share continued the steep descent that had taken hold as the 1970s began.[1]

The generalizations to follow (and the details set forth in the tables) point to growing inequality of incomes, the slow growth of incomes for the bottom four-fifths of the population, the good income growth for those in the top fifth, and the spectacular, even shocking rate of increase of those in the top 5 and 1 percent:

> The economic recovery of the 1980s was unusual in that the vast majority of Americans were, in many ways, worse off at the end of the recovery in 1989 than they were at the end of the 1970s.[2]

> Despite growth in both gross domestic product and employment between 1989 and 1994, median family income (in 1994 dollars) was $2,168 lower than it was in 1989, suggesting that overall growth does not, under current economic circumstances, lead to improved economic well-being for typical families.[3] The 1980s trend toward greater income inequality and a tighter squeeze on the middle class show clear signs of continuing in the 1990s.[4]

> The slow (or negative) rate of income growth after 1979 did not affect all families equally. The incomes of the top 5 percent rose 45.3 percent 1979–89 and another 4.9 percent 1989–94; the incomes of families in the bottom 95 percent fell in varying degree, 1989–94, those in the bottom 80 percent between 5.7 percent and 9.1 percent; the incomes of the top 1 percent rose a stunning 87.5 percent, 1979–89.[5]

57

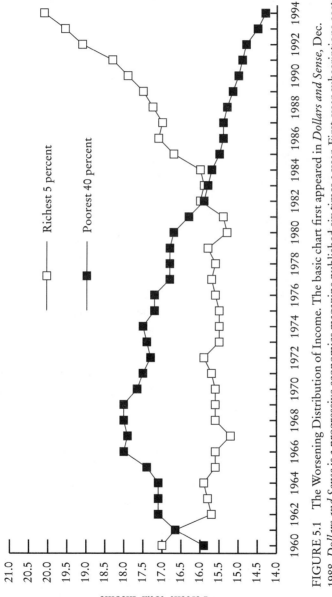

FIGURE 5.1   The Worsening Distribution of Income. The basic chart first appeared in *Dollars and Sense*, Dec. 1988. *Dollars and Sense* is a progressive economics magazine published six times a year. First-year subscriptions cost $18.95 and may be ordered by writing to *Dollars and Sense*, One Summer St., Somerville, MA 02143. The source of the post-1986 data, which gives the figure the apt appearance of widening crocodile jaws, is Lawrence Mishel, Jared Bernstein, and John Schmitt, *The State of Working America, 1996–97* (Armonk, N.Y.: M. E. Sharpe, 1997), p. 51.

The income share of the top 5 percent in 1994 (20.1 percent) was more than a third greater than that of the bottom 40 percent (14.2 percent).[6]

The income of the typical American family grew slowly or declined after 1979, despite the fact that the number of families with multiple jobs rose in those same years to almost half, compared to less than a third in 1967.[7]

A major reason for the growth of those family incomes that did rise is that a greater share of our national income has been in the form of capital incomes; their fast growth is primarily due to strong growth in interest payments . . . caused by high real interest rates.[8] Two-thirds of the value of all stock—which has risen at record-breaking rates over the past decade—is owned by the wealthiest 10 percent; the capital incomes of the top 1 percent doubled, 1979–1989.[9] Such figures make it easy to understand the great pressure for abolition of the capital-gains tax (even though it more than halved in those same years).

Unsurprisingly, then, inequality in 1989 was greater than in 1947[10]; in 1989–1994, it worsened further.[11]

Certainly among the most astounding changes in income distribution in our entire history is the next of the items in this regressive development, summarizing what happened at the very highest income levels:

Within the upper fifth, the top 5 percent gained a greater share of income, while the remaining 15 percent saw their share of total income decline. The unbalanced income growth of the 1980s thus caused the bottom 95 percent of the population to lose income to the upper 5 percent . . . [and] the upper 1 percent of families increased their share of income from 9.4 percent in 1980 to 13 percent in 1989.[12]

And the dervish has yet to stop his whirling, as shown by the details of inequality behind those conclusions, tables showing: (1) *shares* (percentages), (2) *dollar* amounts and ratios between various income groups, and (3) the *growth* of incomes.

Among other unsettling data in Table 5.1 are those showing the *decline* in income shares of the bottom four-fifths of the population—200 million people—when compared with the *rise* of the top fifth, and especially the top 5 percent. Table 5.2 shows dollar amounts (not shares) for the top 5 and bottom 80 percent. Keep in mind that the numbers are *averages* within each category, and that such averages conceal the even greater disparities between the top and bottom that Table 5.3 will reveal. The data in Table 5.2 show the richest 5 percent in 1947 as having $4.90 of income for every $1 received by the bottom four-fifths of the population; by 1967 inequality had lessened to a ratio of $4.10 to $1, but since 1979 inequality has grown and in 1989 it was *worse* than 1947. Current developments in the political economy are unlikely to decrease inequality; if anything, the opposite will occur.

TABLE 5.1   Shares of Family Income Going to Various Income Groups and to
Top 5 Percent, 1947–1993

| | | | | *Income Share Going to:* | | | | |
| | | | | | | | Breakdown of Top Fifth | |
Year	Lowest Fifth	Second Fifth	Middle Fifth	Fourth Fifth	Top Fifth	Total	Bottom 15%	Top 5%
1947	5.0%	11.9%	17.0%	23.1%	43.0%	100.0%	25.5%	17.5%
1967	5.5	12.4	17.9	23.9	40.4	100.0	25.2	15.2
1973	5.5	11.9	17.5	24.0	41.1	100.0	25.6	15.5
1979	5.2	11.6	17.5	24.1	41.7	100.0	25.9	15.8
1989r[*]	4.5	10.6	16.5	23.7	44.7	100.0	26.8	17.9
1992r[*]	4.3	10.5	16.5	24.0	44.7	100.0	27.1	17.6
1993r[*]	4.2	10.1	15.9	23.6	46.2	100.0	27.1	19.1
Point Change								
1979–89	−0.9	−1.1	−1.0	−0.1	3.0	0.0	1.2	1.8
1989–93	−0.1	−0.4	−0.6	−0.4	1.5	0.0	0.0	1.5

[*]r indicates revision using 1990 census weights.
Source: Lawrence Mishel and Jared Bernstein, *The State of Working America, 1994–95* (Armonk, N.Y.: M. E. Sharpe, 1995), p. 36, based on U.S. Bureau of the Census data.

TABLE 5.2   Average Income of the Top 5 Percent Compared with the Bottom
80 Percent for 1947–1989 (1989 dollars)

Year	Average Family Income for Families in the:		Ratio of Average Income of Top 5% to Average Income of Bottom 80%
	Top 5%	Bottom 80%	
1947	60,701	12,357	4.9
1967	89,274	21,915	4.1
1973	109,131	25,919	4.2
1979	118,249	27,317	4.3
1989	148,591	28,743	5.2
Change, 1979–89			
Level ($)	+ 30,343	+ 1,426	21.3
Percent	+ 25.7	+ 5.2	4.9

Source: Lawrence Mishel and David Frankel, *The State of Working America, 1990–91* (Armonk, N.Y.: M. E. Sharpe, 1991), p. 18.

An examination of either the dollar or the percentage figures in Table 5.3 is not merely striking but shocking—especially as regards the top 1 percent. That those already very rich in 1979—with average incomes of $279,122—almost doubled their incomes between then and 1989 (to $523,499), whereas the incomes of the bottom 20 percent of people fell 3.4 percent in those ten years and another 5.7 percent in the five years 1989–1994 is one of the more dramatic repercussions of the policies carved out from the Reagan years to the present. Such contrasts between those best-off more than 2 million Americans becoming much more so while the more than 50 million of their fellow citizens already poor becoming still poorer raise disturbing questions about the nature and direction of our society. Among these questions is, What is it that drives those who are very rich to amass more wealth? Consider that "the average income *gain* of the richest one percent of families in the 1980s is nearly double the average income *level* of the next best-off [and also very rich] 4 percent of the population and is more than 5 times the average family income in 1990."[13] Here the figures have taken into account transfer payments for those at the bottom. That redistribution of income *upwards*, increasing already great inequality, was the predictable outcome of the slowed economy of the 1970s combined with the high military spending, corporate outsourcing and downsizing, and the Malthusian social policies of the 1980s.

Such an examination of income *growth* brings into focus a generalization relating changes in the *level* of the national income to changes in its *distribution*. When economic expansion causes the national income to rise, the biggest *absolute* gainers are naturally those with the highest shares: 10 percent of a bigger pie is of course larger than 1 percent of that same larger pie. In addition to that simple arithmetic of change, those at the top, with their ability to expand their incomes through their income-earning assets, have their fortunes—and incomes—enhanced even more through the economy's successes. On top of all else, the rich grow richer because they are in a strategic position to take advantage of the increased opportunities of expansion.

Table 5.3 also shows that the *absolute gap* between the top 5 percent and bottom 20 percent (in constant dollars) widened from $156,377 in 1979 to $244,489 in 1994, and that the gap between the top 1 percent and the top 20 percent widened from $269,034 to $444,000.

Before looking at the *incomes* of the rich any further, let us turn to Table 5.4 for data on *wealth*, the basis for most very high incomes (with exceptions for those in medicine, law, sports, and entertainment whose high incomes initially derive from their services—and then, also from acquired financial assets).

Wealth measures the sale value of possessions and property. Almost everyone owns something of value (an auto, a home), but the society's income-producing assets, the most vital of which are stocks and bonds, are owned by

TABLE 5.3   Income Growth by Fifth and Among Top Fifth, 1979–1994
(1994 dollars)

	Average Family Income			Percent Change	
	1979	1989	1994	1979–89	1989–94
Average	$45,464	$51,664	$49,883	13.6%	–3.4%
Lowest fifth	10,088	9,741	9,181	–3.4	–5.7
Second fifth	24,527	24,224	22,010	–1.2	–9.1
Middle fifth	38,254	39,031	35,669	2.0	–8.6
Fourth fifth	53,775	57,914	54,287	7.7	–6.3
Top 80–90%	72,210	81,055	77,320	12.2	–4.6
Top 90–95%	91,816	105,674	104,757	15.1	–0.9
Top 95–99%	138,301	171,465	n.a.	24.0	n.a.
Top 1%	279,122	523,449	n.a.	87.5	n.a.
Top 5%	166,465	241,862	253,670	45.3	4.9

Source: Lawrence Mishel, Jared Bernstein, and John Schmitt, *The State of Working America, 1996–97* (Armonk, N.Y.: M. E. Sharpe, 1997), p. 60.

TABLE 5.4   Percent Distribution of Wealth and Income, 1983 Shares of Total

Family Income Group	Net Financial Assets (%)	Net Worth (%)	Income (%)
Upper 2 percent	54	28	14
Next 8 percent	32	29	19
Bottom 90 percent	14	43	67

Source: Lawrence Mishel and David Frankel, *The State of Working America, 1990–91* (Armonk, N.Y.: M. E. Sharpe, 1991), p. 152.

a very small percentage of the population. (As noted earlier, two-thirds of the value of stock are owned by the top 10 percent of households.)

It is also important to note that the considerably greater inequality of wealth than of income distribution (see Table 5.4) is directly connected to an unequal distribution of political power. The wealthy are strategically positioned to affect policies that will enhance their wealth and, with that same power, to neutralize any redistributive income and wealth effects of governmental income, estate, and inheritance taxes.

Table 5.4 shows data for 1983. According to more recent studies, between 1983 and 1989 "the distribution of wealth become significantly more concentrated, and the already limited wealth of the bottom 40 percent fell even further."[14] Beginning in 1975, the United States began to surpass Great Britain as the nation with the largest gap between rich and poor *and* the largest share of private wealth owned by the richest 1 percent of the population. In both respects, the gap has increased substantially ever since.[15]

Given recent tendencies for changes in our political economy to favor the wealthy, most especially those operating in the financial sector, the inequalities for "net financial assets" have of course risen substantially. In 1995 economist Paul Krugman commented on that process: "It's not just that the top 20 percent have gotten richer compared with the rest. The top 5 percent have gotten richer compared with the next 15 percent; the top 1 percent have gotten richer compared with the next 4 percent, and there is pretty good evidence that the top 0.25 percent has gotten richer compared with the next 0.75 percent."[16]

The 1980s were a decade of startling changes in wealth and debt—both rising substantially, the former accumulating mostly at the top, the latter mostly toward the bottom:

> In the 1980s, the financial assets owned primarily by the wealthy grew considerably, while tangible assets, which are spread out more evenly, increased only slightly. This caused the distribution of wealth to become yet more unequal. . . . [The] average net worth of the richest 0.5 percent of families rose 6.7 percent between 1979 and 1989, while the average net worth of families in the bottom 90 percent actually fell by 8.8 percent. This means that the gap in overall financial security between the rich, on the one hand, and the middle class and the poor, on the other, has widened ever further. In addition, there has been a striking increase in the wealth gap between older and younger families.[17]

The growth of wealth was confined to the privileged; debt growth was more democratic:

> Household debt has skyrocketed in recent years. Two measures of the total debt burdens of households—debt as a percent of assets and as a percent of personal income—have each grown steadily since at least 1973 . . . [leaving] families more vulnerable whenever the economy weakens. Household debt leapt from 64.0 percent of personal income in 1979 to 83.9 percent in 1994, and from 13.5 percent of household assets in 1979 to 16.9 percent in 1994.[18]

Moreover, "the lowest fifth of families had an average yearly debt payment of 24 percent of income in 1970 . . . [and] 34 percent in 1983, while burdens among upper income families actually fell off slightly."[19] Even after all that has preceded, what is shown on Table 5.5 will be hard to comprehend: the growth of the very, *very* rich in the 1980s—involving, of course, only a tiny fraction of 1 percent of the population.

Kevin Phillips provides a look at the same development, using his own measures—"millionaires, decamillionaires, centimillionaires and billionaires"— and informs us that (1) in 1981 there were 600,000 millionaires and twice that

TABLE 5.5 Number and Rate of U.S. Millionaires, According to Tax Returns, 1968–1988

	Number of Tax Returns Declaring Income over $1 Million	Rate Per Million Returns (adjusted for inflation)
1968	1,122	51
1978	2,092	41
1985	17,312	186
1987	34,994	338
1988	65,303	595

Source: Andrew Hacker, "Class Dismissed," *New York Review of Books*, March 7, 1991, Table C. Reprinted with permission from *The New York Review of Books*. Copyright © 1991 Nyrev, Inc.

many in 1987; (2) in 1985 there were 38,855 decamillionaires and almost triple that in 1988; (3) there were 400 centimillionaires in 1982 but 1,200 by 1988; and (4) billionaires had increased from 13 in 1982 to 51 by the time Reagan left the White House. Reagan had succeeded at the task he set for himself, which was to make the United States "a place in which you can get rich."[20]

Nothing wrong with that, perhaps, unless it means that increased wealth for 1 percent or so is part of a basket of policies making for the increased poverty of some large multiple of that. The official poverty rate in 1973 was 11.1 percent and in 1979 it was 11.7 percent; but in 1983 it was 15.2 percent, 12.8 percent in 1989, 14.2 percent in 1991—and rising. Those—as we shall see, understated—numbers and much more concerning poverty will be discussed in more detail shortly.

Part of the conventional wisdom—and the heart of "supply-side economics" theorizing and policy recommendations—is that taxes are too high on those who do the savings that finance the investment that makes the economy grow, and thus the taxes thwart a process that is good for all. Whatever else is wrong with that reasoning, two problems stand out: (1) In the 1980s, when such an economics dominated our tax policy and federal taxes on top incomes fell markedly, both savings and productive investment also fell; (2) income taxes on individuals and on corporations in the United States are the lowest of all industrialized countries, and the U.S. growth rate (1980–1987) was lower than many countries with higher taxes.[21]

In order to evaluate such positions more fully, we will first look at *pre*-tax income shares and then go on to data on *after*-tax income shares and on the relatively high tax burden for *lower* income groups.

Table 5.6 is derived from the work of Joseph Pechman (of the Brookings Institution), who was probably the most respected of tax economists. It examines the situation of the top 5 percent from 1952 to 1986. The conclusions Pechman drew from those data are worth quoting at length:

TABLE 5.6   Before-Tax Income Shares (in percent)

Year	Top 1% of Tax Units	Top 2% of Tax Units	Top 5% of Tax Units
1952	8.7	12.1	18.7
1963	8.8	12.3	19.4
1967	8.8	12.3	19.6
1972	8.0	11.4	18.7
1977	7.8	11.3	18.9
1981	8.1	11.5	19.0
1986	14.7	18.2	26.6

Source: Joseph Pechman, *Tax Reform, The Rich and the Poor* (Washington, D.C.: Brookings Institution, 1989), p. 20.

First, between 1952 and 1981 the very rich in the United States did not enjoy larger increased incomes, as defined in the tax code, than the average income recipient. Since 1981, their share of total income has been rising sharply, indicating that their incomes have been rising much faster than the average. Part of this increase reflects a large increase in capital gains, but salaries at the top have also been rising faster than the average. . . . Clearly, this improvement in the income shares of the top 15 percent could come only at the expense of the lower 85 percent.[22]

After noting that after 1979 and even more after 1984 when unemployment compensation and Social Security benefits first became taxable, Pechman added: "Thus, the lower [income] classes have not been able to hold their own in the private economy; even the large increases in government transfer payments did not prevent an erosion of their income shares."

The taxes just discussed have been principally federal *income* taxes (individual and corporate). Their degree of progressivity, although low in the United States, is considerably higher than that of state and local taxes. Thus, in 1991, "the richest 1 percent—average 1991 family income: $875,000—pay 7.6 percent of their income in state and local taxes. . . . The poorest 20 percent, earning $12,700, pay 13.8 percent."[23]

In their table on "The Effects of Tax and Income Changes on After-Tax Income Shares, 1977–96," Mishel, Bernstein, and Schmitt show that for 1977–1989, the bottom four-fifths *lost* 5.2 percent in their share, whereas the top fifth *gained* an equal increase, 5.2 percent, in their share; and the top 1 percent—generally perceived to be highly taxed, had a net gain of 4.6 percent. In the years 1989–1996, there was no change in after-tax income shares for either the bottom four-fifths or the top fifth, but the top 1 percent dropped one-tenth of 1 percent.[24]

In 1995, the very year that our government—all branches, all levels— was undertaking further moves in the direction of the "free market," dismantling an already very flimsy social net, one news story or academic study after another announced that the United States had the highest income and wealth inequalities of any industrialized nation, with the gap between rich and poor widening rapidly, while—part of the same process—taxes on high incomes, on capital gains, and on estate and inheritance were declining.

It was, of course, practicing the ideology of the free market—a euphemism for letting come what may—that allowed median wages to fall and top incomes to rise: Between 1979 and 1995 the median male worker's wages dropped 11.5 percent, from an already modest $31,000 to a mean $27,000.[25] It was the free market that led 55 percent of all women with children under two years of age to get jobs, compared with 31 percent twenty years ago. It was the free market that allowed housing costs for the median family to rise from 23.4 to 31.6 percent of annual income, and house prices to double (in real terms), the cost of utilities to rise from 5.6 to 7.8 percent, health care costs to rise from 4.3 to 6.7 percent.[26] Put differently, only governmental intervention under popular pressure could have *prevented* those costs from rising while in the same years money wages were dropping—and at the same time, the free market pushed the *average* yearly compensation of the CEOs of 424 corporations to $3.7 million.

A recent study estimates that *half* of the growth of inequality between the top fifth and the bottom four-fifths since 1973 can be attributed to the weakening of unions. It has long been understood that if a third (let us say) of workers are organized into strong unions, those who are *not* in unions will also benefit. And *that's* why unions are the interference with the free market most dreaded and opposed by business: Not only do unions bring improved wages, working conditions, and benefits for workers, they lead to increased *power* for workers and reduce that of their employers—a leveling of the playing field, to use a faddish expression.

The past twenty years or so have seen an extraordinary upsurge in the wealth and power of giant corporations and the rich. Those same years have seen close to a fifth of the U.S. population left or pushed into poverty— some for the first time, some pushed back from having recently wriggled out, some never having had a chance to make their way out. Lincoln Steffens wrote a famous book around the turn of the century—still worth reading— called *The Shame of the Cities;* were he to write it today he would have to call it *The Shame of the Nation.* We now examine the who, the what, and the why of poverty in the United States.

Malthus Lives

Published chronologically between the seminal works of Smith and Ricardo was another enormously influential book, one by the Reverend Thomas

Robert Malthus (1766–1834). Unlike them, Malthus opposed industrialization, but his arguments against what we now call "the safety net" helped speed the new system on its way.

His book's disarming title was *An Essay on the Principle of Population as It Affects the Future Improvement of Society* (1798). The influence of Malthus's book, like Smith's and Ricardo's, was greatest in Britain and the United States; after waxing and waning over time, again like Smith's and Ricardo's, its influence has now returned in full force.

Malthus was very different in aims from Smith and Ricardo but quite similar in spirit to those who now bring his policies back to life. However, living at a time when media guile was neither necessary nor possible, Malthus was also considerably more straightforward than today's despisers of the poor: "Instead of recommending cleanliness to the poor, we should encourage contrary habits. In our towns we should make the streets narrower, crowd more people into the houses, and court the return of the plague."[27]

Malthus was an articulate and fervent opponent of industrialization. Warning against both population and economic gluts (later called depressions), he sought in his writings (including a marathon correspondence lasting many years with Ricardo) to turn back *all* the swift currents of modernity flooding toward England from the industrial, French, and American revolutions, each in its way threatening to engulf the economic, political, and social traditions of the agrarian world he prized.

As for the poor, why did Malthus see them with such a steely eye, such a cold heart? One reason was that he was born into the landed gentry and in accord with the "Great Poor Law" of Elizabethan origin his parish (and all others) was obligated to provide food and shelter for its poor (then meaning what we call the unemployed). As the eighteenth century was ending, attempts to amend or abolish the Poor Laws were matters of heated debate: As a result of the Enclosure Movement (which, in "modernizing" agriculture, pushed hundreds of thousands off the land), the parishes of England were awash with countless numbers of "poor"—much like the homeless today—the sturdy yeomen whose "decay" Oliver Goldsmith lamented in his poem "The Deserted Village."

Like those today who, consciously or not, follow in his footsteps, Malthus was much disinclined to have parish "taxes" paid to support the unwashed. He thought it was better to castigate them, to see them as not quite human; or better still, to develop a scientific analysis. He "proved" that because food supplies increase only arithmetically and population grows geometrically, keeping all those licentious (as he saw them) people alive "artificially" would lead them to multiply and not only do themselves in, but all others as well. What might sound cruel, Malthus argued, was a form of benevolence or, as we say now, "tough love."

As has been noted earlier, though population has risen greatly, food supplies have *always* risen faster.[28] There are many reasons to wish to see global population growth slow down, cease, and reverse itself; but—assuming that to be a laudable aim—Malthusian policies, far from contributing to that end, make it unrealizable. The best, perhaps the only, way to slow down population growth is by the spread of education and well-being: *That's* what the facts since 1798 have shown.[29]

Just as Smith can't be faulted for not seeing that industrialization would render his policies atavistic, neither can Malthus be blamed for failing in 1798 to understand the population/productivity effects of industrialization over the next century. Ignorance of what the future will be is close to impossible to overcome; ignorance of the past is less pardonable, especially when there is concern for the present. In that respect not so much Malthus as his current disciples have much to answer for.

Malthus did not content himself with making abstract analyses about arithmetic this and geometric that; he also advocated measures that would break up and punish the families of the poor. His ideas became an integral part of the "Reform Bills" of the early 1830s—laws that took children from their parents (and placed them in factories and mines) and that separated husbands from wives and placed both in "workhouses" (really jails in which one had to work without pay).

Then as now, the word *reform* was the sheep's clothing used to disguise wolfish policies: Thus, the major effective 1996 "reform" of the Social Security Act of 1935 was the abolition of the provision for aid to families with dependent children. The requirement that "workfare" replace welfare flies in the face of a reality that does not and cannot supply the requisite number of jobs, let alone jobs at incomes above the poverty line; and that is by no means the worst of what the law means.[30]

In the first half of the nineteenth century, reform meant unspeakable hardships for innumerable people—relieved only after decades of social misery for a good half of Britain's population. The relief came with the rapid economic development of the new industrialization. Even so, real wages for the average English worker did not even approach acceptable levels until the final decade of the century—and that because the triumph of British imperialism had shifted some of the burden of exploitation to the colonies.[31]

By comparison with our time, two points stand out: (1) rather than in the adolescence of industrialization, we are in a world where muscled TNCs contend with each other for sales over a globe marked by excess capacities in almost all industries; (2) the outsourcing of production to the "developing countries" has already had the effect of *reducing,* not increasing, the real wages of workers in the industrialized nations—while providing starvation wages to those in the poor countries—in a process of global wage deterioration whose bottom has yet to be reached. As with Malthusians in the past, today's reformers are silent concerning the terrible damage this will do to men and women and, most of all, to children, close attention to which will be given in Chapter 6.

Enough of the Reverend Malthus; now our focus turns to the realities of poverty in the United States—its dimensions, its spread and deepening, its causes and consequences. These realities have led to what ranks high among the most shameful episodes in a history that has never lacked for them.

Poverty in the Midst of Plenty

Like other nations, ours tends to see itself as "the fairest of them all," requiring only that we ignore or deny the uglier sides of our reality. Except for an attentive few, that aloofness has always extended to the matter of poverty, as noted long ago and well by Michael Harrington (in *The Other America*, 1962) when he spoke of "the invisible poor."

At the very moment when we were seeing ourselves as "the affluent society" (the title, perhaps ironic, of a 1958 book by J. K. Galbraith), 35 million of our people were living below the official poverty line (as determined in 1964), 20 percent of the population—a percentage lowered significantly in the next decade or so, but toward which we have recently retrogressed.

Earlier, the foolishness of thinking about socioeconomic problems in only quantitative terms was noted; but when those terms are used, their definitions should be accurate and meaningful. The definition of the poverty line set in 1964 was a far remove from such standards, in a manner defying good sense.

Lyndon Johnson had just become president, the Vietnam war was escalating, there was a mounting civil rights and antipoverty movement, and LBJ wished to be known as a liberal leader taking us to his "Great Society"—including a "war on poverty." Although poverty was by no means new in the United States by 1964, it had never been "defined" officially (like unemployment in 1930); LBJ asked his aides to arrive at such a definition.

The resulting definition was—as is our custom regarding social problems—a number: A family of four with less than $3,000 per year was declared as poor. That number in turn was derived from the Social Security Administration's figure, which had been obtained from the Office of Civil Defense, for "a deficiency diet for temporary or emergency use," in turn defined as "a post–nuclear attack period." No comment. (The SSA figure was actually $3,165, based on the estimated cost of food times three; and then rounded off.)[32]

Since then, the number has been adjusted upward—to $15,569 for a family of four in 1995, $12,158 for a family of three—to accord with subsequent inflation, assuming that nothing but prices have changed over more than thirty years. In fact much has changed, most important the cost of housing for the poor, now estimated to equal two-thirds of their expenditures, not, as in 1964, one-third. That change means, of course, that there is less for anything *other* than housing. It is worth adding that "a panel of poverty experts under the aegis of the National Research Council . . . found that changes in consumption, work patterns, taxes, and government benefits all suggested the need for an updated measure of poverty.... [These had the effect of] raising poverty rates by 3.6 percentage points in 1992 (the year on which the panel focused)."[33]

Before discussing the *non*quantitative "definitions" of poverty, let it be noted that already in 1975 the figure of $3,000 (adjusted for inflation to about $10,000) was deemed by the Bureau of Labor Statistics to be just about *one-half* of the amount needed to allow a "*minimum* budget for food, clothing, and housing, with little left over" (emphasis added).

A popular view among those who scorn the poor is that people "remain in" poverty deliberately, and that welfare recipients find that condition preferable to any other they might be able to achieve. Taking only numbers into consideration, that would be a barely credible view. When one considers the larger meanings of poverty, it is an outrageous distortion of what poverty means to the poor.

To be poor is to live in inadequate housing in overcrowded neighborhoods with bad schools and few or no recreational facilities; to be mired down in an atmosphere of hopelessness, of enduring agony over one's children, of poor health, rampant crime, price-gouging in local stores, job discrimination, political underrepresentation, police brutality, and constant insults—not least in the local welfare office. The emotional, psychological— and physical—impact of such conditions can only be imagined (or read about) by those who have not experienced them directly; but it takes little imagination to perceive that for those who are born poor the compounding difficulties of poverty are likely to keep them poor and to have children who will be poor—with here and there a rare and heroic exception.[34]

In the years since World War II, there have always been 10–20 percent of our people living in poverty—in its official understatement. It is a daring society indeed that depends upon singularly exceptional youngsters to save it from the catastrophe implied by such "numbers."[35]

If one stands back from all this to reflect, one asks oneself, Why, in a rich society like the United States, would poverty for tens of millions of people exist and, once revealed, persist? Why would it be, as it has in effect been, institutionalized? In Chapter 1 we saw it useful to ask about such matters: Who benefits? Who pays?

Reasonably decent people's immediate response would be that, well, *nobody* benefits, although quite clearly the poor pay (except for those who fantasize about "welfare queens"). The poor do "pay," of course; and less obviously and less painfully, so do most of the rest of us. But who benefits?

The Beneficence of Poverty

The sociologist Herbert Gans, in his analysis of what he calls "the uses of poverty," has provided some plausible answers to that question, expressed in terms of the functional (as contrasted with *dys*functional) consequences of poverty:[36]

- Poverty means that the society's "dirty work" will be done and, a somewhat different point,
- Low wages for the poor subsidize many activities benefiting the affluent (maids, etc.).
- The poor pay a disproportionate share of (non-income) taxes.
- Jobs for many middle-income people depend upon the existence of poverty (social workers, prison guards, etc.).
- The poor buy shoddy goods others will not buy.

Those are some economic uses of poverty, but there are other uses:

- Those not poor can indulge in a self-defined elevation of their own moral and social standing—not unimportant in a society as concerned with appearances as ours.
- The poor absorb more than their share of socioeconomic change: pushed aside for freeways, urban renewal, etc.
- They also provide more than their share of cannon fodder.
- Subtly, but increasingly obvious these days, the poor are useful in the arguments against liberal social change.

The Facts of Poverty

Books have been written and more need to be written about poverty; here I must be brief. However, it is worth reminding readers that the measurements used in the United States—in ways going beyond those already noted—are systematically understated by comparison with Western Europe.

It is common in Europe to designate as "poor . . . those persons in families with adjusted incomes below 0.5 median adjusted income." Applying that to the United States shows that in 1991 we had (1) the most "poor": 16.6 percent of all persons (Canada at 12.3 and Britain at 11.7 were the next highest; Germany, Sweden, and Norway were the lowest, at 4.9, 5.0, and 4.8, respectively) and (2) the highest percentage of "well-to-do" ("persons in families with adjusted incomes above 1.5 times the median"), with 22.1 percent. For 1993 the adjusted rate was 18.4 percent poor.[37]

As we now examine some of the changing data on poverty, it may be noted that the percentage of children in poverty—to which special attention will be paid in the next chapter—is high and rising. Whatever other rage one may sustain against impoverishment, it is difficult to see why children—incontestably innocent of any cause for their own condition—should be left to such a terrible fate, even were it true (and it's not) that those who are poor have only themselves to blame, being lazy, shiftless, and, as Malthus saw them, sexually promiscuous.[38]

The Arithmetic of Misery

The data to follow are derived once more from *The State of Working America, 1996–97*, this time from chapter 6, whose arresting title is "Poverty: High Rates Persist Despite Overall Growth." Here are some of its findings, quoted directly and at some length:

> The recent debate over poverty has become misguided. The conventional wisdom typically defines the problem in terms of the supposedly counterproductive behavior of poor people themselves, implying that, with more effort, the poor could lift themselves up by their bootstraps; . . . that, because of bad choices about family structure and lack of work effort, the poor have failed to be lifted by the rising economic tide.
>
> [But], when we examine the perceived problem of female-headed family formation, or the question of whether welfare programs have created incentives that increase poverty, or explore the issue of whether the poor choose not to work, we find that the data do not support these explanations for the high and intractable poverty rates throughout the economic expansions of the 1980s and 1990s.
>
> . . . Our analysis of both the government's official measurement and a series of more conceptually satisfying ways to measure poverty reveals that the general finding of the disconnection between economic growth and poverty is valid no matter how poverty is measured.
>
> . . . The heightened inequality of the income distribution, lessened progressivity of the tax system . . . , and, in particular, falling wages—all conspired to keep poverty rates historically high. . . . Moreover, the "safety net" (the social provision of assistance to those in poverty) grew less effective at providing relief to the poor.[39] [And then to some details:]
>
> . . . A major shift in the relationship between economic growth and poverty occurred in the 1980s such that the economic recovery of that decade failed to reduce poverty as much as occurred in earlier periods of growth (such as the 1960s or 1970s). . . . ("Normally" the poverty rate in 1989 would have been 10.4 percent, actually it was 13.1 percent; normally in 1994 it "should" have been 11.3 percent, actually it was 14.5 percent.) Given the size of the population in 1989, this means that over 6 million more persons were poor in that year than would have been the case had poverty rates continued to respond to economic growth as they had in the past.[40]
>
> . . . There has not only been a growth in poverty; the poor have also become poorer [as measured by the so-called poverty gap or the distance in the aggregate or average dollar amounts of a person or family from the poverty line] . . . : in 1995 the average poor family had an income $6,038 below the poverty line . . . : in 1973 . . . the gap was $5,406 (1995 dollars, both years).[41]
>
> . . . [It has usually been suggested that] there is a causal relationship between . . . family structure and the provision of benefits to female-headed families with

children. . . . [But] this correlation between benefits and family structure holds up only to the early 1970s. Beginning around 1972 the benefit sum began to fall. . . . Yet none of the demographic indicators, which have generally risen consistently over time, follow the plunging benefit sum. . . . Falling benefits should have led to a decrease in the formation [of single-headed] families. . . . In fact, participation rates [in AFDC] fell consistently through the mid-1970s and actually appeared to bottom out in 1989. Even in the deep recession of the early 1980s, participation rates continued their downward trend. . . . The trends strongly suggest that female-headed families are forming for reasons other than to ensure AFDC eligibility.[42]

The conclusion we are left with is that two simultaneous effects occurred that kept poverty rates high over [the 1980s and early 1990s]: (1) The wages of those at the bottom of the income distribution fell precipitously, and (2) the system of tax and transfers designed to ameliorate poverty was less effective than in the past. In other words, the primary distribution of market incomes was such that more families . . . were unable to achieve incomes above the poverty level through the wages they earned. . . . Strengthening wage growth at the bottom of the wage scale is perhaps the most important direct way to reconnect poverty reduction and economic growth.[43]

And the children? "The percentage of all children under 18 in poverty in 1979 was 16.4 percent; in 1995 it was 20.8 percent. The percentage of all children under 6 in 1979 was 18.1 percent; in 1995 it was 23.7 percent."[44]

Among the many consequences of the "end to welfare as we know it" accomplished in 1996, it is estimated that from 1 to 3.5 million more children will soon find themselves in poverty with decreased or no assistance. At least one-third of those children will be under six years of age, an age of innocence, if such there be. To that, among connected matters, we now turn our attention.

6

Welfare and Social Security

The Needs of Strangers

In our world, the deepest unmet needs—for adequate food, clothing, shelter, health, and education—which should be seen as human rights, are experienced by billions of people who are now and will always remain strangers to the rest of us.[1] But it is upon us—those societies and their citizens whose own such needs are met—that the responsibility rests to develop and pursue policies to relieve the impoverishment of those strangers' lives. To do so is to practice the ultimate in human solidarity; not to do so, quite apart from ethical and moral considerations, is to imperil our own lives.

The focus of this book is principally the United States, and not only on the poor here. However, given the interdependencies both within and between national political economies, it is reckless to proceed with a "winner take all" economic process, even were "winner" taken to signify half of our own, half of the world's people. However, not even "half" of the people there *or* here are able to meet the basic needs noted above.

"Winner take all" as an outlook has been an inevitable outcome of the economic individualism that has long characterized the United States.[2] Part of the admirable political philosophy of individualism, economic individualism has taken on something of a life of its own, mutating into a genteel name for greed. Because economic individualism is a driving force today, it must be seen more as a social illness than a dynamic making for the strengthening of the economy, let alone for the good of society as a whole.

Our species would not have survived its first millennia had it depended upon the individualistic ways and means common in the United States today. That is not so much a moral judgment as a recognition of the differences between primitive and modern existence: Primitive peoples lived in a "solidaristic" manner—unthinkingly, one may say, but in so living they diminished the number of those who perished and enhanced the number and lives of those who survived. For us, however, because of our considerably more advanced economic conditions, to live with any significant degree of solidarity requires thought and understanding and imagination—lest *we* perish.

The disadvantages and geographic isolation of primitive conditions meant that virtually all behaved in consonance with those they "knew," their principal preoccupation with the meager bounty and great dangers posed by nature. Human ingenuity has learned to "conquer" the rest of nature, to make what earlier was niggardly into a great cornucopia. But in doing that, the species has reached the point where *we* are the danger both to ourselves and to the rest of nature. In that same process, our advanced technologies and economies have provided us with an illusion of independence from others—individuals, groups, nations—an illusion disturbed only when disrupted by social cataclysm.

Such troubles intrude over and over, for what happens to the multitudes beyond our ken—in largest part *because* our advanced conditions tie us to others in ways impossible for primitive peoples—very much affects us, sooner or later: We are, after all, in the same boat; ultimately, there *are* no strangers to our lives. The ancient question, "If I am for myself alone, what am I?" does not depend upon time or place for its resonance.

The facts and tendencies previously and now to be discussed in these pages give many the sense that time is running out; that we cannot afford to wait and see, sit back and hope for the best. As Ignatieff put it, "the allegiances that make the human world human must be beaten into our heads. We never know a thing till we have paid to know it, never know how much is enough until we have had much less than enough, never know what we need till we have been dispossessed. . . . Our education in the art of necessity cannot avoid tragedy."[3]

But how much tragedy can be endured in our nation and our world before we reach a point of no return? Being beaten over the head surely can awaken one; it can also make one senseless. If all those not yet seriously damaged by our callous social institutions must be so afflicted before suitable steps are taken to regain our dwindling humanity, we could well pass through the social equivalent of a global Hiroshima. We cannot afford to take that chance, for neither the people nor the earth can afford much more damage.

In the United States one should not need to be told these things. It would be hard to find a society in which people are led to feel greater shame over their poverty, unemployment, hunger, poor housing, or homelessness, even over their old age, disability, and illness; or one in which the attitude of those who are not in basic need toward those who are is so scornful, insulting, hateful, and—as well it might be—fearful. It is not even grimly satisfying to note that many who were recently in the scorning category have themselves been placed by unemployment or "downsized" jobs among the scorned, standing in lines for assistance where now it is *their* dignity that is being shredded.

In this land of extensive political democracy and the greatest natural blessings of any nation in the world—a world brimming with technological triumphs and "excess" productive capacities—our economic and social horrors can be explained, but they cannot be justified. They endure and deepen because some want it that way, because some have "learned" to think that such problems are incurable, and because some of us just don't give a damn.

But there are many who *do* give a damn, not only among those whose lives are impoverished, but also among the comfortable. Many are inclined to be involved in efforts to move in the needed directions but—given the steady drumbeat of the march into always more conservative policies—wonder if the need *is* deep or have learned to think it may be true that over the long run seemingly decent policies aggravate rather than ameliorate the problem.

Here I seek to show that "decent policies" are both badly needed and practical, beneficial for the economy, for the society, for all. Thus, it *is* desirable and necessary to "end welfare as we know it," but not because it costs too much or because of "welfare cheats." Welfare as we know it should be ended because the system is unfair, inadequate, wasteful, demoralizing, and pretty much hated by all, most especially by its recipients and the social workers who—too often having to function as cops—dispense it. Indeed, let's end welfare as we know it—but by ending poverty as we know it, by going after its causes, not its consequences.[4]

The United States has the highest poverty rate of any industrialized country and the stingiest and *meanest* welfare system. Poor people aren't popular anywhere, but nowhere are they so neglected and demeaned as here; nowhere are welfare programs run so punitively and inefficiently—as measured by cost per person or by "efficiency" in getting people off welfare and back to self-support: in Western Europe, antipoverty programs pulled from 10 to 60 percent of recipients up and out of poverty in the 1980s; in the United States, the relevant rates varied between 0.3 to 0.5 percent, even though our unemployment rates were always lower. Furthermore, regressive taxes on low income groups here pushed more people *into* poverty than income transfer programs pulled out; the opposite was true in Europe.[5]

The welfare system now undergoing change, besides being clearly inadequate to its task, has long been a form of punishment, degrading to its recipients—intentionally so—although such intentions, covered over by habituation, are not seen as such. The observations of two veteran scholars of welfare help to clarify this easily confused matter:

> Most such social welfare activity has not greatly aided the poor, precisely because the poor ordinarily have little influence on government. . . . However, some social welfare programs *do* benefit those at the bottom of the economic order. The most

important are old-age pensions and unemployment insurance. . . . As for relief programs themselves, the historical pattern is . . . a record of periodically expanding and contracting relief rolls as the system performs its two main functions; maintaining civil order and enforcing work. . . . But much more should be understood of this mechanism than merely that it reinforces work norms. It also goes far toward defining and enforcing the terms on which different classes . . . are made to do different kinds of work; relief arrangements, in other words, have a great deal to do with maintaining social and economic inequities.[6]

Those observations apply with special strength to the administration of welfare; but the Social Security Act of 1935, legislation setting up our "relief" system for the past sixty years (AFDC), also provided for the aged (Old Age and Survivors Insurance [OASI]).[7] There have been and remain shortcomings for both the poor and the aged (and their survivors); but there is a substantial difference in the nature and gravity of those defects—a difference worth pursuing for a moment for the light it sheds on our social legislation.

Welfare, providing for those defined as poor, is confined to a relatively low percentage of the population at any time; OASI affects everyone over time, directly or indirectly. Because that difference means there *could* be diminished numbers of poor among us, but that there *are* always-increasing numbers of the old, there have been diverse political implications. There is, however, another defining difference: AFDC is paid for out of general taxation, OASI (now OASDHI) from the prior payroll deductions of its beneficiaries.

Those differences alone explain why the provisions for the aged, although inadequate and foolishly arranged, are at least not punitive. Because the poor, in the Malthusian tradition, are seen as having defects of character that make them responsible for their own condition, it is an easy step to believe they should be punished while being assisted. The old are not punished for their condition, but they are treated unjustly: The better off you were while working, the better off you will be when you work no longer; the greater your unfulfilled needs earlier, the greater they will remain in retirement—if you receive anything at all.[8]

Having earlier discussed the extent of poverty, now we examine the ways in which the needs of the poor are met—or, more accurately, not met. One should remember that the word *need* does not occur in economic theory; it is hardly ever heard in the halls of our legislatures. Were we at least to *use* the word, and were its application pondered sufficiently, perhaps what has happened to the children of the United States, which nowadays worsens their lives, would not have occurred. In the disdainful discussions of welfare and its recipients, the blunt fact that about two-thirds of AFDC recipients are children is seldom mentioned. Therefore, we turn to the poverty and the conditions of American children first, thence to the errors of omission and commission of the recent and emerging welfare system.

Suffer the Little Children

Among the rich societies, ours has by far the highest rate of children living in poverty—four times the rates in Western Europe—and it is the children's rate that rises most rapidly, condemning them to an inhuman life and unnecessary deprivation. Jonathan Kozol (who has spent several decades studying the lives of poor children, especially in their schools) has awakened us to this matter. Here he is speaking of a neighborhood in the South Bronx):

> In the drabness of the neighborhood, the friendliness and openness of little kids . . . seem like the sunshine that has not been seen in New York City during many months of snow and storm and meanness . . . show[ing] us something very different from the customary picture we are given of a generation of young thugs and future whores. There is a golden moment here that our society has chosen not to seize. . . . [It is not until later] that the sense of human ruin on a vast scale becomes unmistakable.[9]

Some of the dimensions of those ruins for today's children in the United States (and an addendum concerning those elsewhere) follow:[10]

- Children in the United States are poorer than children in most other Western industrialized nations because the gap between rich and poor is so large and because welfare programs are less generous here than elsewhere.[11]
- Poor children are more than twice as likely as other children to suffer from stunted growth, severe physical or mental disabilities, fatal accidental injuries, iron deficiency, and severe asthma.[12]
- Poor children are more than twice as likely as other children never to finish high school, even when differences in family structure, race, and ethnicity are taken into account.[13]
- Poor children have significantly lower achievement test scores than children of high-income families.[14]
- In 1993, 46 percent of all African-American children and 41 percent of all Latino children lived in families with incomes below the poverty level.[15]
- Poverty rates among children have increased since 1970 as follows: 1970, 15 percent; 1980, 18 percent; 1993, 22 percent; those living in "extreme poverty"—a family income of less than half that of "plain poverty"—have doubled, to 10 percent, since 1975.[16]
- Child poverty rates grew in all racial categories between 1979 and 1989, and again for white and Hispanic (but not black) children from 1989 to 1994 . . . [when] more than one out of every five children was poor (21.8 percent). For children under six years old, the rate was even higher, reaching 24.5 percent. Black children have the highest poverty rates; in 1989, half of all black children under six were poor. The rates were about the same in 1996.[17]

- More than 60 percent of all AFDC families have a youngest child under the age of five.[18]
- Marian Wright Edelman, president of the Children's Defense Fund, noting that over 16 million children live in poverty in the United States, reports that "every 9 seconds a child drops out of school, every 14 seconds a child is arrested, every 15 minutes a baby dies, every 2 hours a child is killed by a firearm, every 4 hours a child commits suicide, every 7 hours a child dies from abuse or neglect."[19]

And globally? UNESCO's 1995 International Forum on the Rights of the Child reported that 1.4 *billion* children under age 18 live in poverty and 100 million are homeless; in Europe 5 percent are below the poverty line; in the United States, 20 percent. More than 6.6 million children die yearly of diarrhea and pneumonia, because of poor living conditions and, despite vaccines against these diseases, close to 2 million children annually die from measles, tetanus, and polio.[20] In 1993, UNICEF reported that over the globe, every day 36,000 children die from malnutrition and disease (= 13 million every year)—a calamity that could be ended at the cost of $1 a day per child.[21]

*　　*　　*

President Clinton signed the new welfare legislation on August 22, 1996. A bit more than two weeks earlier, Senator Daniel Patrick Moynihan (D.-N.Y.), whose academic work had led to a governmental career centering on the welfare system (beginning with a secretaryship in the Nixon administration), rose to speak to the Senate to warn of the disaster they were creating: "Let me put that in terms of how many children will be cut off. . . . The Urban Institute says 3,500,000 will be dropped from the rolls by 2001. By 2005, 4,896,000 will have been cut off." And commenting on the unlikelihood that government officials would make a good faith effort to meet the work requirements spelled out in the bill, Moynihan went on to summarize the estimate of the (nonpartisan) Congressional Budget Office: "given the costs and administrative complexities involved, the CBO assumes that most states would simply accept penalties rather than implement the [work] requirements."[22]

It would be bad enough if what we have already allowed and now permit to worsen concerning children were an outcome of mere heartlessness, shameful indeed for a society that presumes to value the family. Moreover, there is no sufficient reason for having done and doing all this damage. In the past it has been costly not only to the direct victims but to the society as a whole; Senator Moynihan is by no means alone in believing that those costs will escalate both for all. This combination of pitilessness and mindlessness in our society makes the heart to weep, the mind to boggle.[23]

Perhaps, however, the above is merely the carping of the soft-hearted, based on misleading impressions; perhaps our leaders have acted harshly in past and present because the *facts* demand it, perhaps from this human and social morass there is no better exit? The answer to that question is a resounding "No!"

"Welfare as We've Known It"

The issue is not ending welfare,[24] but the disappearance of work in the ghetto. The problem has now reached catastrophic proportions, and if it isn't addressed, it will have lasting and harmful consequences for the quality of life in the cities and, eventually, for the lives of all Americans.[25]

Has welfare cost too much? Any amount to help the poor would be too much for some but by no means for all;[26] the fact is, as we shall see, that the real dollar cost is low. But what about women who have children *in order* to be on welfare? That too will be shown as a canard. Whether arising from carelessness or misinformation, those generalizations have dangerous political consequences; polls have shown that about three-quarters of us support assistance to the poor but are negative regarding welfare, in great part because of misinformation as to recipients of the now disappearing program. More exactly, all too few know that:

- Whereas the federal budget runs well in excess of $1 trillion dollars annually, combined federal and state expenditures for AFDC amount to only 1.1 percent of federal and 3.4 percent of state expenditures—as compared with the ten times greater budget for the Pentagon.[27]
- In 1994 the average mother with two dependent children received a cash grant of $360 a month—a *decline* of 40 percent (in constant dollars) since the 1970s. Food and nutritional assistance for those same families (food stamps, school lunches, and so on) provided another $120 a month for that same family. Since then, the amount has fallen.
- Contrary to popularized notions about welfare families, their average size has been shrinking, not growing—now 1.9 children, down from 4.0 in 1968, 3.0 in 1978, 2.9 in 1991. But what about all those teen-age mothers? 1991: under 20 years old, 8.1 percent, 20–40 years old, 80 percent. Then what about all the children born—as the quaint phrase has it—"out of wedlock"? Most of those by far are not on welfare; such births linked to those receiving welfare are under 15 percent.
- Still, once "they" are on welfare, they just stay and stay and stay there, no? No. The median period (half above, half below) in 1991 was 22 months; 70 percent stayed less than 2 years; only 7 percent (many of them disabled), more than 8 years. And 46 percent left when they found work that gave them a higher income.

- The impression is widespread that most (or all?) welfare mothers are black; 61 percent are white.
- But wouldn't poor people get out and work if they couldn't be on welfare? In the mid-1990s there were about 50 million poor people (as officially understated), but only about 14 million on welfare. That number has risen about 31 percent since 1989—inverse to the decline of real wages.
- The recent increase of the minimum wage to $5.15/hour in 1997 will not help much, for at least two reasons: (1) working full-time at that wage for fifty-two weeks leaves one at only two-thirds of the official poverty income—if one can find the job; (2) in New York City in 1992–1994 a research team tracked 200 African-American and Hispanic people seeking jobs in fast-food restaurants in Harlem, where the official unemployment rate was 16 percent. The ratio of job applicants to hires was 14 to 1; at the even lower minimum wage then offered, 73 percent could find no work after a yearlong search; moreover, the teenagers for whom those are seen as entry-level jobs found themselves unsuccessfully competing with people in their mid- and late twenties.[28]

Where Are We Going from Here?

And where are we now? The "here" is a set of intersecting processes—economic, political, social—and the "we" is just as complex, including the various spectra of age, color, gender, income, and attitude, as they bear on the manner in which "the needs of strangers" are or should be treated. Our country has done badly up to this point, and the current thrust of things threatens to push us down further into the depths.

Besides the statistics of ill-being that have been noted above are the startling increases in two areas one might have hoped would never rise beyond the statistically negligible in the United States: homelessness and hunger. But rise they have, and to a degree that may yet, indeed may already, exceed their Depression-era existence. Those numbers have already gone well beyond what were considered to be shocking levels in the 1970s—the result then of a disastrous calculation concerning inmates of mental institutions, a calculation bearing all too many similarities with the recent devolution of welfare policy.

The 1960s, it may be recalled was the most successful decade of economic expansion in U.S. history; yet by the opening years of the 1970s, the streets of several major and many minor cities had begun to be filled with the hungry and the homeless. By the decade's end, tens of thousands were thus afflicted, to the utter mystification of most of us.

One cause of this calamity was a badly flawed sociomedical experiment aimed at the "deinstitutionalization" of mental patients—an experiment expected to save much money and be beneficial as well for those patients. They would be given reserpine—in effect a strong tranquilizer—and no longer have to live in hospitals, but would be served by (still to be constructed and staffed) local community centers.[29] A few hundred such centers were built; several thousand were needed. And the released mental patients wandered the streets, as they still do. Now they are accompanied by men and women and some occasional children, there for other reasons: some because of drink or drugs and related problems, many more because the economy has failed to provide good jobs and their government has failed to respond.

This recounting has been prompted by the remarks of Senator Moynihan to his colleagues in December 1995. He predicted that when, after the death of AFDC, the streets fill up with homeless children—as they surely will—there will be "general bafflement" as to why, reprising the bafflement of the 1970s as the mentally disturbed wandered the streets.

Then, as now, fiscal savings and careless or harsh attitudes toward those in trouble were glossed over with claims that the change was for the clients' "own good." It should be pointed out that despite the medical profession's admission of its complicity in a grave error, that error has not been reversed. Can we expect that the human and social costs of thus abandoning the poor to their fate will be dealt with in a better fashion?[30]

It is not just the future that seems stark; the inadequacies of the recent past and present, even *with* AFDC, have caused the streets to abound with homeless. Estimates of their numbers remain only that; it must be assumed that neither the local nor the national governments wish to take the trouble or spend the money for an accurate picture of such a disturbing reality.

That reality is bad enough. We know from private charitable institutions that their support of soup kitchens and shelters has already been stretched to the limit at the very moment the government is preparing to reduce its own assistance. We are thus at what seems to be the edge of a veritable explosion of homelessness and hunger.

Anecdotal though much of our knowledge of the homeless may be, there are reliable data on hunger, which goes along with homelessness. Thus, in California—the richest food-producing area in the world—over 15 percent of the population in 1995 was classified as "hungry" (up 42 percent from 1987), and an additional 10 percent had no reliable source of food.[31] Increased hunger goes along with increased joblessness and poverty; because the weather is more temperate in California than in most of the country, it may be assumed that the hunger and homelessness in less gentle climes are more painful and more dangerous to health—at what could not be a worse time. As will be seen in the next chapter, Medicaid, virtually the sole health provision for the poor, is also being cut severely.

Nevertheless, after two years of hand-wringing, wrangling, and niggling compromises mixed with flights of rhetoric, on August 22, 1996, Congress passed and the president signed the welfare bill, with its reassuring title, "The Personal Responsibility and Work Opportunity Reconciliation Act of 1996."

Blueprint for a (Deeper) Tragedy

The new law mandates the following:[32] an end to sixty-one years of the federal guarantee of cash assistance for poor children and a delegation of authority to the separate states to run welfare programs with lump sums of federal money ("block grants"). Adult recipients of the resulting state welfare programs will be required to find work within two years; there will be a five-year lifetime limit on benefits; aid to noncitizens will be curtailed. More specifically:

1. Most immigrants arriving after the bill was signed have become ineligible for most benefits and social services financed by the federal government.
2. Strict new standards for granting Supplemental Security Income (SSI) to disabled children are going into effect, with the expectation that "several hundred thousand" disabled children will immediately lose support.
3. States were given about a year to rework their welfare programs to meet the new requirements.
4. Within the year after the bill's signing, most noncitizens receiving food stamps and SSI will become ineligible for benefits when their cases are reviewed.
5. As of October 1, 1996, "no individual or family shall be entitled to any benefits or services" under the now defunct federal program Aid to Families with Dependent Children.
6. Also as of October 1, 1996, new Federal rules for food stamps took effect, reducing benefits previously paid.
7. As of January 1, 1997, states were allowed but not required to cut off cash assistance, Medicaid, and social services for noncitizens who were receiving such aid up to August 22, 1996.

There it is in black and white. Some of its meanings over time can only be guessed at; others can be predicted fairly easily. Among the latter, two stand out:

1. No one doubts the likelihood of a recession at some time in the future. But that the legislation's hardships will be "manageable" is predicated upon the assumption that the future fiscal conditions of the separate states will be

no weaker than those of 1996—the fifth and most buoyant year of consecutive economic expansion. As both Republicans and Democrats know, the separate states' coffers fill as the economy expands and empty when it contracts; also known by all is that states are prohibited by their constitutions from engaging in "countercyclical deficit financing": when the economy weakens, therefore, state expenditures *must* decline, unless—as is totally improbable—voters support the floating of bonds for specific purposes (like welfare?), and a consequent increase in their taxes. So, it's back to the fiscal policies of the pre–New Deal era: Each for himself, and God for all.

2. It is generally acknowledged that the delegation of federal funds for welfare to the states in the form of block grants—argued for by its supporters in order to free states from "meddlesome Federal regulations specifying how, why and where the Federal money could be spent"[33]—contains yawning loopholes for state governments to use what are presumably funds for the poor for those who are not. Indeed, in today's climate, such funds are just as likely to be used *against* the poor, directly or indirectly: for prison construction or anti-immigrant fences, for example.

There are two other matters to worry about: The first, as recent conferences of mayors from around the nation have agreed, is that the delegation of block grants to the states will almost certainly lead to *their* delegation of responsibility, but not of their grants, to the cities and counties. The latter will have to scrounge up the money somewhere or, failing that (as is likely), let the poor—two-thirds of them children, remember—suffer. The other matter to worry about jumped into the news almost before the ink was dry on the new legislation: "Giant Companies Entering Race to Run State Welfare Programs: Powers like Lockheed Martin Vie for Contracts." [34] Part of the story went this way: "The jockeying [for welfare contracts] frightens longtime social-service workers and public-interest lawyers. No company can be expected to protect the interests of the needy at the expense of its bottom line, least of all a publicly traded corporation with a fiduciary duty to maximize shareholder profits."

Companies, giant or pygmy, are *supposed* to have the fabled "bottom line" as their guide; although those firms lobbied frenziedly for the new bill, it's not their fault but that of Congress and the White House that their newest area for profits—prisons, education, and health care having earlier been added—will be another of the "uses of poverty."

So much for the poor, except for a final observation. Admirable though the idea of "workfare" may be—and surveys show that the poor also overwhelmingly prefer jobs (at a livable wage) to welfare—sufficient jobs do not now exist, and to prepare people for and create them would require an expenditure of time and thought and money that exceeds the amounts previously spent on AFDC itself. Few if any of those supporting the new act are prepared to devote that much time, thought, or money. As long as that remains true, and the "Personal Responsibility Act" reigns, we shall have to anticipate "children sleeping on grates," in Senator Moynihan's grim phrase. By comparison with the past and present plight of the poor, what will now be shown regarding the present and prospective situation of the old will seem downright reasonable—though it combines unreason and inadequacy in substantial measure.

"The Oldest Hath Borne Most"

The idealization[35] of competition in our political economy has blended easily with personal and group competition—in sports, education, and elsewhere; as doubtless it has played a subtle role in allowing racism to flourish. In the past twenty years or so, there has developed a new competition, even a conflict, between the young and the old.[36] It has arisen out of a belief that there is an institutionalized theft by the old from the young—the theft of the OASDHI payroll deductions from today's young to finance overly generous OASDHI benefits for current and emerging oldsters. The resulting scenario, increasingly publicized and bewailed, is that waiting in tomorrow's shadows—in the year 2010, 2020, 2030, some time—there lurks the total bankruptcy of the Social Security Trust Fund, and an old age to be dreaded for those presently young. So it is said and ever more widely believed.

The demonization of the poor and the caricaturization of AFDC were essential to the "success" of the welfare bill of 1996. Something similar has been under way for some years now for the old and Social Security, and efforts to transform, even to end, Social Security are off the ground and running.

There are of course many differences between the two areas of competition and conflict, not the least that the poor have had no effective lobby but the old do. Among other major differences, one that cuts both ways is that "only" about 50 million are officially definable as poor, whereas everyone at some time becomes old (unless unlucky); another is that almost everyone has paid taxes to finance the benefits the poor have received, whereas Social Security is funded 50–50 by its beneficiaries and their employers—presumably.[37]

Those are some of the most important differences; the most important similarities are in the cultivated prejudice, disinformation, misinformation, and ignorance surrounding the politics of their transformation or dismantling. What is more, as might be expected in our highly commercialized society, not security but money has become "the bottom line."

As noted earlier, social insurance in the United States has lagged behind that of the other industrialized societies. After the disappearance of the social protections of medieval and early modern Europe, there was a long spell of governmental indifference to the adversities of the majority; that began to change late in the nineteenth century—first in Germany, where provisions for the aged, the ill, and the unemployed were begun in 1881, under the guidance of the militarist Otto von Bismarck, who thought it would take the heat out of socialist arguments. Those steps were soon followed in the Scandinavian countries under the leadership of the cooperative movements (their beginnings in agriculture and fishing).[38]

In the United States, despite the efforts of the pre–World War I Progressive Movement to alleviate the terrible housing, health, and hunger problems of some eastern cities, the only governmental provision for social insurance was that for workmen's compensation (for on-the-job injuries—now called workers' compensation), passed in 1911; all else awaited the agonies of the Depression and the legislation of 1935 and thereafter. The legislation, most notably the Social Security Act itself, began with compromises that explain the deplorable status of social insurance in the United States today. The definitive economic history of the 1930s sums up that beginning:

> Chief debate in the planning stage revolved around the relative merits of national and federal-state systems, the social hazards to be covered, and whether financing should be through pay-roll taxes or income taxes. . . . In general, it became increasingly clear that this was to be a modest and partial beginning in social security, and the guardians of states' rights—whether on high or low grounds—made headway.[39]

The legacy of states' rights has persevered, more on low than on high grounds. The decision to finance it by employee-employer payroll deductions, rather than by a progressive income tax, is of more importance to the controversy over and presumed crisis of Social Security, however.

In Chapter 10 the latter matter will receive an extended discussion, advocating a progressive income taxation to finance *all* governmental programs; here a brief comment on the role of payroll deductions regarding Social Security. The present movement toward social conservatism began to take hold in the 1970s. As we have seen, in those years average real wages began to fall; the tax rates on corporate profits and personal income taxes for the top brackets began their steep decline; regressive taxes began their upward acceleration, most notably in payroll deductions for Social Security and falling exemptions for families. It is worth repeating some of the data presented in Chapter 2, for they bear on the abrasive attitudes toward welfare and Social Security: Since the 1950s, the top income tax rate has fallen from 91 to 31 percent; the family (of four) exemption of 1948 was $600; were today's exemption in the same proportion to income it would be $7,781 instead of $2,050; in the mid-1950s, that family would have paid 9 percent for income taxes and Social Security combined, compared to over 26 percent in 1993; corporate income taxes in the same years declined from 27.7 percent of federal tax collections to less than 8 percent.[40]

A closer look at the changing levels of payroll deduction rates provides further insight for current attitudes: In the 1950s, median-income families paid under 2 percent of their income for Social Security; that rose to 7 percent by the close of the 1980s, and now it is 7.65 percent, up to an income of $62,700 (as of 1996). But note that this means "a middle-level manager earning $50,000 a year will pay exactly the same amount as his company's CEO, who makes $5 million."[41] As the result of the conservative shift of tax policy in the 1970s and since:

> If Congress had done nothing since 1977 to alter the U.S. tax code, passed no new legislation at all, nine out of ten American families would be paying less. That is, a smaller share of their incomes would be devoted to federal taxes. Yet, paradoxically, the government would be collecting more revenue each year—almost $70 billion more—if none of the tax bills had been enacted.

Few indeed are those in the United States who know the ugly details of these radical shifts in the burden of taxation. Until recently the great majority has confined its grumbles to highly visible property and income taxes, barely noticing the steady rise of indirect (mostly sales) taxes and payroll deductions. The latter has been noted only recently in connection with the rumored transfer of income from younger to older. The self-interested parties behind the rumors are not characterized by their youth.

The Undoing of Social Security?

What has become something of an uproar over the presumed injustices of Social Security did not originate in the designated victims; it is but the latest variation on the political battle against social insurance that began as that legislation was born. Initially it was the insurance companies that, not without reason, saw the payroll collections of the government as reducing premium payments to themselves. That private insurance covered only a small percentage of the population—and even less well on average than now—as compared with social insurance was not the companies' concern then; nor is it the concern now of the numerous Wall Street companies that have joined the insurance companies' long opposition to Social Security—as we have known it.

In the name of protecting the "baby boomers," a campaign has taken off that only a few years ago would have been viewed as a bad joke: to have a significant share (at least one-third) of OASDHI contributions to the Social Security Trust Fund[42] be invested in common stocks or mutual funds; or, even better, to move toward the total privatization of Social Security. Thus, there being no alternative, individuals would be "allowed" to save on their own in something like IRA accounts, in instruments of their own choosing:

After all, common stocks have risen four times more than the return of Treasury bonds since the 1920s, haven't they?

Indeed they have, but there remain more than a few serious questions to be dealt with, some of which now follow:

1. That Wall Street has been having one helluva boom in recent years might well explain why the number of innocents has multiplied (as they did in the 1920s), but it leaves unaltered the admittedly imprecise but still iron law that "what goes up must go down" and unanswered the question "Who bears the risk when investments go sour?"[43] Treasury bonds do sound a bit stuffy, but in their long history they have yet to go belly up.

2. Few indeed are the savers (nor am I, an economist, among them) who have even the foggiest notion of how to invest in what or when or why; and if those individuals then entrust their savings to professional speculators (in or out of mutual funds), how can they choose among them—especially when assuredly some will turn out to be sharks in a business that often resembles a shark tank? The always too limited regulation of that business is in the process of becoming slighter in the same period in which the movement for privatization of Social Security has gained momentum.

3. Any slack that might in recent years have been taken up by private pension plans can be counted on less and less, not only because such plans are diminishing in the absence of pressure from workers, but also because relatively new governmental tax policies threaten the employer-provided pensions of the one-third of the labor force (41 million) still thus covered. Interestingly, behind those tax policies—which reduce companies' tax deductions—is the effort to reduce the federal deficit.[44]

4. In addition, and among other problems, when a careful estimate is made of how people's incomes have to be invested to assure a satisfactory retirement, the figures come out as astounding, well beyond reach for just about everyone. In a carefully researched essay, *New York Times* reporter Louis Uchitelle found that most

> see themselves caught short, without enough reliable income from pensions or savings or Social Security to maintain their old living standards. . . . If they have to pay their own way, how much must they save? Is it $1 million, $3 million, $6 million? "No one really knows," said . . . the Labor Department's assistant secretary for pensions and welfare benefits. But one 59-year-old woman, with an income from her researcher job of $60,000, because her income will shrink by two-thirds upon retirement, believes she will have to work into her seventies—if she can. Others studied had the same—or worse—prospects.[45]

And remember, finally, that the average income for a family of four is now about $40,000, a family that is sunk in debt, on average, for 15–20 percent of its disposable income. And consider that as of 1994, about 45 percent of Americans sixty-five and over have an annual income of less than $15,000—

including Social Security benefits; 59 percent have a net worth of less than $100,000; only 30 percent have incomes over $25,000 a year. Repeat: including benefits.[46]

In short, the overwhelming majority of us cannot have even the semblance of "security" if it must depend upon savings from an already inadequate income (quite apart from the considerations involving health care, to be examined in the next chapter). Those are just the numbers; there is more to consider.

The Quality of Mercy Is Strain'd

And it does not droppeth as the gentle rain from heaven. Instead, as usual, the Devil squats happily in the details of the quantitative matters just surveyed; but as with the poor, numbers do not by any means tell the whole story.

People who are old today—assume for present purposes that means those in their sixties and over—were born before the end of the 1930s, some before World War I, most in the years between the two world wars. By the time contemporary levels of material well-being took hold toward the end of the 1950s, all were adults, the largest percentage of whom (in one way or another) had experienced at least one of the two worst wars and the worst depression in history. In short, except for a small percentage, life had been anything but easy for the great majority of them and had been very tough indeed for a considerable percentage.

Some earlier numbers have shown that less than a third of all those receiving Social Security benefits have an annual income over $25,000, and that about 45 percent are under $15,000. What qualities of life do such incomes allow? Most who read this will have to use their imagination; others who have friends or family who are old can use past and present observations. They will know that the realities are distinctly different from the popularized notion of the old that calls up scenes in Florida, with old people lounging in the sun, strolling on a beach, shopping, fishing and boating, gambling, and so on. The pictures are not fabricated, but that Florida is for the few there who can afford it, leaving the rest, more than two-thirds of the old, who cannot, wherever they may be—in New York and New Jersey, North Dakota and Missouri, Mississippi and Maine, all over the country (including some living in Florida).

All too many of the old, if they do not live in inadequate furnished rooms, will be found in cramped nursing homes or in one-time private houses converted into small "senior residences," where a principal occupation is wondering who will die next. An already small and always shrinking percentage lives within the family, comfortably or not. An unknown but too large number are homeless. On top of that dreary discomfort, almost all old people come to feel useless and have lost or are losing their dignity—a loss often speeded up by ill health.

Old people are a "problem" in the United States—to the nation, to their families, to themselves. Most Americans would be surprised to learn that that is much less frequently the case in most other countries in the world. In certain countries, old people are prized—in some cases, accurately or not, for their wisdom, in others for their lore, in most because they are "family," important as such, and especially so for the grandchildren. In few countries are the old left so much alone, seen so frequently as a bother, so often allowed or caused to feel useless.

Having a decent income when retired cannot by itself eliminate such sad conditions, of course. Nevertheless, it might at least avert the direct pains of material deprivation and, in doing so, mitigate some connected psychological and emotional problems. It might also, were old people enabled to support themselves decently, lead otherwise nervous and wary relatives to substitute some warmth for too much stiffness. It might, eventually, begin to rehabilitate the family in the United States, in more than a rhetorical version.

And if a "decent income" for the old were seen as a necessary standard, who knows but that the same standard might be seen as a right for all? Perhaps, in the search for the elevation of our society to such standards, we would also find ourselves searching for the means to achieve them.

Those means, as will be discussed in Chapter 10, would take us to a reconsideration of both the expenditure and tax structures of our government and lead us to decide that the beneficiaries of governmental expenditures should be located by their need, and that the payments for those expenditures should be found, not in the current regressive tax deductions from the payrolls of beneficiaries, but in the incomes of the best-off in the country. Social Security deductions could be taken from incomes beyond the present limit and up to the top and from general taxation as well, progressively structured: in the words of our Founders, a tax burden determined by "the ability to pay."[47]

That basic principle is thus not new; nor is it a discovery to note the systematic unfairness of the payroll tax. As noted earlier, the progressive income tax for financing Social Security was first considered in 1935, and a few decades later, it was observed: "Although designated a 'contribution' in the social security law, it is in fact an involuntary tax without exemptions . . . [and] it is also ironical that, although there is a declared war against poverty, the fastest-growing tax should be levied on labor income, without exemptions for families in poverty."[48]

Neither the means nor the ends suggested here are likely to be put in place easily or soon; but just as one can foresee considerable political opposition to both ends and means, especially from on high, one can imagine pleasurable political excitement throughout the rest of society. At least to this observer, there seems to be a deep political yearning among all kinds of us, these days, to have something genuinely worthwhile to work for. We are not, most of us, cynics; may it not be assumed that most of us are fed up with those who are?

7

Health, Education,
and Housing

In 1920, the terrible war just ended had left no doubt that profound changes were on their way. R. H. Tawney, perhaps the wisest and most profound social critic of industrial capitalism, cautioned and advised in words that ring true as much today as they did seventy-five years ago:

> It is obvious, indeed, that no change of system or machinery can avert those causes of social *malaise* which consist in the egotism, greed, or quarrelsomeness of human nature. What it can do is to create an environment in which those are not the qualities which are encouraged. It cannot secure that men live up to their principles. What it can do is establish their social order upon principles to which, if they please, they can live up and not live down.[1]

The Eighth Deadly Sin

On the face of it, it is amazing that so many people have come to believe that "safety net" programs are unduly generous and should be cut back or even abolished. It is amazing because the life experiences of many might well have taught them to conclude the opposite; amazing, too, because many who think that way are now or soon will find themselves in need of a significantly *stronger* safety net than has existed, to say nothing of the shreds that may be left after ongoing cuts. Most amazing of all, the process that has taken us to today was actively or passively facilitated by many of these same people.

Undergirding such self-harming attitudes is the twisted version of "individualism" now passing for socioeconomic wisdom in the United States: free marketry. The artillery battery serving this ideology, now camouflaged, is composed of what were once deemed "the seven deadly sins": anger, covetousness, envy, gluttony, lust, pride, and (for this purpose, mental) sloth.

Those sins are practiced by persons; what is put forth here as the "eighth deadly sin" is our society's: the commodification of all aspects of the social process. That is, each person's access to any good or service—irrespective of degree of need (or its absence)—is in principle to be determined by purchasing power, by nothing else.

Commodification has not yet been total even here, but for those who sing the praises of the market, that is a consummation devoutly to be wished. In the absence of a widespread political effort to reverse present tendencies, that ideal is moving within reach and, were it not for the coming socioeconomic disasters, could soon be grasped.

The grip of commodification was already strong by the late eighteenth century, when land and labor—long sheltered by deep traditions[2]—were careening toward submission to free markets. By the beginning of this century, particularly in Great Britain and the United States, almost everything was coming up for grabs—a process slowed and reversed for several decades by the Depression of the 1930s. That Depression revealed society's susceptibility to catastrophe when economies are ruled over by unrestrained clashes for profits and power.

There is surely justification for commodification of some goods and services; indeed for the largest part of both. If we accept the notion of sin (at least metaphorically), there is something also to be said for an occasional fling with one of the seven deadly sins, that is, for being human: no anger, or lust, ever? never a gluttonous evening or lazy afternoon? Still, the commodification of *everything* (that's what Friedman advocates and what we are moving toward)[3] should win the grand prize among the eight—not least because it and its associated behavior patterns are vital partners to socialized greed and deepening racism, which in turn are exacerbated by rampant consumerism and growing job fears.

In the United States commodification has gone considerably further than in Western Europe for at least two reasons, the roots of which are in the long separated histories of the two areas: (1) the United States has had virtually no encounter with the socially protective institutions that went back to the Middle Ages (and that persisted long afterwards); and (2) the United States has never had a strong labor movement (as distinct from a trade union movement);[4] that is, never an organized Left. (Further examination would show that the two "reasons" were much intertwined as they evolved over time.)

The United States, alone among all nations, came into history *as* a capitalist society, with no meaningful anticapitalist opposition from church, labor, or state—until, as regards labor, well after the Civil War. Then the opposition was not to capitalism as such, but to its greatest excesses—most especially to the consequences of the commodification of labor.[5]

Because our history has been relatively incognizant of the needs for and benefits of social insurance (and associated institutions), we must in some sense learn that alphabet. Only then can it become "natural" for us to see the clear distinctions between those goods and services for which commodification can be a virtue and those for which it can amount to a crime.

Of course it's advisable to have access to goods like autos and skis, oranges and chocolate bars, personal computers, woolen scarves and overcoats, books and records and movie tickets, houses, and a very long list of other things determined by purchasing power. In fact, what we are really talking about is the impact of buyers' choices, not only on the disposition of their incomes, but on the quality and pricing of those goods as well. *But,* if some of those things are essential to a decent and healthy life (some foods, some clothes, some books, some housing, perhaps—as things now go—easy access to a computer), it should be easily comprehended that society should ensure that indispensable goods and services be available to those *without* the requisite purchasing power.

That should be, but too often is not, true for health care, education, and housing. As we examine the whys and wherefores of that generalization, it is useful to note that these three areas are only the most vital services, and developing guidelines for them can accustom us to a language that, thus learned, can be translated to other deserving needs.

Health Care

The leading economies of the world are those of Western Europe, the United States, Canada, and Japan, followed by the other members of the Organization for Economic Cooperation and Development (OECD). Of those countries, the United States spends the *most* on health care (in the aggregate and per capita) at the same time that it provides the *least* coverage to its citizens. None of those other countries has a significant percentage of its population with *no* coverage or such inadequate or fragile coverage; all have higher longevities and lower infant mortality rates.[6] Yet Americans have been told and most probably believe that ours is "the best health care system in the world": That is, we may pay more, but we get more and better health care.

Would that it were so. It is of course not so for the 15–20 percent of Americans who have *no* health coverage—private or public (including Medicare/Medicaid). Setting them aside, we will look into what we are getting for our money: "What America Buys for the Extra Money":

Amenities: impressive lobbies in hospitals catering to the well-insured (but not others), 2-bed rooms, compared with the more normal 4-bed rooms of the other countries.

Higher Incomes for Providers: doctors (whose high median incomes of the early 1980s rose even more, at a rate [1984–1990] of 12+ percent compared with 6 percent for full-time employed women and a *decrease* of 3+ percent for men); plus higher costs for drugs and equipment here than elsewhere.

More People Working in Hospitals: comparing Paris with New York, for example, New York had 40 percent more patient-care staff, 155 percent more *non*-patient-care staff, and 327 percent more financial and billing staff.

Extra Administration and Hassles: "the hardest to defend. . . . The General Accounting Office estimated in 1991 that the American insurance system created costs of $67 billion over and above what the United States would pay if it had Canadian-type institutions . . . , about 1.2 percent of GDP."[7]

White concluded his study: "Americans do not need more information. They do need the clarity of understanding necessary to overcome the obstacle course of the political system, the propaganda of entrenched interests, and above all the ideology that says that responsibility is fending for yourself, not standing up for each other."[8] What follows is an attempt to move in that direction, although I disagree with White's first phrase: I think Americans *do* need more information in order to correct abundant misinformation.

We shall examine (1) the evolution of the U.S. health care system before 1965 (when Medicare/Medicaid were born), (2) the combination of improvements and failures that emerged up through the 1980s, and (3) the 1990s—including the blunder/miscarriage/folly, call it what you will, of the 1993–1994 Clinton Health Care Plan (hereafter: CHP) of not so fond memory.

The Good Old Days

Before 1965, there was, of course, health care—doctors, hospitals, and pharmaceutical and equipment companies—but there were no national or state or local "programs." Almost all cities or counties provided some emergency medical assistance for the poor and/or for the destitute old, usually in hospitals associated with medical schools; health care insurance of any kind, even for those in the middle and upper income brackets, was very much a rarity until after World War II: One had a family physician (or one didn't).[9]

By the end of the 1920s there were 6,850 hospitals in the United States; of that small number, 800 had *closed* by 1938. It may be assumed that already inadequate medical care for the average person was declining in those same years, as purchasing power collapsed. Directly and indirectly, the war changed that lamentable condition, as it did for so much else—at lamentable costs, of course.

Just as the war was ending in 1945, the new president, Harry S. Truman, as part of his "Fair Deal," proposed a universal health care program: National

Health Insurance. Like an associated proposal, the nationalization of the housing industry, that for universal health care never even made it to the floor of Congress (although Truman proposed it more than once in later years). What did get there and passed in 1946 was the Hill-Burton Act, the bedrock of subsequently provided funds for thousands of hospitals, clinics, public health centers, nursing homes, and rehabilitation facilities—prompted initially by veterans' needs but soon extended to others.

The war also facilitated the strengthening of industrial unionism, partly as a continuation of union growth in the 1930s. Wartime arrangements—although leading to wage and price controls—made it easier for unions to organize and to recruit workers; at the same time the wartime arrangements assured high profits for corporations. The effects of these arrangements were felt most especially in autos, steel, and electrical products—the heart of military production. (The auto and electrical industries, in addition to their production of motors and military vehicles, also produced aircraft engines and even whole aircraft, as with Ford's B-24 bomber.) One of those effects was the beginning of health care benefits for workers: Because wages could not be legally increased and skilled workers were short in supply, companies sought to attract workers through such benefits.

In the 1950s, when U.S. unionism was at its maximum numerical and political strength and was under strong leadership—especially that of Walter Reuther, head of the United Auto Workers (UAW)—there was a successful push for broadened benefit programs, including and going beyond health care. These successes paved the way for the unorganized, pulling up wages and spreading the adoption of health benefits by employers beyond unionized industries. (Note that the decline of union strength has had the symmetrical effect of falling wages and benefits throughout the economy.)

Paralleling those wartime developments were the first successful attempts to establish group health care organizations—most notably in New York City and in the San Francisco Bay Area. In the latter, the cutting edge was provided by the Kaiser-Permanente health plan and hospitals, an outgrowth of two developments: The high accident rate in coal mines, along with owners' liability for workers' compensation, had led to the establishment of an accident and hospitalization program ("Permanente") as a means of spreading and reducing costs to mine owners. During the war, that program was extended to the thousands of Kaiser shipyard workers in the Bay Area and became "Kaiser-Permanente."[10]

The response of the powerful American Medical Association (AMA) to health care organizations was fiercely negative, both in medical schools and in the political arena: The mantra was "Group practice is incompatible with good medical care." Doctors who signed up to work at Kaiser or emerging similar plans found that in doing so they were threatening their future medical careers (most effectively by the denial of access to hospital use—a kind of blacklist) if they moved on. This was also the era of McCarthyism, and not a few doctors had doubts raised about their loyalty in the same process.

Such organizations nonetheless grew in the United States. The principal power behind that growth was that part of the business community (mostly large firms) that found itself insuring the health needs of their employees. Beginning in the 1950s, group practices of one sort or another multiplied, leading to changing attitudes in the 1960s and the creation of Medicare and Medicaid under President Johnson in 1965.

Much Better than Nothing

The beneficial effects of the progress up to 1965 were almost entirely confined to those with relatively good jobs. Most numerous and important of those left out were the old and the poor, who had no job or one that left them in poverty. In 1965, as LBJ sought to focus public attention on his program for a "Great Society" (and away from Vietnam)—having just won a landslide reelection (along with a Democratic Congress)—he was able to make a major addition to the Social Security Act of 1935: health insurance for persons over sixty-five, Medicare.

Initially, Medicare included two plans, basic and supplementary, the first financed by increases in workers' Social Security payroll deductions, the second by deductions ($3 a month, at first; more than ten times that now) from beneficiaries' Social Security benefit checks. The basic plan essentially covered hospitalization (up to 90 days), home nursing visits, and nursing home stays (both up to 100 days). The supplementary plan covered most other major medical expenses (physicians and surgeons, but nothing for troubles with the eyes, the psyche, the teeth, or for prescriptions).

Medicaid, also enacted in 1965, is a federal-state-county program (50 percent federal financing) that provides health care for the poor under sixty-five, as well as to disabled adults, children of families on welfare, and the blind. As of the early 1990s, however, Medicaid and other public health care programs covered only *half* of the poor, and because only a small percentage of those had private coverage, that meant at least one-third of all the poor were totally without access to medical care—except at emergency rooms. The latter have been in decline over the years, a decline now precipitous.[11]

A decisive improvement was thus provided by Medicare/Medicaid, inadequate though it was originally and remains. But those programs also had serious side-effects that have occupied an important role in creating what already by 1990 had come to be called our "health care crisis." It is instructive that those who originated that term and who use it incessantly have been referring rarely to the inadequate health care coverage of tens of millions of us, but very much to the explosion of costs for those who pay for them—employers, HMOs,[12] insurance companies, governments and, of course, us.[13]

The health care crisis we live in is one of inadequate coverage *and* extravagant costs. It is striking to note that already in 1992 we spent $839 billion for health care (over $1 trillion now), a 39 percent increase over 1987 (adjusting for inflation), equal to a rise from 10.8 to 14.0 percent of our GDP—nearly 1.5 times the level of Canada (the next highest among the OECD countries), more than twice that of Germany. Perhaps more informative are the dollar figures for an average family in the United States: The average cost of health insurance for an employee and family (in 1991 dollars) rose from $1,806 in 1980 to $4,464 by 1991, while employee out-of-pocket expenses for health care rose from $248 to $1,300—a rise much faster than wages or business receipts or government revenues, despite the declining rate of insurance coverage in those same years.[14]

Why are our costs so high, and how did they get that way? The answer is not pretty. Although the evolution from there to here has been complex, its guiding dynamic has been simple: king bottom line. All those for whom the costs of health care are their source of income have been beneficiaries of a system of health care insurance whose political construction (accompanied by intense lobbying in 1965) assured from the beginning that the sky would be the limit: for hospital care, doctors' fees, medical equipment, and, over time, anything and everything, as the following breakdown of its component parts reveals.[15]

We may begin with one source of high costs that everybody who has coverage of any kind knows all too well: the "paperwork syndrome." There are 1,500 or more separate for-profit health insurers in the United States; their administrative costs amount to one-quarter of total health care costs. By way of comparison, Canada has *only 1* insurer, and its paperwork costs are under 40 percent of ours. Covering 25 million people, Canada's health care system has fewer administrators than Massachusetts Blue Cross (covering 2.7 million). Those who advocate that "single-payer system" for the United States have shown that Medicare, whose standards and procedures could be the initial basis for a universal health care system, has administrative costs as low as Canada's.[16] But that's not the half of it: there are also the doctors, the hospitals, the pharmaceutical companies.

Doctors. According to the OECD, U.S. physicians' average annual incomes—about $156,000—were the highest in the world in 1989: almost twice those of physicians in Canada and Germany, more than three times those in Japan and the United Kingdom. The average had risen to $177,000 by 1994—years in which wages were standing still. And these are incomes from doctors' medical work, taking no account of investments or increase of after-tax incomes by the now frequent practice of doctors' incorporating themselves to lower their taxes on a given income.[17]

What accounts for the relatively high incomes of U.S. physicians? The first component is one of the negative side-effects of Medicare; another is the "intensity of use" in U.S. health care.

The AMA and the American Hospital Association (AHA) have long been against any interference with the free market for health care—other than their own, their control of medical schools and of hospital access. So, although in 1965 President Johnson had an easy time getting the health reform legislation through the Congress, it was much more difficult to get it accepted by the medical profession:

> Many doctors publicly swore that they would destroy the program by not participating in it. . . . To win the doctors over [LBJ] allowed them to set their own fees under Medicare . . . and they did that by hiking their fees. . . . As a result of the higher fees and the increased number of patients of Medicare in 1966, the average physician's earnings rose 11 percent to its highest level ever. And of course their earnings have continued a steady climb ever since. "Losing" the Medicare fight was the greatest thing that ever happened to them.[18]

Thus the rise in physicians' incomes is a result of their being able to raise their fees. The intensity factor is a different story. The United States has a much lower rate of utilization of health care services (far fewer days in hospital, fewer visits to a doctor) than other countries.[19] But "intensity" refers to the number and type of services received when someone *does* visit a doctor or hospital; in that respect the United States is far in the lead. Why? Because, as Rasell pointed out, "we have many fewer primary-care doctors, and many more specialists than other nations; and insurance companies pay more for procedures and tests than for equivalent amounts of time and levels of skill devoted to physical examinations, thinking about solutions to medical problems, talking to patients, or 'just' prescribing medicines."

To put it in the language of politics, the custom of "you scratch my back, and I'll scratch yours" is evidently more advanced in our medical profession than elsewhere. Not that it is always a bad idea to have that X-ray, or CAT-scan. But as many who read this will know from their own experience, it is unlikely that *so many* such procedures are advisable.

Members of the medical profession claim that the reason for this "intensity" is the constant threat of malpractice suits, plus the aging of the population; but studies have shown that "defensive medicine" accounts for only about 2 percent of the increase in health care spending, and that most of the effects of the aging population are yet to be significant. Moreover, life expectancy at birth for females here is below the level in seventeen other countries, that for men lower than twenty-one other countries; and twenty-two countries—including Italy, Spain, Hong Kong, and Singapore—have a lower infant mortality rate than ours. We must be doing something wrong.

Hospitals.   Since 1965, the decay and the actual or threatened closings of public hospitals have been in the news. These were the same years in which private for-profit hospital giants came to be household names: Humana, National Medical Enterprises, Hospital Corporation of America among them. Although the funds for hospital expansion—beginning with the Hill-Burton Act of 1946—have come from the general public, at least 60 percent of all revenues from government sources have gone to private hospitals. The latter have the latest in technology and have been the primary source of demand for equipment companies, real estate and construction firms, drug companies, and financial institutions, all of which have fed at that trough. Those hospitals, however, despite their public funding, limit their in- and outpatient population to people who are not poor and who are well insured; they rarely have emergency rooms these days.[20]

The AHA has seen to it over the years that hospitals are unregulated; and they still are—except, of course, by themselves. That there is poor care is the subject of countless anecdotes.[21] It has also received careful study by, among others, Harvard Medical School. Their findings go beyond the shocking to the frightening: The Harvard study counted 7,000 deaths from poor hospital care in New York State alone in just one year. And later research showed that "3.7 percent of all admissions studied were injured by the hospitals ... and that 14 percent of those patients who were injured by the hospital died."[22]

It is said that hospitals have always been dangerous places; they have become more so as the bottom-line pressures from insurance companies, HMOs, and Medicare and Medicaid move them in the direction of further cutting quality: replacing full-time with part-time nurses, nurses with orderlies and assistants, and lowered total numbers of these and other health—as distinct from administrative—personnel. According to another Harvard Medical School study:

> On an average day in 1968, American hospitals employed 435,100 managers and clerks while caring for 1,378,000 patients. By 1990, the average daily number of patients had fallen to 853,000, but the number of administrative personnel had grown to 1,291,600. ... Administrative costs ranged from 20.5 percent of total hospital spending in Minnesota to 30.6 percent in Hawaii, with New York, at 25.1 percent, near the national average.[23]

The foregoing discussions of doctors and hospitals has dealt essentially with the conditions that emerged over the years after Medicare/Medicaid were instituted, in which the numbers of doctors more than doubled, from under 300,000 to over 600,000, along with the great increase in private nonprofit (= no taxes to pay, but good incomes for the staff) and for-profit hospitals, the HMOs that use them, and the insurance companies that are seen to pay the bills.

Where that left us when President Clinton first entered the White House will be discussed shortly; clearly the situation could not handle the looming problems now posed by the new welfare reforms. In 1996 a *New York Times* headline read, "Hospitals Look on Charity Care as Unaffordable Option of Past: Squeezed by Managed Care and Reduced Aid."[24] It is a mark of how we use language today that such a title leads one to believe that the problem is suffered by the hospitals, not by poor people.

There are three elements of that unaffordability, the third of which we have yet to examine, the cost of medicines—not to hospitals or doctors, but to those who need them. Like the other two elements, this one qualifies as scandalous.

Pharmaceuticals. If you have had an appointment with a doctor (the term *your doctor* is becoming an anachronism) in recent years, you will have noticed that in the waiting room with you has been someone with a substantial briefcase: He or she represents a pharmaceutical company. Probably that person will see the doctor before you do, and not always because of an earlier appointment: First things first.

The pharmaceutical industry, faced as it is with criticisms because of its high profits—15.5 percent as a percent of sales (an extraordinary figure, as any economist will allow) compared with 4.6 percent for all industries—even discounting that it has to do with often desperate human needs, will explain (patiently, for it has much experience in this) that such high profits are absolutely essential to assure that research continue, and do so successfully. A persuasive argument.

Except for some stubborn facts. The facts are that prices for prescription drugs rose 152 percent 1980–1990, compared with the overall price inflation increase of 58 percent; that research and development costs for pharmaceutical products (in 1991) were $9 billion, a lot to be sure, but not as much as the $10 billion the industry spent on marketing (those briefcases you see) and, interestingly, twice the sum spent in beer and cosmetic advertising, *ten* times that for average consumer products.[25]

Prescribed drugs are not among the "consumer" products that the free market should control. Perhaps it should have some influence in that area, but be decisive? No, not for life-saving medicines. Some will remember that during World War II there was price control and rationing, and that the controls and the rations were meant to see that purchasing power *not* be the determinant of who should have how much of certain products—gasoline, meat, tires, and so on.

There was a war on then, of course. But about a century ago (with earlier wars in mind), the philosopher William James asked that we find a "moral equivalent for war." In our social thought and our public policies some such equivalent has been sought, but not persistently enough to be found. Until it is found, we shall remain unable to find a decent answer to the following kind of question: Is not the pained life of that child with Down's Syndrome, that of a cancer or an AIDS victim (and other sufferers), worth the same consideration as the pains of a war veteran? And a related but different kind of question: What is it about pharmaceutical companies—aside from their money and lobbying power—that makes their products so different from the rationing of gasoline by vital need rather than purchasing power as in World War II?

Writing about fifteen years ago, the sociologist and health care scholar Paul Starr came to the following conclusion:

> The failure to rationalize medical services under public control meant that sooner or later they would be rationalized under private control. Instead of public regulation, there will be private regulation, and instead of public planning there will be corporate planning. Instead of public financing for prepaid plans that might be managed by the subscribers' chosen representatives, there will be corporate financing for private plans controlled by conglomerates whose interest will be determined by the rate of return on investments. That is the future toward which American medicine now seems heading.[26]

And that is the future where now we dwell.

The Nineties

When Clinton was elected president in 1992, the approximate size and distribution of the annual $1 trillion income from health care in the United States was as follows:

Hospitals, $410 billion; doctors, $200 billion; nursing homes and home health care, $110 billion; drug companies, $100 billion; insurance companies, $65 billion; others, such as dentists, optometrists, physical therapists and pharmacists, something over $100 billion.[27]

Bill and Hillary Clinton wished to change that for the better; since then, however, deterioration has been rapid—for patients and doctors, that is. The insurance companies, most especially the Big Five, Aetna, Cigna, Metropolitan, Prudential, and Travelers, are better off. Unquestionably some of the intentions of the Clintons were admirable, but those were done in by the poisonous mix of political ambition into which they were stirred.

The result of the CHP was to weaken not only health care but the Clinton administration, and to facilitate the "Gingrich revolution" of the 1994 election. Clinton and the Democrats have recovered from that;[28] an always dangerously inadequate health care system has been pushed further into a deep morass.

The old saying has it that there is no use in crying over spilt milk. True, if it is a cup or glass that has been spilt; but the CHP was a milk tanker; its spilling over not only halted health care reform but also placed the country on a track of retrogression whose end is not yet in sight. We cannot make believe that the disaster did not happen, nor can we let it pass without seeking to understand how and why it happened, if we are ever to reverse it.

The trouble began before the CHP came into the public eye. The idea of national health insurance (NHI) had been planted first in 1945, as noted earlier. Well before 1992 there were many in the medical profession, untold millions in the general public, and a goodly number in Congress who saw NHI as the only acceptable path to follow. Perhaps—one is inclined to guess, probably—the Clintons were of the same persuasion. But, to quote Colin Gordon in these respects:

> Let us speculate about a scenario that never emerged. Instead of his 1,340 page monstrosity, imagine if the President supported the McDermott-Wellstone single-payer bill. With perhaps 150 votes in the House and, maybe, a dozen in the Senate, he could have faced the voters on November 8 [1994] as the champion of a people's health care plan. Is it not possible that the reactionary triumph could have been avoided? Remember, exit polls found the voters still designating health reform number one among their concerns. More importantly, would not some portion of the 61 percent of the electorate who didn't vote be finally moved to participate?

Instead, Gordon goes on to say:

> Finally [1995], the health issue has moved into a new phase. With the mergermanic corporations successfully taking over the hospital chains, HMO conglomerates, and doctors' groups, we are now living through a classic confrontation: the market-driven solutions against the humane, socially-just premise of a not-for-profit, government-facilitated insurance plan.[29]

Be it remembered that when the president first began to proclaim the need for health reform, it was with the express goal of universal coverage. The promises soon became compromises, and well before the time the public was let into the backroom debate, what had been four possibilities had been reduced to three; the single-payer possibility was dropped with absolutely *no* comment. The remaining three, with varying degrees of *im*probability for achieving universal coverage, were called "employer mandate," "individual mandate," and "no mandate."[30]

All the "mandate choices" as they then were discussed had an element presumably directed toward universal coverage but—unlike the single-payer plan—none guaranteeing it. The employer mandate, which would have built on the existing system of private coverage, was simultaneously the linchpin and the major compromise of the CHP. However, as James Tobin (one of the few genuinely deserving Nobel prize winners in economics) and law professor Michael Graetz pointed out, "The biggest flaw in the Administration proposal is the requirement that employers pay the premiums—a mandate whose awkwardness and unfairness stand out starkly in a system dedicated to universal coverage . . . [, a requirement] that no one would choose now if given a clean slate."[31]

Like the other two mandate plans, the CHP made it into but never out of committees. All the plans, in Gordon's image, were "dead on arrival." Gordon also underscored the unhappy truth that after the single-payer plan was silently shelved, the CHP came to be seen as the "plan of the Left," with all subsequent compromises veering to the Right. For diverse, mostly opposing, reasons, neither political party was willing to support a full set of compromises; the whole notion of health care reform, sagging under its own weight, finally expired from compromise poisoning.

For the main beneficiaries of the rising costs of health care, however, reform had not so much died as been successfully assassinated—by them. If we add up only the admitted amounts spent by health care interests to sway Congress and the public in 1993–1994 (political action committees [PACs], TV ads such as "Harry and Louise," lobbying, and the like), it comes to over $120 million.[32]

Once the NHI disappeared into the mists, the public debate was over one form or another of what stood as the center of the CHP, "managed competition." The defects of such an approach were pointed out by numerous health care experts; what was not discussed was what would happen if—and when—the whole effort collapsed into a black hole of dithering and finger-pointing.[33] What has happened is clearly worse than the CHP itself for the important reason that after the failure of the administration's effort at reform (and the *way* it failed), the gates were opened wider than ever for private interests to speed ahead on their own terms.

The health care industry, now clearly dominated by the Big Five insurance companies, has since 1994 been experiencing mergers in all its dimensions. The most important consequence has been that the main unhealthy tendencies in the system before 1994 have been exacerbated: Assured excellent care for the rich (as ever) and little and declining care for the poor—with rising uncertainty and fears for those in the middle, who see their costs rising for the same or fewer services, whose quantity and quality are both at increasing risk.

Those risks are rising most especially for the old and the poor who have been covered by Medicare and Medicaid. The pressures on and by Congress to cut both have been strong—for the old in part because of misinformation about the incomes of Medicare's beneficiaries, for the poor because—it is tempting to say—well, because they're poor, that being much of the attitude behind "welfare reform" legislation. Again, a look at some facts: The strong public impression is that a high percentage of Medicare beneficiaries are mostly well-off people who are taking advantage of a bumbling system. Earlier, the economic condition of the overwhelming majority of Social Security beneficiaries was shown to be weak; ditto for Medicare recipients (they are, after all, very much the same people): The number of Medicare beneficiaries with annual incomes over $50,000 is only 5 percent; those with incomes below $25,000 number 78 percent. And the average out-of-pocket spending on health care by those sixty-five and older in 1994 was $2,803. Nothing enviable there, and no sensible margin for reductions.

As for Medicaid (the health coverage for those under sixty-five and also poor), its fate is in the same dark region as AFDC and other forms of relief: Federal monies are now delegated in block grants to the states, which have substantial discretion as to how to dispose of those grants. Many states have already made clear that cuts in Medicaid are likely. The undoubted decrease in Medicaid is occurring just as other developments have increased the need: "From 1992 to 1993 an estimated 3 million children lost private health insurance" when their families lost jobs or employers stopped providing health insurance; although in 1988, 66 percent of all children under eighteen had private coverage through family employment, that had dropped to 39 percent by 1994, raising the Medicaid need from 16 to 26 percent.[34]

None of that occupies the attention of the expanding insurance giants, as they briskly gobble up or crush the smaller companies—as was to be expected even had there been (as part of the doomed CHP) a governmental overview. As Woolhandler and Himmelstein argued in 1994, the giants

> have the capital to assemble the sprawling provider networks demanded by big employers and regional health alliances, and the clout to extract discounts from hospitals and doctors by threatening to withdraw a large chunk of business . . . [shifting] costs to smaller plans, driving their premiums up and subscribers away. . . . Already, 10 insurers control 70 percent of the H.M.O.s.[35]

"Managed competition" there is and will be: between the mammoth companies on one side, and the patients, doctors, and hospitals (even the drug companies) on the other. Among the insurers themselves, however, there will be what economists call "oligopolistic competition"—that is, not the cost and price-reducing presumed to accompany competition, but constrained rivalry among the few for a larger share within defined limits. Those limits collectively safeguard the interests of the giants (spending on advertising instead of cutting prices and passing on the costs while increasing profits).

There is a ray of sunshine in that cloudy sky, although a feeble one: Now that an always larger majority of Americans will have agonizing health care fears and realities, now that doctors find themselves simultaneously losing income *and* professional dignity (diktats from insurance companies replacing their medical judgments), now that hospitals and even pharmaceutical giants find themselves up against a variety of ceilings set by profit policies—all that happening to the clear and sole benefit of giant insurance companies and their allies—perhaps a coalition of injured parties will be patched together to work toward a system that, though containing imperfections, will have more health care, not more profits, as its chief goal. Perhaps.

But that "perhaps" depends for its realization upon a reevaluation of priorities and standards by actual and prospective patients and by the doctors and nurses who do the medical work. Leadership in a promising direction has not come from on high, and we should not depend upon that in a democratic society—if or when it contains a reasonably educated and political citizenry, that is. That takes us to the next section.

Education

The structures and processes of private and public education in the United States, K–12 through college and graduate school, are mostly determined by the wrong people, mostly in the wrong ways, mostly for the wrong reasons—people whose ways and means and reasons have too much to do with individual and institutional gain, prestige, and power (and not rocking the boat), painfully too little to do with human and social (and nature's) needs and, tragically, young people's possibilities. Contemplating this sad state years ago prompted the child psychologist Erik Erikson to identify a ninth deadly sin:[36]

> Some day, maybe, there will exist a well-informed, well-considered, and yet fervent public conviction that the most deadly of all possible sins is the mutilation of a child's spirit; for such mutilation undercuts the life principle of trust, without which every human act, may it feel ever so good and seem ever so right, is prone to perversion by destructive forms of conscientiousness.

However, as Jonathan Kozol made clear in his 1991 study, *Savage Inequalities*, that "some day" is at least as far distant now as it was decades ago, or farther:

> Liberal critics of the Reagan era sometimes note that social policy in the United States, to the extent that it concerns black children and poor children, has been turned back several decades. But this assertion, which is accurate as a description of some setbacks in the areas of housing, health and welfare, is not adequate to speak about the present-day reality in public education. In public schooling, social policy has been turned back almost one hundred years.[37]

The preceding section, on the inadequacies of health care, was very long; this section on education will not be. That is not because health care is more complex than education, and certainly not because our educational system is more adequate than our health care system. Indeed, education has been immersed in a swamp for as long as one can remember, a torpid condition interrupted substantially only once in this century for some improvement, interrupted more recently by a slide into something much worse.

The welcome changes, unsurprisingly a consequence of war, were an outcome of the GI Bill, the educational grants to veterans of World War II. Those grants—covering tuition, fees, and books, plus a small but vital monthly living allowance—changed the lives of millions of veterans, greatly expanded the number of students and faculty and institutions, and made college education into mass education. There were more college degrees granted annually toward the end of the century than high school diplomas granted at its beginning—measured in both absolute and relative terms.

All the differences between the pre- and postwar educational systems will not be listed here. But not only did so many millions get more—much of it better—education, but their families' lives were much altered, more for the better than the worse, one can assume; and in the process the society had a large chance to change for the better in all its dimensions. That it both did and did not change for the better was, of course, a consequence of the fact that society moves in ways prompted by considerably more than its educational system. That makes the latter all the more important.

Mass education has always served to train and to socialize the young, whatever else it might do. In a safe and sane and decent society, the educational system should also be the means by which human beings could realize their constructive and creative promises. The educational system can also reduce the tendencies toward cruelty and violence and bigotry allowed to prosper by ignorance. That is, our education should be where we learn to understand and to appreciate our society, ourselves, Mother Nature, and our culture; where we learn who we and others are and can be. Such an education should continue throughout our life, be "womb to tomb," as was said for the British NHS in its beginnings.

The reality, but for a small percentage, is that our educational system is mostly one of training and "tracking"—what a term for educational activities!—that teaches children to recoil from school and to distrust teachers. Many of course stick with studies, because of the influence of family and/or an inspiring teacher. They are likely to be called "sissies" at school and "eggheads" later on—even by the president of the country.[38]

All that connects with a fundamental fact, namely, that the educational system always both reflects and shapes the society in which it exists. The society being reflected in recent decades has been one pulling at its seams: wealth accumulating and spectacular incomes on a grand scale for a few while a large majority's real incomes and meager wealth stagnate or fall; racism becoming more virulent; poverty spreading and deepening; violence of all sorts in all areas; and an evident shallowness, emptiness of feeling: in short, a social tinderbox.

In those same years, we have done much more to expand shopping malls than schools and have produced children inclined to rush from rather than to school. Many of the schools are like disciplinary barracks, even jails. Probably children have "always" been bored by school, which indicates that education has always served the status quo, not children's human needs and possibilities: There has never been a golden age of education.

So educational shortcomings did not begin here or recently; but those shortcomings now plumb new depths, sucked down in a swirling whirlpool whose dynamic is the deteriorating larger social process. An improved educational system is not by itself sufficient to lift us up and away from that condition, but it is necessary. Are we then faced by an insoluble dilemma, where for education to save and itself be saved, so must too much else be saved first? It is neither a dilemma nor insoluble; it is just like much of life, and the real villains are not those of complexity so much as apathy, subservience, and confusion.

Above all else, the resolution needed for education is one involving a re-shaping of priorities. As earlier, we may begin with numbers, on the simplest level of difficulty: "The Government Accounting Office [in 1995] cited $112 billion in pressing construction needs in the nation's 80,000 existing schools at a time when [locally funded] school districts are spending $5 billion a year to repair and expand buildings."[39]

That is not a lot for a nation that spends over $250 billion annually on military goods and services (and, as will be seen in Chapter 9, has spent over $10 *trillion* since 1946 on that same military). Meeting school construction needs could also provide a lot of good jobs as well as sales for construction and building materials companies. Nonetheless, when in 1995 a bill asking for $100 *million* for such construction reached the floor of Congress, it was handily defeated.

Just as the inadequacy of health care deepens while spending on health care rises, K–12 public education suffers similarly. Average expenditures per pupil (in 1992 dollars) increased from $2,626 in 1970 to $5,412 in 1993.[40] That most public schools rely heavily on local property taxes for their funding, however, contributes to substantial inequality in the funding for affluent as compared with poor districts (with ratios differing as much as 9 to 1 per pupil).[41]

Despite inadequate spending and the social problems bearing negatively on education for the poor, it is striking to note—and important to understand—that the general view of the poor (especially blacks) as breaking all records for dropping out, low scores, and the like, does not match the reality. The facts show that a high percentage of those given the least break by the larger society are doing very hard work to overcome that disadvantage: High school graduation rates in 1989 were 87 percent, as compared with 10 percent in 1910 and 73 percent in 1969; school drop-out rates have been declining or are stable for every ethnic group. Of those who do drop out, about two-thirds are white; two-thirds are from two-parent homes; over 40 percent are from suburban schools; nearly three-quarters never repeated a grade; 86 percent are from homes where English is the native language. Math and verbal SAT scores have increased for all "racial" groups but one since 1976, with the largest percentage increase in the African-American students. The one lower-performing set is among those classified as white. Finally, the performance of twelfth-grade students in science shows no difference between public schools, private Catholic schools, and private non-Catholic schools.[42]

That despite all these problems, children continue to survive the public schools is a summons to reduce their obstacles—not to give up or to place children in costly private schools (as some who are *not* well off do, requiring painful sacrifices). The rest, children and parents alike, must struggle beyond any reasonable level—especially unreasonable in a society as rich and as proud of its democracy as this one.

That the poor have done so well would come as a surprise for most. But that relatively good news should not lead to the mistaken conclusion that all's well in K–12, for it is not. It should lead to other conclusions: that young people, not all but most, given half a chance will struggle to do what humanly can be done, even—perhaps especially?—when they are children. Think what they could do under better conditions.

The foregoing has concerned schools K–12. Before our brief remarks on desirable reforms on that level, however, I shall make a few remarks on college education. Going beyond high school has become essential for getting and keeping a decent job, in addition to other needs and possibilities it may serve. But two other developments run alongside that need: (1) The yearly costs of a degree (tuition plus room and board) at both private and public universities continue to rise more rapidly than the rate of inflation. At public colleges "tuition soared by 234 percent between 1980 and 1994, while general inflation rose by 74 percent. . . . On average, the costs of private universities now exceed 50 percent of median family income, overall (1996–97) more than $18,000, and for the top schools, $26,000 annually. Though public colleges and universities are cheaper, they are not cheap: The average is over $7,000 a year, for the nine million (two-thirds of the total) who attend them." (2) Meanwhile, public aid to college students has "plummeted. . . . In 1979, a student from the highest quartile was 4 times more likely to earn a B.A. by age 24 than a student in the poorest quartile. By 1994, that individual was 19 times more likely."[43]

Those data are the meat and potatoes of the existing educational system. Whatever the grave inadequacies of that system from the viewpoint of needs and possibilities, it is what we have; it ought to be funded sufficiently in the aggregate and, at least as important, with a rock-bottom minimum of racial discrimination and a substantial increase in funding for the poor. So much, once more, for numbers. What about the qualitative situation?

There is no point in putting forth a series of recipes; a cafeteria list of what we must do will have to suffice:

- An easy first step (just begun in California): smaller classes, at all levels, especially important in the first years. Usually by the time really small classes—seminars—are the norm, at the Ph.D. level in the university, they are nowhere near as necessary.
- A not so easy next step: a substantial reduction of bureaucratization in the public school system, with more part in decision-making for teachers and parents. Not only is much of the bureaucratization more in the nature of sludge than lubrication, it is also a large part of what was meant earlier by "the wrong people. . . . " Few indeed are those who get to the top levels of the bureaucracy because they have a strong interest in learning.
- De-bureaucratization within the thousands of school districts must be accompanied by long overdue development of national standards for education: a child in one state or county should not be educated to lower standards than one elsewhere. Never should that have been true; in this day and age of blurred geographic boundaries for jobs, it is a sentence of mediocrity for the children who come from areas with low standards: and some are very low indeed.
- There must be a lessening of the differences in quality of education available simply because one is from a white, or a rich, or an anything family: For educational purposes, if not yet all others, how about trying on the notion that we were all created equal and deserve to be allowed to stay that way, if we don't blow the opportunity.
- In the name of the future of both the children and the society, the schools must cultivate the possibilities of learning, not only or even mostly training; of appreciation and understanding of all that we hold dear, past and present and hoped-for; schools must be made places where the young cherish the time spent.
- No more nostrums, but one more question: Can we not put ourselves in the mind of those whose lives are cramped by the stinting of their educational opportunities, and that because of the accident of their birth? Can we not learn to act on the practical implications of the ancient wisdom, "there but for the grace of God go I?"[44]

Housing

The discussion of housing will be even briefer than that on education; the needs are also great, but their origin and their solution are simpler to understand and to enact. In fact, a reasonably good solution has already been "done" once—and since undone.

FDR's second inaugural address, one of his many noteworthy speeches, contained the memorable statement that "one-third of the nation is ill-clothed, ill-fed, and ill-housed." He expressed his determination to change that for the better. Concerning housing, earlier steps had been taken for those not already ill-housed but threatened financially of becoming so, those with homes they might lose, a relatively well-off minority of the population. In 1934 the Federal Home Owners Loan Corporation (FHOLC) was established to refinance what otherwise would have been defaulted home loans, saving hundreds of thousands of small owners' homes (and their banks' investments).

More important over the longer run was what occurred regarding the so-called thrifts or S and Ls (savings and loans). In one form or another such banks had existed throughout the nineteenth century; in the 1920s there were 12,000 in operation in the country. But even in that "prosperity decade" (which wasn't prosperous for most), by 1928 there had been 75,000 home foreclosures, a number the Depression inflated to 275,000 by 1932.

All those foreclosed homes meant a lot of family misery; it also meant the failure of at least 2,000 thrifts—a terrible problem not only for the small bankers but also for their very small depositors.[45] The FHOLC helped banks to refinance existing loans; then, also in 1934, the Federal Savings and Loan Insurance Corporation (FSLIC) was established. In ensuring the thrifts' depositors against loss, the FSLIC was also "ensuring" that the process of small savings and of small borrowings for homes could pick up once more, sometime; as it did. Thus, "savings and loans [banks] occupied a special place in America, making home ownership affordable for the emerging middle class through 30-year fixed-rate mortgages ... [and] provided the fuel for the home-building engine that for almost half a century [after 1934] acted as the fountainhead of America's dynamic domestic economy."[46]

There was of course much else—not least war and cold war—driving that economy; still, the S and Ls were decisive for the process by which two-thirds of Americans "owned" their own home by the 1960s. The war was also involved in that evolution: Veterans' subsidized and guaranteed home loans, together with cold war economic stimuli, led to a boom in the residential construction industry after the war.

Before the war both the construction industry and those with inadequate housing had been helped by the U.S. Housing Act of 1937, put in place after FDR's address. It authorized assistance to local communities "to remedy the unsafe and unsanitary housing conditions and the acute shortage of decent, safe, and sanitary dwellings for families of low income." In 1947 that evolved into the Public Housing Administration; in 1965, the Housing Act renewed the program of housing for those living in substandard homes with a $7.3 billion appropriation for housing construction.[47]

Today, with one-third of Americans living in overcrowded or substandard conditions, public policy is going in the opposite direction.[48] Already in 1983 it had been estimated that "approximately 50 million people live in the deteriorated and socially dysfunctional areas called slums."[49] In the decade following, the shortage of affordable housing has moved toward doubling—although there is still a "public housing program."

So what went wrong? Many things. (1) The definition of "public" has been drastically altered: Though still governmentally assisted through subsidized interest payments (which normally amount to at least 50 percent of costs over the life of a mortgage), the public has changed from "families of low income" to families with incomes averaging $75,000 or more. (2) Earlier-constructed housing projects for the poor have been left to decay and rot—many of them standing vacant, some of them simply blown up. (3) Programs such as Section 8 are being cut back or abandoned. And during the 1980s, (4) "federal appropriations for low-income housing fell by 81 percent (allowing for inflation)."[50]

Among the results: "Up to 7 million were homeless at some point in the late 1980s." In 1991, "34 percent of the nation's homeless were families with children (up from 25 percent in 1985) . . . , the fastest-growing segment of America's homeless population." Notwithstanding these grim numbers, in fiscal 1992, "total state appropriations for emergency housing programs for the homeless were cut 10 percent (adjusting for inflation)." All relevant changes have moved in the same direction in the years since, the number of homeless has risen, and appropriations continue to fall.[51]

In the face of such conditions, in summer 1995 the Gingrich Congress eliminated rent subsidies for 60,000 new housing units, the most recent cut in a process that has seen the annual average of about 290,000 in 1977 fall to about 74,000 in 1995. Finally, although "there are nearly two poor people for every unit of low-income housing [in New York and Connecticut and more than that in New Jersey] . . . , all sides agree that a sharp reversal of the Federal role in directly creating more affordable housing is under way."[52]

Many of those saddened or angered by the squalid (or no) housing of literally millions of our people are nevertheless beset by hopelessness in terms of dealing with that problem, not only because of the decline of funding for public housing, but also because of the failures of that housing when it has been funded. Some place the blame on the infamous "high-rise projects" over much of the nation; others put the blame on the residents. Doubtless it would be better all around if public housing were composed entirely or largely of smaller buildings with much space between them (as some are here and many more are in Europe). And some of the blame can be put on the residents, but only if we acknowledge a prior responsibility of those who initiated the policies setting up the largest number of projects after World War II. As Nicholas Lemann pointed out,

> [In] the late 1940s, the nation embarked on the course that led to the perception that public housing doesn't work: the construction of enormous high-rise proj-

ects. It wasn't the architecture, or the mere presence of government subsidies, that caused these places to go so horribly awry. There was also a big change in the tenant population, from carefully screened working people to the very poor. Because of changes in Federal rules, people who got jobs actually had to leave the building, and it became nearly impossible to kick out tenants who were criminals. Even so, it's not all public housing that doesn't work. It's just the large-scale, all-poor, severely isolated projects that invariably fall. . . . [T]he real estate industry, by and large, supported the construction of the worst projects . . . [in] the 1950s and 60s when African-American migrants were streaming into the big cities, and part of the reason for the building of the projects was to contain them within the existing ghettos so as to avoid residential integration.[53]

Lemann added that recently HUD has begun to demolish about 30,000 of the worst high-rises, hoping to replace them with community development projects that screen tenants, create a mix of working and very poor people, and oust criminals, while providing security forces for ongoing confidence and safety. The funding for this initiative, however, must come largely from that very Section 8 program that is now being pushed into oblivion.

Finding ourselves in what seems to be a vicious circle of substandard housing and substandard lives, it is well to realize that the circle is the result not least (or only) of a political economy that makes good jobs always harder to find at the same time that public policies make surviving without a good job always harder. Such problems have been produced by our society, and they can be resolved by our society.

Chapter 10 will offer a broad program for putting us on a path of socioeconomic improvement, one that happily need not be original: It will echo many others now being put forth. Here we may partially anticipate those suggestions and recall the thoughts of William Julius Wilson, noted in Chapter 6. The disappearance of jobs in the ghetto led to the poverty and dreadful housing of a substantial percentage of those afflicted. A vicious circle worked to bring about that effect also: The deeper ghettoization of many big cities (in the 1950s and 60s), as Wilson made clear, also became a process of wiping out small businesses and jobs in those ghettos. If one puts that together with "downsizing and outsourcing" and their offspring, the picture becomes one of very high odds against people of low incomes, and even higher odds that they will be pushed down further—into lower or no incomes, worse education, worse housing. And so on. And then they will be blamed for their ills; all of them, for all their ills.

8

Environmental Deterioration

Earth, Air, Fire, and Water

Western culture and science had their beginnings among the Greek philoso-
phers about 2,500 years ago, for present purposes most relevantly in the
thought of Empedocles (c. 493–433). The four components of the subtitle,
earth, air, fire, and water, were seen by him as "the original roots or elements
of all things, mixing and separating under the influence of two forces, attraction (love) and repulsion (hate)."

"Love" was defined by the Greeks much as Erich Fromm would have it,
embodying not only romantic and familial love but also "concern, understanding, respect, and compassion"—and hate stood opposed in all those respects. Nature, of which we are but a part, has already been damaged terri-
bly, and the time is all too close when currently accelerating damages will
end life as we know it: There has been too little "love" and too much "hate"
by us of the "earth, air, fire, and water" that created and sustains us.

The Greeks who planted the seeds of modern rational thought are not
likely to have imagined our species' having either the powers or the impru-
dence that would bring nature and society to today's ugly pass. But even at
the middle of this century, Rachel Carson, who combined scientific training
and sensitivity to a rare degree and who wrote several pathbreaking books,
including *Silent Spring*, did not think that Mother Nature had reason to fear
the inhabitants of the earth:

> Man's attitude toward nature is today critically important, simply because of his
> new found power to destroy it. . . . In the days before Hiroshima I used to won-
> der whether nature . . . actually needed protection from man. Surely the sea was
> inviolate and forever beyond man's power to change it . . . ; vast cycles by which

water is drawn up into the clouds to return again to the earth could never be touched. And just as surely the vast tides of life—the migrating birds—would continue to ebb and flow over the continents, marking the passage of the seasons.

But I was wrong. Even these things, that seemed to belong to the eternal verities, are not only threatened but have already felt the destroying hand of man. Today we use the sea as a dumping ground for radioactive wastes, which then enter the vast and uncontrollable movements of ocean water through the deep basins, to turn up no one knows where. . . . The once beneficent rains are now an instrument to bring down from the atmosphere the deadly products of nuclear explosions. Water, perhaps our most precious natural resource, is used and misused at a reckless rate. Our streams are fouled with an incredible assortment of wastes—domestic, chemical, radioactive, so that our planet, though dominated by seas that envelop three-fourths of its surface, is rapidly becoming a thirsty world.

We now wage war on other organisms, turning against them all the terrible armaments of modern chemistry, and assume a right to push whole species over the brink of extinction.[1]

It is of course we of the industrially and scientifically most advanced societies that can and do increasingly poison, misuse, waste, and destroy the bounty of "earth, air, fire, and water" for ourselves; and for the poor countries, as much or more. The satirist (and math professor) Tom Lehrer caused many an uneasy laugh in the 1950s by singing (in an anti-nuke song), "We'll all go together when we go." It wasn't truly funny then; now it seems more like a funeral dirge, now that the possibility of an ecological Armageddon in the next century has ceased to be a remote one.

The Effluent Society

That such a man-made ("anthropogenic") catastrophe looms on the horizon and that so much damage has already been done is the consequence of complex and dynamically interacting quantitative and qualitative developments in all dimensions of the social process—scientific, economic, political, cultural, demographic, and geographic. Intertwining swiftly and ubiquitously at an accelerating pace as this century opened, those developments reached their "critical mass" after World War II, as the political economy of contemporary industrial capitalism took hold and deepened over the globe. In the post–World War II decades, concerns over ecological/environmental dangers were raised to the level of popular consciousness.

World War II brought to fruition the qualitative side of the matter, invention and innovation in the areas of chemistry and physics—synthetics, electronics, and nuclear physics. The war was ultimately instrumental for the renovation, modernization, spread, and deepening of industrialization and the associated quantum leaps both in the patterns and levels of consumption and production and in the dependence upon their heedless growth. Massive damage to the environment caused by—among other contributors—petroleum, its byproducts, and their numberless applications has ensued.

E. F. Schumacher, in his influential *Small Is Beautiful,* understood that "modern man does not experience himself as a part of nature but as an outside force destined to dominate and conquer it." Writing in 1974, he was among the first to identify that arrogance—what the Greeks called *hubris*—which had its practical realization in the decades following World War II:

> The next four or five years are likely to see more industrial production, taking the world as a whole, than all of mankind accomplished up to 1945. Partly as a cause and also as an effect, there has also been a unique qualitative jump. Our scientists and technologists have learned to compound substances unknown to nature. Against many of them, nature is virtually defenceless. There are no natural agents to attack and break them down. It is as if aborigines were suddenly attacked with machine-gun fire: their bows and arrows are of no avail. These substances, unknown to nature, owe their almost magical effectiveness precisely to nature's defencelessness—and that accounts also for their dangerous ecological impact . . . [because] they tend to accumulate, and the long-term consequences of this accumulation are in many cases known to be extremely dangerous, and in other cases totally unpredictable.[2]

The qualitative aspects of these processes are quite complex, but the quantitative dangers are easy to comprehend: When a few factories emit quantity X of a pollutant in the air or a river every day, nature cleans it up quickly; when some thousands of factories multiply X by a million (or a billion), nature is defeated—all the more so as the toxics become more potent, as the pollutant is not itself part of nature, but man-made, such as chlorofluorocarbons, plastics, pesticides: nonbiodegradable. You can't fool Mother Nature, but she can be beaten. She is being beaten.

A common belief is that the quantitative side of the matter is the nub of the problem, and among all the numbers "the real problem is that there are too many people." In other words, Malthus was right, after all, if perhaps for the wrong reasons. Because that is both a plausible and a widespread position, what may seem a detour is needed here.

It is easy to agree that rising population exacerbates most other social problems, that the world would be a more comfortable and safer place if population were to cease rising and, if possible, undergo a natural decrease over the long term; all constructive steps to assist that are desirable. But the problems exacerbated by population growth have their origins elsewhere; rapid population growth is an outcome, not a cause.

Population experts all agree on one matter, if not all others: As biologist Josué de Castro made clear already in his *Geography of Hunger* (1952), population growth takes place least rapidly in the rich countries and most rapidly in the poorer ones (and among the poorest in all countries); population growth slows down as material well-being increases, and rises with poverty.[3]

There is also substantial, if by no means universal, agreement that the population of the poor countries—with a good 80 percent of the world's people and the highest rates of population growth—suffer increased impoverishment along with a battering exploitation of their natural resources as and *because* the interdependence of the poor countries with the richer ones escalates. Traditional economic systems (especially the customary balance between self-sufficient agriculture and petty industry) are disrupted and ruined, leaving vast numbers of people to migrate to cities (or other countries) to search for nonexistent or poverty-level jobs—or to become criminals.[4]

There is nothing new in this; it happened most dramatically in the nineteenth century in India (the Irish famine was equally dramatic, but in smaller numbers over the long run), when British imperial controls forced India to open itself to free trade, especially British cotton. The Indian (pre-factory) cotton textile industry, thriving and exporting in the eighteenth century, was destroyed, and India in the nineteenth century became instead a grower of cotton for those "dark satanic mills" in England. Thus ended what had been a stable and interdependent cotton textile and agricultural sector; thus was initiated the process that produced India's massive population and widespread urban poverty. Now it's happening all over.

It is *not* that there are too many people or that we are industrialized or that science and technology move ahead always more rapidly. It is how people live—have learned or (especially in the poorer countries) been forced to live; the reckless ways and means of industrialization; the structures of production and consumption creating and depending upon too much and always-more-destructive waste; pursuing too much of what we don't need and too little of what we do; the ways in which science and technology are used.

Few indeed are those who are against modern industry (nor am I one of them). The problem's core instead is who decides what is to be produced, in what ways and quantities, and for what purposes; that is, the problem is the location and use of social power—in the economy, in government, in the realms of education, the media, and entertainment.

Of course the planet could not be threatened were the global population stabilized at 1 or 2 billion, living an agrarian existence, with barely a sprinkle of science and modern technology. But that world is neither possible nor desirable. What is both possible and desirable—and imperative—is to change our ways and means and, it needs adding, some of our ends. But those are matters of politics and morality, not of numbers or of economics. Were we to move along sensible lines in those respects, population would cease to increase and would then decrease for positive reasons—and Malthusian theories could finally be ensconced in a fine and private place with the eternal rest they so richly deserve.

Thus it is not our extraordinary numbers that must be dealt with; it is what we all do, how and with what it is done, and where, how often, and, usually, why. Now we summarily explore those whys and wherefores. Not here, but in Chapter 10, resolutions to ecological problems will be examined that are not only workable but also job-increasing. Some of those resolutions are to keep and strengthen what exists that is being weakened: the Environmental Protection Agency, the Occupational Safety and Health Administration, the Clean Air Act—put in place not by "liberals," but by the Nixon administration.

The Self-Endangering Species

What must be reversed was summarized in largest part by Murray Bookchin as he saw matters a quarter of a century ago:

> What is at stake in the ecological crisis we face today is the very capacity of the earth to sustain advanced forms of life. The crisis is being drawn together by massive increases in the "typical" forms of air and water pollution; by a mounting accumulation of nonbiodegradable wastes, lead residues, pesticide residues and toxic additives in food; by the expansion of cities into vast urban belts; by increasing stresses due to congestion, noise and mass living; by the wanton scarring of the earth as a result of mining operations, lumbering, and real estate speculation.[5]

Writing today, one must of course add in the operation and the intractable wastes of nuclear plants, the disappearing ozone layer and global warming and the dangers they entail, and other matters more recently come to light. The following examination of that litany of troubles in terms of which activities are responsible will serve as a point of departure.

It is, of course, important to remember that we are not exposed to the harm of each of these dangers separately—Monday, poison in the air; Tuesday, poison in the water; Wednesday, your detergent may be causing testicular cancer; Thursday, a spot of skin cancer from the ozone hole; Friday, a radiated fish; Saturday, smog alert; Sunday, an extraordinary—warmer-earth caused?—storm; and, in the next week, Monday? Don't ask.[6]

Of course we do not endure these one at a time (and some we are not conscious of enduring at all), though that is the manner in which the dangers are too often discussed and analyzed. It is all of them, all the time, all increasing, interacting, multiplying. We begin with the most dramatic.

Nuclear Energy

The horrible consequences from nuclear fission, whether from nuclear bomb testing or use, as in Hiroshima and Nagasaki, are well known and need no discussion here. But connected matters do. The two main offenders in the nuclear arena are the military and the energy/utilities companies. (For the military see Chapter 9.)

The peaceful uses of nuclear energy create at least two large and unresolved problems: (1) they are very dangerous (some will still remember the Three-Mile Island near-meltdown in Pennsylvania, and that of Chernobyl in the former USSR); and (2) what can safely be done about the disposal of nuclear wastes has now been discussed and acted upon in a manner resembling the game of musical chairs. Every solution—bury it, burn it, sink it in the seas, pay the Indian reservations or the poor countries to put it someplace, don't worry about it, who lives forever?—if not already found wanting has yet to be shown as safe. In fact, lots of spin is put on any public discussion in order not to face the enormous fact that there is still *no* waste that has been safely disposed of after more than fifty years of dumping it somewhere—whether by us or the other countries that have risked the development of nuclear facilities. Radiated materials, no matter where they're put, are going to radiate for hundreds or thousands of years, and there's been no real (as compared with putative) wall or other device yet they can't get through before their half-lives are used up.

Another point is relevant to the budget-balancing discussion of Chapter 2: the largest number of nuclear power plants have two characteristics, of which the first is welcome information: (1) they either never have been or never will go into operation or they are being "phased out"; less welcome is that (2) they have come out with much higher than predicted per kilowatt costs (instead of the lower costs touted), and capital expenditures running into many billions of dollars have routinely been underestimated. You may be sure that somehow, especially if you live in a region that has had or still has a nuclear power plant, you will pay for all that dangerous folly.

☞ In 1966, during the "Atoms for Peace" years[7]—"when nuclear electricity [was expected] to be 'too cheap to meter'"—then-Governor Rockefeller (N.Y.) "encouraged a private company, Nuclear Fuel Services, to build a plant near Buffalo to take in spent reactor fuel, chop it up and dissolve it in acid, and recover uranium or plutonium for re-use." The factory was shut in 1972, leaving until today "a rusting tank holding material that contains about half as much radiation as was released at Chernobyl." The plant cost $32 million to build; cleaning up the waste it left behind will cost $1.5 *billion*. (That is only the first estimate.) It will be paid to West Valley Nuclear Services (of Westinghouse), 90 percent by the federal and 10 percent by the state government. "'It was somewhat [!] costly and took quite a period of time, but at least it's not going down Cattaragus Creek and into Lake Erie,'" said a spokesman for the cleanup company.[8] The new canister arrangement is presently expected to be placed in Yucca Mountain (Nevada), where it is hoped all will be well for some thousands of years, when the radiation's half life will have ended.

Air Pollution, the Ozone Layer, and Global Warming

"Pollution" seems very much a euphemism for what happens to the poisoned air we all must breathe. What are the most important problems and what are their sources? The air has become dangerous to our health (among that of other flora and fauna) in countless ways: by the spewing into the skies of industrial contaminants from products using new chemical combinations, with consequences both known and as yet unknown; by leaks large and small of this and that; by the continuing decline of public transportation and the proliferating uses of internal combustion engines *and* their increasing number (*and* an *increasing* consumption of gasoline because the most popular category of new cars is the "sports utility vehicle" that guzzles gas in the manner of the 1950s Cadillacs); and the increased use of synthetic materials (especially those based on petrochemicals) in almost everything, including construction, the waste and dusts from which, one way or another, foul our air. Whatever else all this entails in terms of lung and heart disease, it has already created a large and rapidly growing "hole" in the ozone layer and initiated a process of climate change toward global warming.

With respect to the ozone layer, "the destruction . . . (technically, [of] the global sheath) is worsening, with the ozone practically destroyed in one level of the atmosphere." "We're looking at a possible new record for ozone destruction."[9] The ozone layer filters the sun's ultraviolet radiation. With the layer intact, the sun's rays, powerful enough to penetrate the layer on the way in, but having been weakened by bouncing off the earth's surface, are unable to "bounce back" into space.

The "hole" began (or began to be noticed) in the 1970s, with the rising use of chlorofluorocarbons (CFCs) in spray cans:

> In 1979, after a bitter struggle with corporate and political special interests, spray cans using CFCs—mainly DuPont products—were banned in the United States and a few other countries. Most nations, however, continued to use them. As they were phased out in the U.S., DuPont and other corporations began to push CFC use as a refrigerant . . . , as a foaming agent . . . , and as a solvent, especially in treating computer chips. . . . [Now] CFC production [and use] is said to be increasing world-wide at the high rate of 5 or 6 percent each year.[10]

In early 1996, scientists from NASA and colleagues at the University of California (Berkeley) announced that CFCs were "guilty beyond any reasonable doubt" of destroying the earth's ozone layer and thereby letting in damaging ultraviolet radiation from the sun. And in October 1996 the warning was once again issued: "Any sustained surge in radiation reaching the earth could lead to a rise in cancer in humans and animals, lower crop yields and affect the marine food chain, according to experts."[11]

And then there's global warming, caused by the heat-trapping "greenhouse" gas, carbon dioxide (CO_2)—from our use of fossil fuels (oil, coal, and gas)—whose astonishing increase is perhaps the most worrisome matter of all for scientists who follow its course. Like the dangers of the depleting ozone layer, those of global warming have been pooh-poohed as minimal or nonexistent or "theoretical." To which, the nonworriers add, what dangers there might be wouldn't be realized until well into the future. Unless, that is, you believe that already observed and decidedly peculiar climatic changes over the globe of the sort warned against are due to, well, global warming—as did the authors of a report in *Scientific American*, in 1989:

> The world is warming. Climatic zones are shifting. Glaciers are melting. Sea level is rising. These are not hypothetical events from a science fiction movie: these changes and others are already taking place, and we can expect them to accelerate over the next years as the amounts of carbon dioxide, methane and other trace gases accumulating in the atmosphere through human activities increase.[12]

Perhaps all these consequences, way out in space or here on earth, are, after all, way off in time (cross our fingers) or will affect only others? Evidently not. In a dry, technical, and authoritative MIT study, such points were examined:

> Where are the greatest risks to humans and over what time frames as a consequence of global and environmental changes? Similarly, where are most humans at risk? . . . In the case of a global rise in sea level, this [study's] approach would recommend a selective focus on places such as New Orleans, Alexandria in Egypt, and Bangladesh. In the case of ozone depletion, it would pinpoint fair-skinned people in the high latitudes or any other populations at high risk for skin cancers. . . . Rising temperatures should mean less precipitation, more demand for irrigation, and increasing risk of desert encroachment. Under the human conditions just specified, one ought to be highly motivated to begin finding out.[13]

Well, the insurance companies have begun to take such matters seriously in the United States, evidently prompted by the nineteen tropical storms of 1995 (including eleven hurricanes). Given that the affected companies have something under $250 billion in relevant assets, and that for the first time the $1 billion damage mark was passed in 1989 (Hurricane Andrew in 1992 cost $16 billion), one can say it's about time:

> In a classic case of "strange bedfellows," gray-suited insurers are seeking advice on global warming from the in-your-face environmental group Greenpeace.

"We have to be viewed as the odd couple," acknowledged Franklin Nutter, president of the Reinsurance Association of America and a leader of the insurance industry's anti-greenhouse movement. [By September 1996, after 8 tropical storms that year] the insurance industry [had] awarded 15 research grants to scientists who will study hurricane and typhoon threats around the world.[14]

Water Pollution

As for our water supplies, what shall we look at first? The streams, the lakes, the oceans, the rain? the drainoff from poisoned soils? And how shall we count them? Which pollutants of what toxicities shall we cite? Rachel Carson's alarm bell in the night was concerned principally with the direct and indirect consequences of pesticides on underground waters. Not yet visible, but just around the corner, other fearsome developments were under way.

The means of production and our cleanliness are among the principal causes of water pollution: the disposal of industrial and bodily wastes, of our soaps, and the washing away of *urban*-applied insecticides and herbicides. There are the increased runoffs of water from filled-in swamps and denuded hillsides, the closing off of local for distant water supplies, as the major cities become more crowded and more extended into vast suburbs, then reach out for "reliable" water. Put all this and earlier noted factors together and it becomes easy to understand why, as early as 1967, President Johnson felt impelled to declare that "every major river system in the country is polluted." So are most of the lakes and bays and significant parts of the oceans.

Quite simply, through organic and inorganic chemical residues, sewage and heat and algae, clean water is rapidly becoming a very scarce resource—though it, along with air, is classified in the econ textbooks as a "free good." It was free to business, as it made profits from our reckless development, but not free to the population, which must finance the remedies, where there are remedies. Some of the causes of water pollution—for example, the disposal of industrial and bodily wastes—cannot be done away with; but they and all the other causes can be constrained, and some *can* be eliminated.

With all her insight, and frightening though her first book was, Rachel Carson could not anticipate the sort of massive tragedy in India where it was the *production,* not the use, of insecticides and herbicides (for the fabled "green revolution") that was the problem. In 1985 a malfunctioning storage tank of methyl isocyanate at Bhopal released its deadly poisons into the air of a surrounding and densely settled neighborhood. The immediate deaths were over 2,000, accounted injuries over 200,000, disabilities serious enough to prevent work, 30,000–50,000. Union Carbide is still wrangling over the degree and nature of its responsibility. One wonders if such a catastrophe in the United States would have left Union Carbide still in business: The answer is a qualified yes. After many thousands of asbestos workers were shown medically and judged by the courts to have been severely, even fatally, afflicted by their work, the corporation responsible—Johns Manville—detached its asbestos division, which promptly declared itself bankrupt. The suits go on; the plaintiffs die off.

There are various reasons for "outsourcing" and foreign plants. Among the most persistent is that where there is very cheap labor there are likely to be few or no environmental controls. Weak as the latter are here, they are weaker (or nonexistent) in the poorer countries. Carson could not discuss, though she did anticipate, another production disaster of a more slow-moving sort: the many casualties from the (long-denied) chemical wastes poured into New York's Love Canal, which polluted both the air and the water. Doubtless we shall hear of others in due time.

What *is* it about our civilization that it has found so many ingenious ways to do harm to itself? What *is* it, even worse in a sense, that when the harms have been explained and even *have come to pass,* the system sails blithely on, almost always denying or explaining the harm away, even lying about it? What *is* it that ensures that when a problem has been recognized and laws made to contain it, there are insufficient personnel to enforce those laws, or else they are repealed?

What lies at the center of the problem was suggested in Chapter 3, all too briefly: our dependence upon and virtually total belief in economic growth as the main source of our well-being and main solution to our problems. It "goes without saying" that otherwise profits and jobs must fall. Compounding the problem, we have been taught—increasingly—to find our main sources of satisfaction in buying and having, made possible, we have been taught, by that selfsame economic growth.

That we—the whole family—must work more as we gain always less satisfaction from our purchases, that economic expansion has already caused the loss of jobs—40 million in twenty-five years—and the addition of few good but many worse ones, that the simple arithmetic of ecological relationships signals a brick wall for both expansionism *and* consumerism within the lifetime of the next generation—all of that and more cannot persuade us to change our ways except, at best, to slow down the rate of *increase* of the problem. It is not implicit in the foregoing litany of troubles that we can save our planet and ourselves only by living badly. Although we (let alone the entire world's population) cannot continue to consume at the present per capita consumption levels of the OECD countries, we and all others could live better than we now do, were we to achieve sustainable development instead of continuing on the path of unsustainable growth.[15] As will be argued in Chapter 10, acting on an informed view of our needs and possibilities makes possible a *better* quality of life for all—although it also requires that those now on the very top of the pyramids of income, wealth, and power be reined in significantly in all three respects. To that later; here and now there is yet more damage to be noted.

All Creatures, Great and Small

The silence of the spring Rachel Carson warned us about was the absence of birdsong—owing to the absence of birds. Birds subsist mostly on insects, which, as farming has been "modernized," have been killed off by insecticides: organic phosphates such as parathion, and chlorinated hydrocarbons, such as DDT (used lavishly in Indochina to destroy crops and forests, but which also harmed people, including many thousands of U.S. soldiers, who are still suing). It is noteworthy that the initial research and development of insecticides was during World War II and was for disabling or killing enemy soldiers. Thus, their dangers were known by their inventors and financiers from the outset. As insects (including harmless species) were poisoned, birds too were poisoned, or starved, and/or disappeared.

Meanwhile, by the 1970s, the exploitation and disappearance of the Amazon forest—the largest in the world—had come to endanger not only the oxygen supply but also a good part of the bird population of North America, not to mention the fate of the native peoples of those devastated areas. But not only those people.

The aforementioned Love Canal disaster came from the seepage of toxic wastes into the gardens and water supplies of the people living nearby. The insecticides used in farming find their way into the food chain directly and indirectly, as they move into wells and streams and rivers, and into the bodies of fish and ducks and grazing animals slated to be eaten one day.

It is not only the little ones, the insects and birds, that are disappearing, of course, so are the big ones. *The* world authority on tigers[16] estimated that there were but a few hundred still running free, and that (except for those in zoos and circuses) tigers would be extinct very soon.

> *Tiger! Tiger! burning bright*
> *In the forests of the night,*
> *What immortal hand or eye,*
> *Dare frame thy fearful symmetry?*

No immortal hand, dear Blake, the hand of man, the hunter and the destroyer of habitats.

In the United States there was a horrifying preview in the nineteenth century of what could happen with no "good reason": the virtual extinction of the buffalo. You probably didn't learn about this in your history courses: In a process as astonishing as it is abhorrent, the buffalo population of North America shrank from 65,000,000 in 1800 to 1,500 in 1900. Suppose that estimate for 1800 was too high by a factor of two, that, say, there were only 30,000,000 or so in 1800. Still. . .

What happened? It wasn't the indigenous tribes. They had long depended upon the buffalo for food and warmth, of course, but their killings fell much below the buffalo birth rate. The slaughter was a squalid, twisted game that had nothing to with food or warmth. It had several variations, all involving killing buffalo (an animal that will walk up to you so you can place your gun between its eyes). Perhaps the most revolting were the excursion trains (with benches looking out to both sides) moving over the plains as dozens of men shot thousands a day, and left the buffalo there to rot; just for the hell of it. The buffalo slaughter also disturbed the natural balance of survival for the tribes—perhaps *that* was intended. That disturbance, along with the slaughter and confinement of the natives, pretty much took care of "the Indian problem."

Times change. Today the buffalo is being nurtured back into existence: to be eaten, of course. However, at Fort Wingate (N.M.) you can buy a license to kill aged bull buffaloes; better yet for some, near Yellowstone National Park for $250 (1989 prices) you can do the same and have your picture taken with the dead animal.

There are many endangered species, of course. All too many have passed through danger and become extinct; some hundreds become extinct every year. Each time the alarm is sounded for one or more of the species in the gun sight, defenders of the status quo cry that they are maintaining jobs: Is preserving the spotted owl worth one job lost? And the public has been taught to assume those are the only alternatives.

Not only are there constructive alternatives, there are also many other areas of deep concern not even noted here except in passing. Among the most damaging to people, as contrasted with the rest of nature, are the environmental problems in our cities: congestion, dirt, daily mountains of garbage (a high proportion of it nonbiodegradable)—remember the Homeric-like journey of the ship loaded with New York garbage that for six months no port would accept in 1987?—air pollution, lead and asbestos poisoning in the crowded dwellings of especially, but not only, the poor.

The problems of the cities are of deep concern because that is where most of our people live and/or work, where most of the poor reside, and where a particularly vicious circle has been at work for many years: The pains and fears of city life, real and imagined, have driven numberless families to what were expected to be pristine and safe suburbs. This process steadily gutted the tax base of the cities, causing the problems to intensify steadily, and around and around it has gone. Now parts of many cities resemble war-torn areas; now, however, life in many suburbs has deteriorated and seems worth something less than the commute.

Such matters must be left at that, as we turn now to a less visible but critically important source of our environmental problems: sheer waste—monumental in quantity and, much of it, destructive in its effects. Were we merely to reduce by half our wasteful practices—in both consumption and production—we would go far toward reducing environmental damage.

Wasting Away

U.S. industrial capitalism has simultaneously been the most efficient and the most wasteful productive system in history.[17] The contradiction arises from the great contrast between the high efficiency with which a modern *factory* might produce and "package" a product (such as autos or toothpaste) and the contrived and massive inefficiency of the economic *system.* That system induces people to pay for toothpaste a price that is almost completely (more than 90 percent) dependent on the cost of marketing and profits, not on the production of the dentifrice. So, toothpaste isn't all that important. But autos are, and taken together, the car and the toothpaste well exemplify the wasteful characteristics of the manufactured consumer goods industries. The automobile industry is the leader in that wastefulness.

Until recently, about 15 percent of all jobs in the United States were directly or indirectly connected with the production and use of motor vehicles. Under investigation in 1939 by the Federal Trade Commission, General Motors presented figures showing that a Chevrolet with a market price of $950 had *production* costs of only $150; the rest went for advertising, distribution, and profits. Moreover, one-third of production costs are caused by the annual model change—getting you nowhere, serving much the same function as the packaging of toothpaste.

These kinds of waste, and others to be noted, began to spread throughout the U.S. economy in the 1920s, and spread like a pox. The process was led by American Tobacco ("Reach for a Lucky Instead of a Sweet") in cigarettes, and by General Motors (GM) in autos. GM was first with the annual model change and related trade-ins, extensive advertising, and consumer financing. The model change constituted—and in the industry was called—"deliberate obsolescence." The latter came to be a way of life in the production of consumer durable goods, just as living in constant debt slowly but surely became a way of life for the population.

What was waste for the economy was a way of increasing or maintaining sales and profits for companies. In the nature of the capitalist process, however, not only was there no turning back once begun, but worse, the waste like consumer debt *had to* spread and deepen continuously. What saved the economy from the seemingly endless Depression of the 1930s was the greatest waste of all: war.

The new consumerist economy of the 1920s had fallen flat on its face as the decade ended—pushed there by the inability of at least two-thirds of the population to get the credit or the cash to pay for the cars, the fridges, the gas and electric stoves, whatever; that, taken together with a collapsed global economy and a giddy Wall Street that boomed along spectacularly—even as (like today) business slacked off and wages fell—and then crashed even more spectacularly.[18]

Although the bandages and blood transfusions of the New Deal reduced the pain, the economy did not arrive at full production and employment until 1942. The achievement was not hard then, with 16 million passing into the armed forces and the government buying half of the GNP (as it did, 1943 and 1944).

There was much waste during the war, most of all of lives. But overall production, by comparison with what ensued later, was at maximum efficiency; and at least, for better and for worse, the military production was being put to some use. The cold war institutionalized large-scale expenditure on the military; an always high and increasing share of that is sheer waste, facilitated by corruption (see Chapter 9). And the Pentagon, as the eighth-largest user of oil in the world (exceeded only by seven *nations*, including the United States), has of course been a great contributor to the numerous damages done to the environment by petroleum products.

But that's just an introduction to the dimensions of waste. A reputable study of how matters stood at the beginning of the 1980s[19] concluded that useful output was about *half* of total output in 1980—even when counting 70 percent of military output as "useful" and taking no notice of "deliberate obsolescence." We cannot pursue these matters in the detail they deserve; however, here is a partial list of the dirty laundry.

☞ Advertising: In 1980, 2 percent of GNP went to advertising, more than doubling the percentage of 1950, and rising (by another 50 percent in the 1980s). All the numbers about advertising are appalling, as is a great deal of what's *being* advertised. When advertising serves the purpose of information (as it always has, but barely so, now), it can be useful, telling us what, where, how much, and so on. But that is not the main purpose served now. Instead, as Paul Baran put it, it is "to teach us to want what we don't need and not to want what we do."[20] And the resulting process contributes to wasted production (materials, equipment, work) and, among other things, to the mountains of garbage.

☞ Transportation: A good transport system would meet the standards of safety, convenience, comfort, speed, and the efficient use of resources. A transportation engineer asked to design such a system in engineering rather than profit terms (and after distinguishing between cargo and passengers) would have us fly very long distances, go by rail between city and suburb and between cities only two or three hundred miles apart, use public systems within cities (electrified underground and surface rail), and private (or rented) autos only for recreational and some few other purposes, while making all possible speed toward setting stiff minimum miles-per-gallon standards and the achievement of the (quite clearly feasible) manufacture and common use of autos powered by nonfossil fuels.[21]

Such a system would be safer, more convenient, faster, and more resource efficient by comparison with (especially) the "system" in the United States, where we are moving away from rather than toward a sane transportation system. That is happening despite the knowledge that, for example, (1) for one person to go from Boston to New York City requires ten gallons of gasoline by air, seven by private car, and two by rail (assuming each vehicle to be half full); (2) the dependence upon the private auto instead of mass urban transit causes consumption of 50 percent more fuel than is necessary; (3) it takes six times as much fuel to haul a ton of freight from Los Angeles to New York by truck than by train.

In addition to using more oil and gasoline, current practices of course also pollute and warm the air more than the "engineering alternative." How did our wasteful and foolish system come about? It did not just happen. It was created deliberately; indeed, it required the undoing of the more sensible system preceding it.

A telling example: When in 1939 the San Francisco Bay Bridge was opened, its upper deck had five lanes for autos and its lower deck was divided between a two-way truck road and an electric railway system (25 cents to cross the bay, cheap even then). At the end of the 1950s, both decks were being used for cars, buses, and trucks, and the clean, swift, safe, and cheap electric trains had disappeared. The public, never consulted, didn't know it was happening until it was done. How?

General Motors, in conjunction with Standard Oil of California (now Chevron) and the Firestone Tire Company, set up a holding company, National City Lines, purchased (and soon dismantled) the train system, put buses in its place (GM is the largest diesel bus manufacturer; guess who made the tires and the gas?), and when that bus system was sold to a local company, it was with the (free market?) stipulation that the purchase of new equipment "using any fuel or means of propulsion other than gasoline" was strictly prohibited. You may think all that sounds like a conspiracy; so do I; but it was all legal, and it certainly made good business sense. And that group did the same, in one form or another in forty-five metropolitan areas.[22]

The endless traffic jams of buses and cars on the bridge created the necessity for public transport *not* on the bridge; the underwater Bay Area Rapid Transit (BART) system was built at enormous cost (something like the "Chunnel") in taxes, and traffic on the bridge is still bumper-to-bumper. Los Angeles went through the same process: a really great public rail system was replaced by throughways, bumper-to-bumper almost all the time. Like San Francisco, L.A., too, is going underground.

☞ Energy and Petrochemicals: The wastefulness and dangers of the transportation system are almost the Siamese twin of the problems of the energy system (setting aside nuclear energy production and wastes). The most powerful companies in the world today are "energy," not oil, gas, or coal, companies. The largest energy companies are owned and controlled by the major oil companies; the latter are already or soon will be the major natural gas, coal, and uranium companies. Thus, no matter *what* happens that might cause a shortage or price increase for any source of energy, the energy companies benefit.

Waste in energy began and continues at the point of production. The pattern of land ownership in the United States led to "competitive drilling" for crude oil, as compared with the "unit field" system in Saudi Arabia and elsewhere. What might cost $15 a barrel to extract in Texas costs perhaps $2 in the Middle East. Moreover, with competitive drilling, about two-thirds of the oil is left in the ground or can be gotten out only at even higher costs: Instead of being pressured out by natural gas (as in the unit field manner), it has to be pumped out. Similarly, about half of underground coal has been left in the mine. None of this takes account of subsequent wastes in distribution, conversion, and use. And the public is told daily of the preciousness of those energy supplies while those who make the pronouncements are participating actively in throwing the energy supplies to the winds.

And then there are the petrochemicals. Every day and night, almost everyone in the leading industrial countries (and a rising percentage of all others) is eating something, wearing something, cleaning oneself or car or house with something, sleeping on something, and surrounded by something made from petroleum: petrochemicals and their endless products. They have taken the place of something natural or organic—cotton or wool, steel or copper or wood, animal wastes (for fertilizer)—or they are put into otherwise natural products to preserve them or make them more attractive, such as additives in foods.

Pity Mother Nature (which includes us): detergents in the rivers, bays, and oceans quite simply *never* disappear; plastic containers never rot, nor do those aluminum cans in their billions. All these and many others must somehow be disposed of, somewhere, somehow.

Some people believe that our society has created this demon by reverse serendipity, that is, that an unstoppable technological process of undeniable goodness has somehow become cancerous, metaphorically and actually. But that is only a good cover story; the truth is that all these (and other harmful) products are quite simply more profitable for the giant companies to produce and sell than their natural or organic predecessors, even though synthetic products are more dangerous and, ultimately, more costly to people and to nature.

We began with Rachel Carson, and no birdsong: bad enough, taken alone. But the *whole* ecological process, damaged, scarred, poisoned, destroyed in each of its many dimensions, is now in peril. It is hard to believe, but the foregoing has but scratched the surface, and it must be left at that.

In brief, we are in a terrifying crisis. We have recovered from depressions and wars, however great their social and physical damage and destruction. We shall not recover from an ecological system that is destroyed by a stronger alien power. That power, to repeat, is the gospel of expansionism and accumulation, by companies and by consumers. The bell is tolling.

What has yet to be said and done in this book relates to the policies and programs needed and desirable and practical to reverse these awful processes. Those will be summarized in Chapter 10 and linked—as they must be—to the other areas of social need and possibility.

9

Expenditures on the Military and Crime

"Where Angels Fear to Tread"

Federal, state, and local governments spend about $350 billion annually on the military and crime. The most important similarities between milex and crime expenditures (crimex) are that (1) both rely all too much on the threat and use of force to surmount complex problems of international rivalry and domestic crime; (2) because the origins of those problems are in social and political processes, the problems are more likely to deepen and spread than be mitigated by forceful "solutions"; (3) in the same process, milex and crimex seriously deplete and misuse the precious human and natural resources and capital equipment required to deal effectively with many other critical domestic and global needs and possibilities; finally, and quite apart from any other consideration, (4) all this is done in a breathtakingly wasteful manner, dramatically more so than much-maligned social expenditures such as those on children and health care.[1]

That milex and crimex are viewed as vital for good jobs and high profits is a major reason for their perpetuation, despite what should be seen as strong reasons for the decline of both: The cold war ended some years ago, and increases in crimex are coincident with—even among the causes of—increases in crime. Moreover, it has been shown that governmental expenditures on education and construction, for example, produce "more jobs for the buck."

The main differences between milex and crimex follow: (1) Milex are financed by the federal government, whereas most of crimex—almost 90 percent—are the responsibility of states and localities; and (2) milex are about three times crimex (although the latter now rise more rapidly). Accompanying both areas of expenditure has been a strong level of support by politi-

129

cians, the media, and the public; opposition, though significant and increasing, remains marginalized. Support for milex and crimex is a consequence of a long-sustained discourse mixing nationalism with economic, ideological, military, and racial fears in a rapidly changing and confusing world at home and abroad.

Throughout our history resort to militarized means of resolving real and imagined problems has been routine, but the enduring high status of milex and crimex since World War II has been qualitatively different from anything earlier. The quantum leap for both occurred after World War II—milex from the late 1940s, crimex from the late 1960s.

As those developments took hold, what President Eisenhower dubbed "the military-industrial complex" as well as what has come to be called "the prison-industrial complex" grew with them. Their lobbying efforts have been decisive for the long-run rise of milex and crimex—and have contributed significantly to corruption in both business and government.

The hundreds of billions spent each year for these purposes have been harmful in and of themselves, as we will see; they have also been deeply harmful in terms of what economists call "opportunity costs"—the alternative uses of resources thus foregone. We will now look more closely at all these dimensions, first for milex, the more familiar of the two areas, and we will begin within the dispute-filled framework of balanced budgets and deficits.

Milex: The Political Economy of the Big Stick

The goal accepted by both the White House and the Congress in 1996 was to balance the federal budget by the year 2002. The means of doing so were to include substantial reductions of social expenditures, most notably in the areas affecting children, health care, education, and infrastructure (the more vital "opportunity costs"). Meanwhile, Congress voted to increase milex about 5 percent *more* than the White House had requested.

Suppose, instead, that milex were *cut* by 10 percent each of those seven years, working with the fiscal 1997 military budget of $266 billion—greater than the milex of the hot cold war year 1980 (in today's dollars). A rough calculation indicates that after seven years annual milex would be down to about $127 billion annually—more than 50 percent; instead of an aggregate of $1,862 billion, milex would be $1,248 billion over that period (a saving of $614 billion), with a consequent release of $139 billion annually in years to follow. And the magical balancing of the budget would have ensued sometime *before* fiscal 2003 without slashing needed social expenditures. But then, for all too many who wish to slash social expenditures, budget balance has been the excuse, not the reason.

For decades our milex have exceeded the GDP of all but twelve nations; today our milex are equal to that of the next ten military powers combined (most of them allies), amounting to 40 percent of world milex, three times those of Russia, twice those of Britain, France, Germany, and Japan combined. Meanwhile, with substantial government support, private arms exports (including some to potential enemies), subsidized to the amount of $7.6 billion annually by our government, provide more than half of the world's arms supplies.[2]

Less than half the current Pentagon budget would leave both friends and foes still a distant second to us in milex and weapons technology. Of course approval for such cutbacks either from Congress or the White House now would be difficult, to say the least: Genuine and supposed economic, political, and strategic reasons hold both back from even considering—even *mentioning*—such a move.

It is almost forgotten that cold war policies met with more skepticism and opposition than support when first aired after World War II. Is it inconceivable that the White House and Congress could provide leadership for a markedly different set of conversion programs, with the advantage of costing less and yielding vital economic and social gains? President Eisenhower had the courage and good sense to speak of what he called a "peace dividend" in the 1950s, before the cold war had metastasized further into more deadly realms. And now the cold war is over—in fact, if not in habits of mind and policy. It remains reasonable to be concerned with military matters in today's unstable world, of course; but it is quite unreasonable to act as though there were still—was there ever?—an enemy justifying John F. Kennedy's "any sacrifice."

Astutely appraising his fellow citizens, LBJ deflected attention from the horrors of the Vietnam war with policies claimed to provide "both guns and butter," setting off a lively debate as to whether both were possible simultaneously. They were, of course, in the Vietnam as in other wars. As is true for most economic arguments, however, it should not be numerical calculations, but qualitative conditions and dynamic consequences, that are defining.

Thus, as only one major example of what is meant by the latter, Seymour Melman, an industrial economist who is an expert on these matters, showed even in the record-setting general prosperity of the 1960s that a main cost of our milex programs was a steady weakening of our overall industrial efficiency, both in itself and in comparison to other nations. That was no surprise given the large percentages (estimated as over 60 percent by Melman) of engineers, scientists, and highly skilled workers working for the military-industrial complex.[3]

Though numbers standing alone are insufficient for understanding, they are necessary. Now we look at some of them,[4] and at some of what lies behind them. We begin with a snapshot of those who gained in monetary and other terms, thence to those who paid.

The Winners' Table

What are the dimensions of milex? Here, as with other official data, it is necessary to be careful with definitions. Government figures show that from 1947 to 1991 milex totaled $8.7 trillion (in 1992 dollars). If we add in milex for 1992 through 1996, we get to $10–10.2 trillion—a very large sum indeed, but also a very large understatement, by about 50 percent.[5]

As suggested earlier, a reasonable accounting of milex should include the interest on that portion of the national debt stemming from milex—debt incurred for past, current, and future military strength. When conservatively estimated at about 50 percent, that would add about 15 percent, or $1–1.5 trillion, to the official $10+ trillion.

Neither do the official data take any account whatsoever of the military and paramilitary expenditures hidden away in "energy" "foreign aid," "space research," and, among other matters, the military component of covert (and much of the overt) activities of the CIA's top secret budget ($38 billion annually, by conservative estimates)—leaving aside the inanity, dangers, and wastefulness of the recently revealed (by the House Permanent Select Committee on Intelligence) $5.6 billion spent by the CIA for "keeping secret documents secret." That was for 1995 alone and was seen by Representative David Skaggs of the committee as "surely an understatement."[6] Nor does any of this take note of the U.S. Army and CIA "schools" for training those who became or worked with dictators—especially in Latin America.[7]

It was only recently revealed that squirreled away in the Energy Department's budget were $3.9 *trillion* spent on nuclear *weapons* by the Army and Navy since 1947 but never before admitted.[8] Now also assume—very conservatively—$10 billion annually in the half century 1947–1996 for the combined military share of foreign aid, space research, and the CIA, that is, about $500 billion; if we add that to the official total plus interest's share, we have something between $15 and $16 *trillion.* Senator Everett Dirksen (as GOP Senate leader in the 1950s) once quipped, "Add a billion here and a billion there, and pretty soon we're talking big money!" Child's play; were he quipping nowadays, it would have to be "Add a few hundred billion here . . ." For what and to whom does it go?

☞ Over 130,000 separate firms contract with the Pentagon; 25 of those firms receive about half of all contracts and farm them out to still other thousands of firms—which, along with about 3 million civilian arms-plant workers, over 1 million civilian workers on the Pentagon payroll, and over 1 million reservists (with income supplements), constitute a formidable political support system for milex.[9]

☞ Profit rates for military production are two to three times those for all production. And why not, given "cost-plus contracts" and virtually assured payments for cost overruns? The mother of all cost overruns (one hopes) is that for the B-2 ("Stealth") bomber. The original contract, for ten bombers, was obtained at the (itself outrageous) price of $400 million each, $4 billion *in toto*. By 1990 the price was $870 million; in 1994 it had risen to $2.2 *billion* each, more than five times the original price, $22 billion *in toto*. And there is a story lurking behind those figures that deserves the name of institutionalized corruption.

Standard Pentagon contracts allow payment for correction of defects. The first B-2 had 110,000 defects. The second had 80,000. (After a decade, there is still no third.) The payment for the correction of defects would seem to be a strong incentive to *make* defects, given that contracts are cost-plus. But 110,000 defects? And on the second try, still 80,000? Be that as it may, although the Pentagon declared that ten B-2s were enough—as the original two continue to struggle with their defects—Congress in 1996 appropriated enough for twenty ($44+ billion, at the present going price).

For better or for worse, the B-2 has yet to be used in combat. That may surprise many who followed the Gulf war and learned of the Stealth's combat triumphs. Thereby hangs another sordid tale: The Stealth *fighter*, the F-117A (at $106 million each), *was* used, twice, in Panama and in the Gulf war. However, Panama, one of the last places in the world where high-tech stealth was needed, was the occasion for the 117A's low-level bombing, and "collateral damage" to ordinary Panamanians was very high. The target—presumably General Noriega's hideout—was never hit. The F-117's use in the Gulf war was even more problematic; scandalously so, as the excerpt from a July 1996 General Accounting Office (GAO) Report revealed:

> The Pentagon lied about the performance of its most advanced weapons systems, particularly the F-117A Stealth fighter. . . . For example, the Air Force told Congress that the Stealth fighter had an 80 percent success rate on its bombing runs [as compared with a real rate of 40 percent, and that] commanders defined "success" as *launching* a bomb or missile, not hitting a target. The Report's authors said these lies were told to help persuade Congress and citizens to buy the next generation of weapons: newer, stealthier fighter jets, newer smart bombs and missiles. Perception management . . . made the weapons of Desert Storm look better than they were, as part of a strategy "to justify future weapons spending. . . . " "The better the F-117 looks, the better the B-2 looks."[10]

The war news never made clear that it was not the B-2, but the F-117, in action. The source of the report was the GAO's Program Evaluation Division. The *New York Times* story concluded with the terse statement: "The division is being dismantled, destroyed by budget cuts imposed by Congress this year and last. In a few weeks it will disappear." That takes care of *those* spoilsports.

☞ In an editorial entitled "The Pentagon Jackpot," the *New York Times* noted that "The Senate Service Armed Services Committee tossed $1.3 billion into its budget bill to order an LHD-7 amphibious assault ship the

Navy does not want. The vessel will be constructed in Mississippi, which is represented by Senator Trent Lott, a committee member and the Republican whip."[11] When Bob Dole resigned as majority leader, Lott succeeded him in the considerably more powerful post.

☞ And then there is procurement fraud, the current term for the corruption link between the Pentagon and its contractors. In recent years twenty to thirty of the top contractors have been guilty of such fraud; none has been or is expected to be barred from further contracts.

☞ In the "Defend America Act of 1996," Congress sought to revive Reagan's "Star Wars." The cost was estimated by its sponsors, then-Senator Dole and Representative Gingrich, as one-eighth or less of the $60–70 billion estimate provided by the Congressional Research Service. The act promised to deploy a fully operational national missile defense system—regardless of cost—by 2003.[12] The act was passed by both houses of Congress, over the objections of both the White House and the Pentagon. That this seems a big boondoggle for a few at a time when the many are pushed toward austerity is one matter; that such a program violates the 1972 U.S.-USSR Anti-Ballistic Missile Treaty is a dangerous something else.

Such reservations are reinforced when we examine the reasoning of Speaker Gingrich, who supported his and Senator Dole's proposal in this way: "One day, mathematically, something bad can happen and you ought to have a minimum screen on a continent-wide basis, and it's doable."[13] Just as "doable," the American Physical Society had opined (in 1987) as "deflecting a bullet in midflight by firing one of your own." The society deemed that to be impossible at prevailing levels of technology, adding that "another ten years of research would be required to learn whether it might *ever* be feasible."[14]

☞ Then there are innumerable expenditures so outrageous as to be downright funny—so much so that one wonders what, if any, kind of controls there are over the Pentagon's past and present fiscal activities. Intermittently the following kinds of follies have been brought to light: The Pentagon pays $750 for a toilet seat; $2,034 for a 13-cent nut; $1,500 for a screwdriver; $3,100 for a common wrench. And we must assume that countless toilets seats, nuts, screwdrivers, wrenches, and the like were bought at those prices.

All of that would be bad enough if it were only a sad or enraging tale of money, of greed, corruption, waste, and foolishness. It is that. But in addition to the greedy behavior on the part of its principals, there was also much more and worse than financial misfeasance and malfeasance.

Decades of large-scale militarized production required not only a militarized economy but also a society whose attitudes have become significantly militarized, whose responses to complex problems have come increasingly to be military responses. Given the many years of huge milex, it is not surprising that we fought or encouraged and financed (and often trained others to fight) many wars—in Asia and Central America and the lesser-known conflicts in Africa and in the Middle East (such as those in Angola and Afghanistan). Thousands of U.S. soldiers were casualties of those wars, as were millions of others, both military and civilians, in the countries involved.[15]

It is not easy to find justification for all that bloodshed and misery. Strong arguments have been made that most of those wars occurred when and where they did not as a means of defending our country but as a virtually inescapable part of the cold war and its military-industrial complex, whose main participants gained greatly thereby. That position will be seen unconvincing by some and as an understatement by others. In either case, there remain serious questions needing serious answers from us as a nation regarding the questionable ways and means of milex: its money costs, its financial crimes, misdemeanors, and associated corruption, and its larger effects on the social process here and abroad. We return now to some narrower and less complex aspects of milex: What about the losers?

Who Paid and Who Pays?

The "payment" has taken many forms: taxes, distortions in the economy, pressures to curtail or deny needed social expenditures, diverse tendencies toward the shallowing of political discourse and behavior and the contamination of relations between government and business, and, not least, the damages done to those directly involved in warfare. Here we confine our attention to a relatively narrow band of economic matters. First, taxes.

Among the many things about our nation in which we take pride is the high level of our per capita income. Until recently it was the highest in the world. That the GDP ($6+ trillion) into which our population (260+ million) is divided to get that "per capita" includes milex ($400+ billion annually by our calculation) is seldom if ever remarked upon by economists. One cannot, however, eat a hand grenade or mow one's lawn or get to the supermarket with a tank. But, those economists might add, milex stimulate the economy over time and in more than a one-to-one fashion: A dollar of fedex will ultimately result in $2–3 of national income. Probably so.

However, many studies have pointed out that $1 of fedex yields much less in income and jobs from milex than if it were spent on education, infrastructure, or health care—and that in yielding higher incomes it would make higher taxes feasible.[16]

Consider some of the tax data: In California, the average household pays over $3,000 annually in federal income taxes, of which half is for milex (as officially calculated). Comparing taxes paid with milex (and its associated incomes) in their areas, New York City had a net *loss* of $8 billion, and

Chicago and Los Angeles each a net loss of $3 billion; calculated by family, the loss was $3000+ per family—a result common to nineteen of twenty-five major cities. Funds thus diverted from public and private investment also meant a significant loss of jobs in past and present.[17] Some areas must have gained, of course, mostly in the Sunbelt states of the Southeast and Southwest (excluding California), notably Georgia and Texas.

If we look at milex with a different measure—the *relative* importance of milex in total fedex—we find a major distortion when comparing official with more realistic numbers. Thus, it is officially stated that milex usually count as 25 percent or less of fedex. More accurate measures, such as those earlier calculated, yield a percentage of fedex over 50 percent. That is so even if we neglect to take into account the budgetary sleight of hand of President Johnson in 1966 (mentioned in Chapter 2). The Vietnam war had begun to get out of hand—financially, militarily, and politically. In addition to hiding $10 billion of milex from his own budget chief, Johnson initiated the custom of including Social Security in annual budget calculations—thus automatically reducing the percentage of milex to fedex.

But Social Security always has been and remains outside the realm of fiscal policy. The taxes and expenditures that constitute fiscal policy and determine the dimensions of the federal budget are decided upon by Congress and the White House each fiscal year. Social Security collections and payments go into and out of the Social Security Trust Fund and are independent of the budgetary process. Congress, which legislated Social Security, can of course—and often does—change the terms of its operation, but the Social Security Act placed the trust fund where it remains, *outside* the realm of fiscal policy. To give it the appearance of being inside that process is to camouflage government operations.

On top of that, despite the deliberately created public impression, Social Security has for many years run a rising surplus (now between $50–75 billion annually); and for those same years a portion of that surplus has been shifted from the trust fund to the Treasury. That means the Treasury need *not* borrow from the public to that same amount, thus creating the illusion of a smaller annual deficit. The present rate of that legal deception is near $50 billion annually, and rising.

As in many other governmental deceptions, those just noted have been practiced by both parties in the Congress and the White House. It is worth repeating that when the regular surplus of the trust fund becomes instead a deficit (in about twenty years), the Treasury will have to borrow from the public—sell bonds—to "replace" the amounts shifted and raise taxes to pay the interest. Those politicians who regularly deplore the "perilous condition" of Social Security, and the "thievery" of today's elderly from today's young fail to mention their own role in heightening that peril. Corruption makes strange and bipartisan bedfellows.

Waste, and Want Not?

The pressures on political leaders to maintain milex come from both the public and business. Economically, it is of course true that cuts in milex cause problems for enterprises and workers and their communities. The cuts up to now have been disproportionately in milex going to people rather than to corporations: Many bases have been closed and the armed forces reduced, whereas weapons expenditures have been increased. Whether or not that difference was calculated to preserve popular support for milex, that is its effect. Meanwhile lobbyists ensure that the maintenance of milex favors weaponry. There can be no blinking at the fact that "conversion" entails not only physical facilities and supply-demand relationships, but also habits of mind and procedure, including slovenly habits of management and production.

Must we choose between milex and some mix of chaos and stagnation? No, we need not. The intricacies of conversion have for many years been the focus of discussion and study by the relevant parties: engineers, economists, businesses, unions, and civic groups. The literature is both abundant and solid.[18] "Beating swords into ploughshares" is feasible and it would have immense benefits of many kinds over both the short and the long term. There is no question of whether it can be done; it *was* done after earlier wars, most notably after World War II, when there was a will to do it.

Nevertheless, it is important to recall that the processes of conversion after World War II were much eased by several conditions that contrast sharply with the current situation: (1) World War II brought "overfull employment" (less than 2 percent unemployed, 1943–1945) at home as factories expanded, *and* 16 million were serving in the armed forces; the last two decades of the cold war, the 1970s and 1980s, were marked by relatively high unemployment. (2) Through the combination of rationing, bond sales, price controls, high incomes and high profits, personal and business savings were substantial and growing throughout the war, thus creating an aggregation of "pent-up" demand from both consumers and businesses; savings in the cold war years were in steady decline, and now the levels of business and consumer *debt* are both worrisomely high. (3) That earlier pent-up demand combined with cold war milex and expanded exports to stretch production facilities, leading to rising business investment and (in particular) consumer durables, along with a boom in construction—residential, commercial, and road (the latter much stimulated by the superhighway program of the 1950s).

When all that coincided with (4), the economic stimuli provided by Truman's Fair Deal and pressures from then-strong unions, there developed a U.S. version of the "social wage" (pensions and health care for a significant share of workers with a program of subsidized public housing). What lay ahead in the 1950s was thus strikingly different from now: two decades of growth that stimulated and supported processes of rapid technological and socioeconomic change. When a different era took hold in the late 1970s it was characterized not by "pent-up" but by sagging (or debt-financed) levels of consumer and business demand; marked more by recession *plus* inflation ("stagflation") than by easy growth; weighed down by social and political controversies, fears, and the beginnings of political "gridlock," which blocked the processes of beneficial change.

In sum, future reductions of milex require a degree of social concern, imagination, understanding, and intelligent leadership not required for the post–World War II milex increase. There is another, if subtler, difference between the end of World War II and the end of the cold war, as regards conversion. The appropriations for and the granting of military contracts in the cold war era were (and are) done with a shocking casualness. The resulting waste and corruption blot the political economy; they cannot be repeated in this age of heightened sensitivity to fedex (although that sensitivity does not cover milex and crimex). It should be assumed that a substantial process of conversion will not permit either amusing instances such as $750 toilet seats or the larger economic crimes attending the built-in institutionalized fraud of multibillion cost-plus contracts or their connected and predictable processes of corruption between capital, labor, the Pentagon, and Congress.

In Chapter 10, the conversion of "swords to ploughshares" will be examined more carefully, as we explore alternatives to current structures of consumption and production. It is still believed by many that ordinary working people have a stake in the continuation of the milex status quo, lest a worse fate befall. They might ponder but one example plucked from a large selection: From 1992 to mid-1995, while the CEOs of six of the largest military contractors were cutting 178,000 jobs, their own average compensation more than tripled—from $1.3 million in 1989 to $4.0 million in 1994.[19]

In the military-industrial complex, as in the rest of the corporate economy, profits and CEOs' incomes are coming to be inversely related to the jobs and incomes of workers: Like a seesaw, the former go up as the latter go down (except that a seesaw normally goes back the other way, which the present process shows no sign of doing). Any conversion program, instead of carrying with it cost-plus contracts and the other thievery of milex, must ensure that its benefits are justly divided between those who pay taxes and those who own the enterprises.

Crimex: Solution or Part of the Problem?

Just as the United States is Number One in milex, so it is in crimex. Ah, but we are such a large country, it may be said. But our leading position is relative, as well as absolute: Average incarceration rates for the United States in 1991 were 426 per 100,000 of population; second was South Africa (mostly blacks, this before its recent conversion to a democracy), with 333; then the Soviet Union with 268. Even Northern Ireland, with its ongoing conflict, had a rate of less than a third of ours: 120. Equally interesting are the figures at the other end of the scale: France, 81; Japan, 45; Netherlands, 40; Philippines, 22. And that was in 1991; the number of our imprisoned had risen 16 percent by 1994.[20]

In 1995, the Justice Department reported that the number in federal and state prisons and local jails rose 6 percent, and that since 1980 the total number under correctional supervision (probation and parole) had "almost tripled, from 1.8 million to 5.4 million, with an average annual rate of growth of 7.4 percent."[21] Those are the very years in which crimex accelerated to their present spectacular rate of increase. An objective analysis might well conclude that the side effects of crimex are exacerbating the disease they presumably seek to cure.

Although it may not have been used consciously, the military-industrial complex has been a model for what has now become the prison-industrial complex. As this is written, forty-four of the fifty states are building new and expanding old prisons; prison construction is the most rapidly rising item in state and local budgets. The money-making aspects of the federal grants for that process have become so obvious that a major weekly subtitled a piece on appropriations for prison construction: "An Anticrime Program Smells a Lot Like Pork."[22]

Federal grants to states and localities are rising for prisons while they have been falling for social expenditures. That decline is scheduled to continue and accelerate—especially now that federal grants for social entitlements have been changed into "block grants." The latter is a euphemism for increased leeway for the states to use (probably reduced) federal funds as they choose; and the choice is likely to veer away from health, education, and welfare and toward crimex. As with CEOs' salaries and bonuses in relation to jobs and workers' wages, as crimex (or milex) go up, social expenditures must go down.[23] The most spectacular example of that process is in California. Once the state that led all others in its fiscal devotion to higher education, California is now low on the list in terms both of expenditures and achievements: In 1996 crimex edged out expenditures on higher education for the first time.

Measures touted as reducing crime neither begin nor end with prison construction, of course; the latter happens to be the most profitable—as advanced weaponry is among milex. The comparison is quite close in some respects: In the 1980s, California's prison construction (the most costly in the nation) boasted new prisons whose *minimum* security cells would cost $100,000 each (half for construction costs, half for interest). Then there are the additional costs for food and clothing, guards, and medical care, amounting to $25,000 per year per inmate. Make what you will also of this (still in California): While industrial workers' wages were declining in the 1980s, those of prison guards rose from $21,000 in 1982 to $43,000 in 1991—plus pensions, medical care, and the like. Teachers and nurses should be so lucky.

As noted earlier, crime became a lively political issue in the late 1960s, and crimex began their rise soon thereafter. Before long, so too did crime. In 1973, there were 500,000 inmates in U.S. prisons and jails; by 1995 that number had tripled to 1.6 million. In California, the leader in crimex among the states, the number of inmates quintupled in the same years.

It wasn't just prison construction that had increased in that period; so had other supposed remedies: fewer restrictions on police, longer sentences, harsher treatment, twenty-three-hour incarceration, and reinstitution of the death penalty and (in Alabama) of the chain gang and rock busting. Meanwhile, training and education and other rehabilitation efforts were decreased—despite the view of an overwhelming number of prison wardens that "cutting back on amenities" was a mistake.[24] Between 1990 and 1995, the number of prison guards and wardens doubled. In those same years—as both crimex and crime were growing rapidly—violence *within* the prisons exploded: The number of assaults on guards rose fivefold.[25]

These changes, followed not just by higher costs per prison and per prisoner but also higher rates of recidivism, would be seen as dramatic signs of failure were they to take place in the business world. Instead, none of this having reduced crime, the latest experiment is "three strikes, and you're in for life"—requiring, of course, more prisons, more crimex.

It would be comforting if stupidity were the reason for this rush toward counterproductive policies. The reason is not that benign. As an article in the *New Yorker* [26] put it: "Politicians are well aware that cutting prisoner education programs will result in higher recidivism rates and contribute to a need for more prisons. . . . Right-wing politicians consider additional prison construction not a necessary evil but a necessary good." (For "right-wing" it might be more accurate to say "politicians beholden to the prison-industrial complex.")

All this occurs in an environment of deteriorating socioeconomic conditions: long-term joblessness, double-digit joblessness for the young, deepening racism, drug use, demoralization, and despair. There is almost universal agreement among criminologists and sociologists that neither the prevention of nor the cure for crime will be found principally—if at all—in crimex; in particular, prison wardens almost universally advise that prison work programs reduce violence, help discipline, and reduce the high rate of recidivism; that present tendencies increase violence within and outside the prison walls. They should know, and they can't be seen as "soft on crime."

There is strong, if not unanimous, agreement among criminologists and sociologists that significant reductions in crime could be expected with better education, housing, and job opportunities for *all*. But such experts can offer only judgments; they cannot afford lobbyists. Their views, if they are ever to prevail, would need widespread political support.

In the immediate future the changes are going in the wrong direction: Using California again as representative, since 1991 prison expenditures have risen by 11 percent as AFDC has gone down by 9 percent and as state university fees have risen by 20 percent to offset the fall in state expenditure. The "correctional" budget, which was $300 million in 1980, had risen over ten times by 1995, to $4 billion; the average monthly AFDC payment (in California) was $630 monthly and falling; the average monthly cost per prison inmate was $2,000, and rising.[27]

If there is a causal connection between desperate social conditions and crime—and there is surely *some* significant connection—the wrongheadedness of current priorities is quite startling. But practicality is not the only matter: Well over half of all AFDC payments are for the support of children; as these payments fall, along with other patterns of deterioration in the lives of children, fundamental questions as to our society's future are raised.

We Must Do Better

The American Dream has already become a nightmare for the tens of millions whose lives are blighted, dangerous, desperate, without hope. There are more in that plight today than there were twenty years ago; we could, were we to muster the will, find the way to reduce those numbers toward the vanishing point. A sample of what we could do was captured by Melman when, after exposing the folly of our weapons programs, he noted that such "valueless military parts of the proposed 1996 to 2002 budgets would save at least $875.7 billion. He added: "With these savings, we could improve America's infrastructure while creating two million-plus jobs—more than enough to offset the jobs lost by ending these military programs. This combined with local advance planning for economic conversion would reduce the fear of lost jobs that manacles communities and their members of Congress to a cold war mindset."[28] Further steps in that and other directions will now be examined, in our concluding chapter.

10

Needs and Possibilities

Toward a Square Deal

Echoing the New Deal of FDR and the Fair Deal of Harry S. Truman, Adlai Stevenson—running for president against Eisenhower (and losing to him twice in the 1950s)—saw Ike's first term as a "big deal" and the White House as staffed mostly by "used car dealers." After Nixon had been in office a while, his policies came to be dubbed the "raw deal." And that's what most Americans have had ever since from the wheelers and dealers who have increasingly dominated our social process.

Now the time is overdue for something very different from any of those "deals." We need a socioeconomic program that has the well-being of the overwhelming majority of our people and of the earth as its *direct* focus: a square deal—no more trickle down, no more pie in the sky, no more jiggery-pokery. Too many millions have been too badly damaged by the failed promises of those years; the society can't afford it any more—if it ever could.

But we cannot become a just and sane society easily or quickly. There is too much debris to be cleared away, too much that is new to us to be constructed. The cleaning up and the new construction will not be done by those who have made it necessary. Those who hold economic, political, and social power will not change their ways; they must be dislodged—a difficult job, but not without a modest precedent or two, as recently as the 1960s. After that brief period of minimal power sharing, the nation resumed its march toward a greater concentration of power. It should come as no surprise that the power has been used to the rising benefit of those who hold it, at the cost of an always higher percentage of Americans.

Put differently, it should be clear that substantial socioeconomic betterment *for* those outside the charmed circle of power must be wrought *by* them. That requires much more thought and political work than usual by the ordinary people of this society; it means much changing of the mind about social causes and effects, doing that "more political work" with ordinary people like ourselves, trusting one another more and trusting less those who time and again have betrayed the trust they were granted. A government *for* the people quite literally must be *of* and *by* the people. Even those of us who haven't been very trustful have been too lazy.

Some who read these words will agree but go on to say that real reforms are unlikely and would in any case not be enough; therefore we need a whole new society, a noncapitalist society, a democratic socialist society; capitalism *can't* be reformed. Even assuming that to be so—and there are good arguments to be made both ways—the stubborn fact is that there is no existent movement for such a social revolution in this country, nor even a wisp of smoke signaling one over the horizon.

But there is a widespread sense of unease, worry, fear, and anger at what is, as many feel that worse is on its way. Although, by the society's standards of measurement, the economy is doing well, most of the people don't believe *they* are doing well, do not believe their children will do even as well as they have (even when that hasn't been all that great). And if current tendencies continue, the probabilities are that "most people" are right.

This is surely *not* a revolutionary moment in the United States, but it almost surely *is* a period in which a substantial reform movement could—as it must—be constructed. The first signs have been evident in numerous ways, like the crocuses that peep through the snow as winter ends. The crocuses don't need our help, but significant reform does; it depends upon a major change in political attitudes and a broad movement to realize them in practice. But can that happen?

In forbidding times like these, it is helpful to recall earlier times of difficulty; thus one often finds just how surprising the social process can be. As the Depression of the 1930s took hold, questions concerning possibilities for beneficial change could have been asked by all workers, as a tough minority fought for unionization against terrifying odds; by the unemployed and the old and the otherwise desperate, never represented in Congress; in the politically insipid 1950s—when young people were called "the silent generation"—questions could have been asked by young and old, black and white.

Most Americans in the early Depression years, if asked what the prospects might be for what came to be an AFL-CIO or a "New Deal" or, if asked in 1959 whether the next few years would bring significant social reform, would have answered with a groan or a laugh, or turned away in scorn. The changes that in fact took place in all those periods of reform were neither as broad nor as deep as were needed, but they were considerably more so than had seemed possible to virtually all before they happened (myself included). Thus, FDR, now remembered as one of the great "liberals" in our history, was a classic economic conservative in his first administration, indistinguishable in economic policy from the outgoing president, Herbert Hoover: Balance the budget, give business a freer hand, save the banks, do little or nothing for the 25 percent officially unemployed—and it was Hoover, not FDR, who began price supports for farmers.[1]

Nonetheless, despite the threat of being fired, injured, even killed, workers began to fight fiercely for union recognition and better wages and working conditions. And political groups all over the spectrum appeared, with substantial numbers on both left and right.[2] In late 1935, with another election coming up, FDR's closest advisers (among them his wife, Eleanor) warned him that discontent was becoming politicized and that for his reelection he had to change course, develop policies for "the common man," as the saying then went. And so he did: By 1936 the Second New Deal—the "real" New Deal—was under way, leaving behind traditional "relief and recovery" measures and replacing them with "reform."

In the 1960s, LBJ's steps toward his Great Society were clearly prompted by the political activism of the (mostly) young blacks and whites for civil rights and against poverty—against the background of a growing antiwar movement—along with the power of organized labor, then still strong, which was pushing successfully for health and pension programs. Those are the ones now being cut back or eliminated.

That is, when powerless people have ignored the odds against them and organized for an effort to change the society, they have sounded a responsive chord in many others, have become in some degree powerful, have brought about a different structure of power. And there is no other way. These are not original observations, of course. History is filled with axioms such as In union there is strength.

However, there could well be a different kind of question from those familiar with recent developments in Western Europe. There, many of the reforms noted earlier and to be advocated below have been in place for some time, but in Germany, France, Italy, and even Sweden, those reforms are now under attack and are being undone.

What should be noted in that respect is that both attack and undoing are coming largely—though not entirely—from the top layers of those societies, especially (as here) from the financial community. But there are at least two other important points to be made: First, the economies of those countries— all of them—have for the past twenty years or so become always more closely integrated with the U.S.-led world economy, a dynamic that pushes them toward becoming increasingly like our market-driven socioeconomy.

That development has been accelerated by the emergence of the European Union (EU, now fifteen countries, and growing) and the pressure for institutionalization of the "Maastricht Agreement, its single currency and unified monetary and fiscal policies."[3] All the leading (and some of the lesser, notably the South Korean) economies have developed patterns of production and consumption that increasingly duplicate one another and, having become so, remain largely unchanged in structure. They (and we) all must do more of the same, run faster to stay in the same place; that is, all must produce and sell more of the same things in competition with one another at home and abroad, and all must find ways to lower costs to maintain profits.

The easiest costs to push down are those of labor and environmental protection. Now the Europeans, like us, are going through the same dreary and punishing patterns of trying to keep up profits (before *and* after taxes) by pushing down the real incomes of the large majority, downsizing at home, outsourcing to cheap labor and "cheap environment" in the poor countries.

The second important point concerns European politics. For those same twenty years or so, the working class and its allies in Western Europe have coasted on their oars, have become less and less active politically,[4] leaving the vital political work to be done (or left undone) by *their* leaders (in unions and left-wing political parties). And in Europe (and Canada), as here, their leaders have become better at making deals.

Union leaders in the United States have long dealt with the companies in decreasingly combative ways (with some few exceptions). Meanwhile, the liberal Democrats have come to behave the same with the conservatives as the latter move steadily to the right. In Europe, what have been socialist or social democratic unions and parties now resemble the once liberal wing of our Democratic Party. And there as here, the free marketeers and budget balancers have taken up the slack.

The attempt to stop the retrogression in Europe has already begun and will most likely become stronger in the immediate future. Because the Europeans have an organized past and the political habits and institutions that go with it, their path seems easier than ours: It is easier to save reforms than to construct them. However, the U.S. economy is much stronger in many ways than theirs, even in combination (given their warring histories and often bitter quarrels). As will be seen later, the United States has considerably more *economic* room in which to maneuver toward a "square deal" economy than the European countries do; in the long run that could ease our way more than theirs to do what is needed.[5] Nevertheless, the relative importance of our economy in the world economy means that unless *we* are maintaining a reasonable level of economic health, all others' troubles will be deepened. This takes us to a relatively abstract but essential set of points concerning economic growth, domestic and global.

Economic Crossroads

Capitalist political economy by definition has at its heart a system of production whose economic strength depends upon general profitability over time. What the *average* rate of profits must be—and over time has been—is variable, in both good times and bad; and it varies with shifts in political power as well as with market changes. From 1992 through 1996, corporate profits rose (underlying the stock market boom of those same years). However, their base was fragile, dependent upon a tenuous debt structure and diverse sporadic developments; as 1996 drew to a close, "what analysts [were] arguing over ... [was] how much more slowly earnings will grow."[6] We can have and in the past have had a vigorous economy with lower after-tax profits (as in the "Great Society" 1960s); the current leveling off, far from accompanying a "developing" socioeconomy, a rapidly expanding world economy, and a stimulating war, confronts opposite tendencies everywhere.

When, in the next section, restructuring and its constituent elements are discussed, it is important to keep in mind that the reasons for those proposals go beyond the aim of making a better life for the majority of our people, desirable in itself though that is. Such a set of changes, it can be argued, are also necessary to forestall a deep economic and sociopolitical crisis.

Economic "restructuring" is another term for economic *development*—a process underlying but analytically quite distinct from economic *growth*. Growth, as noted in Chapter 3, is a quantitative process, whereas development means *qualitative*—structural—change. Furthermore, any society that has undergone the structural changes constituting *economic* development has ipso facto undergone structural changes in its *sociopolitical* sectors.[7]

Most relevant to the present discussion is that economic growth becomes fitful and sluggish in the absence of developmental changes—as is now seen in all the industrialized nations. That is a way of repeating something said a bit earlier; namely, that all the national economies are trying to do more of the same in their own and one another's economies. The almost frantic consumerism now gripping the leading economies sprang from that process; it is also integrally related to the types and levels of waste now common.

Ours is by no means the first period in capitalist history when the need for restructuring has occurred; there have been several disastrous predecessors. Thus the need was great at the turn of the century, but not even in retrospect can one discern a sufficiently widespread and politically realistic basis for that need to have been fulfilled. Instead, the consequence of developing weaknesses was that nationalism and imperialism combined with unfulfilled national economic needs to bring on World War I.

Between that war and the one that began in 1939 various nations moved in one or another unpromising direction (those "unpromising directions" included Hitler's), with economic structures changing mostly, if at all, in the direction of the military. In the United States—the most affluent of all, especially in resources—one structural change took hold in the 1920s, but inadequately: the beginnings of the mass production and associated (and indispensable) mass consumption of durable goods (autos and household appliances). However, the distribution of income and purchasing power soon set a limit to that development, a limit reached all the sooner, given passive federal and state governments and a collapsing world economy.

It must be understood that the widespread prosperity of industrial capitalism for the two decades after the 1950s depended upon the reemergence of that same system of mass-produced and -consumed durable goods in, but also outside, the United States—critically assisted by the economic stimuli of the cold war and the U.S.-revivified world economy—the most widespread and sustained period of "positive restructuring" in this century.[8]

The preceding paragraphs have been concerned with the disastrous consequences of *not* restructuring compared with the relatively beneficial consequences of having done so. One cannot be certain, but the present seems to be another turning point in the history of industrial capitalism: The economic growth of the United States has for at least a generation become increasingly frantic, dependent upon our extraordinary military spending, the accumulation of debt in all quarters (personal, business, governmental, international) in a dangerous mix with feverish speculation, and the functional combination of all that with widespread excess productive capacities, here and over the globe. In short, the time for "positive restructuring"—rather than the chase after endless growth—has come again. The question arises as to which structures should change in which ways to maximize social and planetary health. That is what the next section seeks to ascertain for the United States.

Just before that, it is important to make one more generalization regarding the European situation. The path toward industrial capitalism for all the European members of the OECD (and Japan) has always been shaped by (among other matters, of course) the inadequacy of their natural resources relative to the needs of industrialization—spectacularly so, when compared to ours.[9] They *must* import a high percentage of their raw materials, and they *must* export in proportion; therefore, they *must* be more sensitive than we are to all the elements of the world economy.

The Europeans' (and Japan's) economic flexibility is thus substantially constrained. For them to have *our* structural flexibility, they would have to move in one or both of two directions: away from capitalism, and its critical dependence upon property incomes, toward socialism and/or toward deeper integration of their national economies, not just in trade and finance (the present direction), but also in resource and production policies, that is, to become something like another United States. To the degree that that perspective is valid, the path ahead for the Europeans (to say nothing of the Japanese) is both steeper and more slippery than ours need be.

Some Principles and Elements of a Restructured U.S. Economy

Throughout this book, implicitly or explicitly, discussion has moved back and forth between one "structure" or another and the processes flowing through and among them, affecting and affected by them. We have dealt with structures of production (and employment), consumption, foreign trade, income and wealth, and the triad of economic, political, and social power. One can think of such social structures and processes as analogous to the those of the body, as an organic whole of bones, muscles, and organs, of physiology and psychology, all in dynamic interaction.

For present purposes, note the similarity between the functioning of the society and that of the body in that in neither case can significant change take place in one function without dynamic alterations in the others. But one of many differences between the two "organisms"—which suggests why speaking of society as an organism is a metaphor—is that major changes for the human body often occur as the result of a change *outside* the body; major social changes (except when induced by natural disaster) are the result of purposive actions, deliberately initiated from *within* its structures and processes.

The proposals now to be examined constitute "deliberate" changes, which, were they effected, would alter the structures of society in one degree or another. Such important steps require principles if they are to become and remain desirable. Those now to be enunciated are by no means esoteric or novel; they are indeed the principles to which this country has always presumed to adhere but seldom has, and never fully. Those principles have given the United States the "glow" that has made it so attractive to others and to ourselves.

Restructuring should be guided by standards moving us always closer to the achievement of increased economic, political, and social democracy, toward more equality and greater freedom. Of course such ideals have been routinely expressed by those in and out of the various seats of power from our beginnings, but their realization has been just as routinely obstructed. The sources of that obstruction have been institutionalized in our history; restructuring thus has much to *undo*: economic autocracy and political oligarchy, chronic racism and sexism and numerous de facto and legal constraints on the freedom of individuals. Moreover, such ideals cannot be realized within a society stricken by militarism and violence. There is as much to be unlearned as learned, as much to be undone as done.

Before particular restructuring programs are specified, one further caution is needed, perhaps uniquely relevant to American habits of mind. Given the troubles plaguing our society, a certain impatience and determination to reach our goals are of course essential; it is equally essential to cultivate the habit of patience, to recognize that the resolution of deep-seated social problems *cannot* be speedy, that significant social improvement requires a different mind-set than athletic events.

Our history has of course been marked by difficulty and tragedy; compared with other nations, however (and except for those Americans enslaved or crushed), we have had an easy time of it.[10] Because of our history, we are a people with a limited view of the complexities and snags of the social process, too confident that minimal political efforts (voting or an annual demonstration, for example) can realize our hopes; too likely to suffer disappointment and disillusion when stubborn realities impose themselves. We must learn to be pleased while also being dissatisfied with partial forward movement and to keep working in moments of seeming defeat. This is the opposite of a counsel of despair; it is based instead on the belief that continuous hard work is both necessary and sufficient to our ends.

Now comments on the structures whose change is essential for a just and stable society. As we treat one after the other, remember that the structures' continuous interaction makes deliberate changes in all of them necessary, at the same time that such interaction also provides momentum for further progress. In a "primer" such as this, only the surface of each structure can be skimmed; much more reading and research and discussion are necessary.

Production

The patterns of production determine the patterns of employment, and their levels rise and fall together—if at different paces, in accord (mostly) with technological change. What is produced is also what will be consumed—here and abroad—except insofar as it is used for further production (or stockpiled). We begin with the structure of production narrowly defined, leaving in temporary abeyance those other closely connected matters.

Changes in the structure of production are needed to rid us of what is currently amiss there: too much waste and inefficiency and damage, too much production of socially useless or harmful goods and services (or as in agriculture, too much restricted production), too much misuse and waste of labor in those respects; and, the obverse of all that, too little of what we need and what makes good sense. As an illustration, we produce too much of certain commodities—most spectacularly autos and weaponry—in terms of resource costs, wastes, and environmental damage and too little of certain others, such as mass transit and housing. We have too many of some services—advertising, finance, and the military—and too few in health care and education. And we have too many millions of people jobless and underemployed (part-time workers who need full-time work, or those with unused or undeveloped skills), "the worst waste of all."

The constant refrain that "we cannot afford to produce" a list of socially useful goods and services rests upon the assumption that what we now produce is produced efficiently and serves some useful social function and that there is no "give." Careful studies show that neither belief is valid; least of all, as we have seen, for military expenditures.

☞ In addition to what has been noted in Chapter 9, consider only this: The modern military man or woman has been well-trained for accomplishing a broad number of complex tasks—most of which have more than a military applicability. *Suppose* that half of those in the armed services were working at jobs in the civilian sector using their existing skills (with slight modifications, requiring only adaptation). They could increase the production of useful goods and services, earn incomes like those of their civilian counterparts, and become part of an expanded consumer market. In terms of their real income while in the service (receiving food, clothing, and health care and accumulating pensions and so on), they are well above the poverty line; they could be at the same level as civilians—with a restructured economy. The costs of the military would of course go down, allowing the government to spend on other needed goods and services—or to lower taxes. Note that the focus on production has just shifted easily to jobs, as it will now to consumption.

Consumption

Our producing so much that serves no socially or humanly useful purpose has another consequence, that we do *not* produce enough of what is badly needed—needed to assure that there will be no "ill-clothed, ill-fed, ill-housed," nobody without adequate medical care or the custodial care needed by many of the aged; to assure that a dedicated and imaginative educational system will nourish the young and the rest of us, throughout life. These generalizations should produce a sense of the resilient relationship between production and jobs and consumption and therefore between them and incomes (and purchasing power)—that is, between three separate but interacting structures. But a significant share of production needn't be bought here if it is exported, as a significant part of what is consumed here may be imported. Thus, there is a fourth structure, world trade. Also, some critical percentage of what is produced doesn't go to consumption here or elsewhere, but to business expenditures on equipment or buildings ("real investment"). That occurs when businesses expect expanding markets at home and/or abroad.

Now we must pause and adjust the focus to examine the processes within those structures that have created what may well be history's greatest problem: the threat to the earth's ability to support its flora and fauna—including us. It is not merely that we produce much that we do not need and therefore waste precious resources. In that same process we have developed products and ways of life that not only waste but destroy: (1) To sell that toothpaste, to produce and use those autos, to have that vast military (and so much else), we and the other industrial nations have recklessly pursued economic growth that eats away at the very basis of life on earth. Using all that paper and other materials to market and sell toothpaste (and many thousands of other products) is not only wasteful in itself, but it also has been part of the process of destroying forests—and the oxygen supply and the creatures and the soil they nourish and the flood prevention they assist. (2) All those autos require all that oil and steel and rubber and cloth and paint and glass, and poison the air and warm the atmosphere and cause deaths. Their thirst for oil (which gave rise to the petrochemical industry and its numerous hazardous products) has made it the largest of our imports, by far. (3) The military (see Chapter 9), the eighth-largest user of oil in the entire world, is a major polluter of the air, a major cause of the distortion of our structure of production, of our politics, a massive scandal within a decades-long set of processes of waste, destruction, and corruption at home and abroad—all in the name of patriotism. The list could go on but will not. But remember that in order to do all this and so much more that is wasteful and destructive and foolish beyond measure, we have also been part of that invasion of the societies *not* industrialized and have used their resources and their people, destroying them as we destroy ourselves. Who was it who said, "Whom the gods would destroy they first make mad"?[11]

To slow down, halt, and reverse those senseless processes, we must change not only the structures of production, jobs, consumption, and world trade, within which the processes have been created and function but also, and most decisively, the presiding structure of economic, political, and social power. Without an alteration in the structures of power, little else can be accomplished. That potent triad is simultaneously the consequence of and the ongoing basis for the heedless chase after profits and power. The chase is led by those few in society who both have that itch and have been in (or able to get in) a position to scratch it.

Because we live in a capitalist world, the attempt to understand the structures of power takes us to our earlier examination of the distribution of income and wealth. In Chapter 5 it was noted that wealth and its accumulation are a largely self-propelling process: Wealth (here, income-earning assets) produces income and some of the latter is used to gain greater wealth. That a very high percentage of wealth comes, not from contributions to production, but from inheritance or speculation or other socially unproductive sources, is not difficult to show. Nevertheless, accumulated wealth is virtually sacrosanct, more envied than criticized.

Any proposal to decrease the highly unequal distribution of income—let alone the even higher inequality of wealth—faces not only great opposition from the powerful, but even more widespread outrage among the non-self-serving populace. A page or two, much less a paragraph or two, cannot undo that reflex, but a start can perhaps be made here by considering a few points.[12]

Wealth

When industrial capitalism was first taking hold in Britain and here, the economists' argument encouraging the accumulation of private wealth was that it was the source of public well-being: Those who accumulated profits from their enterprises would ordinarily "plow it back," thereby producing expansion, more goods, more jobs and higher real incomes, more wealth, and so on, ad infinitum. That view persisted even after the traditional single proprietor (or partnership) mutated (after mid–nineteenth century) into the corporation and then into the giant corporation and now into the super-transnational corporation—whose owners (stockholders) most often cannot even list the products of the company they partially own.

Leaving aside any comment on the original argument and its time and place, it may be said that the ownership of and dividends from the contemporary corporation are, and long have been, sharply separated from the functioning of that corporation[13]—except insofar as its CEOs now regularly receive bonuses in the form of stock options (etc.) that make some kind of connection thereto. Only rarely, however, are those bonuses (etc.) connected to any specifiable performance of the company or the recipient, and even then the definition of "good performance" bears no demonstrable relationship to social contribution.[14]

Of all the policies advocating some containment to the accumulation of wealth, at least one has been somewhat honored over time, here and elsewhere; that is the taxation of inheritances. Although it is pleasant to agree that wealthy parents should be able to leave their offspring in some kind of considerable comfort when that can be accomplished through an estate, is it not equally pleasant to argue for some limit? But what limit?

The specific level of the limit is not so important as the principle itself, but for purposes of thought and discussion, let us propose a maximum inheritance of $500,000, with increasingly steep taxation on anything above that, moving toward confiscation above, say, $1 million net. Some who accept the principle would say those numbers should be higher, others lower. At this state of our history, it is acceptance of a considerably less generous set of figures than the status quo that is important. Let a hundred arguments resound.

Income

Similarly, it seems reasonable for our society to consider both a floor and a ceiling for incomes. We have in effect considered a floor in our antipoverty and welfare legislation—a floor, however, now moving toward zero. It will be suggested later that we should see to it through a jobs program that there be *no* poverty (and thus no need for welfare payments) in this very rich country; on the path toward that objective, defining a livable wage and setting a minimum income (for families and individuals) would be a useful first step.

Taking the standard family of four as the focus, it may be suggested that the present definition of poverty—just under $16,000 annually—would be funny were it not so cruel. As has been said by critics, nobody would agree with that figure had they tried to live on it with a family of two, let alone four. Twice that would seem reasonable.

But a *ceiling* on incomes? The word that pops into most minds when such a point is raised is "incentives." We have come to believe that *any* ceiling on incomes would be socially counterproductive, for reasons taken so much for granted it seems foolish to question them. Here again is one of those remarkable phenomena—as with Americans' believing that they have the best health care system in the world while worrying themselves sick about paying for their own health care. Who knows how many of us accept a notion we do *not* live by, irrespective of our own incomes?

Everyone wishes to have an income allowing comfort and security, of course; but how many doctors, scientists, baseball players, entertainers, teachers, or even businessmen went into their occupations—and the training for them—with only, or mostly, an unlimited income as the reason? Well, nowadays that is becoming increasingly common—multimillion dollar incomes for some of the above, and an avaricious struggle to lift them even further. But almost all who go into those areas of work do so because the nature of the work (its usefulness, its acclaim, its interestingness) attracts them.

Only those who do not have enough money to survive easily are likely to choose a job for money incentives alone, or principally. And one must ask whether you would select a doctor who had a very high income and wanted it higher and that was her/his reason for becoming a doctor, or look for another who had *being* a doctor as the incentive? A teacher? Or if you owned a company and sought a manager, whom would you select, someone endlessly hungry for money or someone who, naturally liking money, liked also the nature of the work even more? Few of us know—or would want to depend upon—someone whose principal motivation in life is to make money.

All that reasoning could be wrong. Assuming that it is not *all* wrong, what would such a ceiling be? How would we determine it? As with wealth, a proposal for an income ceiling at this time can be seen only as a way of beginning discussion. Let's begin with, say, an annual income of $200,000 after taxes as reasonable—in the specific sense that anything above that is difficult to justify, and that having such an income even now places one comfortably in the top twentieth of the population.

Is this a proposal to take money away from the very rich and distribute it among the poor? Not at all. I for one would be opposed to such an idea on various grounds. It is a proposal instead whose implementation would make sense only as part of a cluster of other proposals, in which "money would be taken away from the rich" only as taxes and used to help finance services not for the poor—who, were the proposals enacted, would be few—but the larger society. After all, those with the greatest ability to pay taxes are also those whom the society has most generously blessed.

The "cluster of proposals" (regarding jobs, health care, and so on) will occupy the sections to follow. The largest part of that program would be publicly financed but privately produced—as with milex, in both respects. The financing by the government would in turn rest almost entirely on (federal, state, and local) taxes, the largest part of which would be from federal estate and inheritance and progressive income taxes.[15]

The ratio of taxes to the national income in the United States is the lowest of all the industrial capitalist nations; so are our various governments' social expenditures (as noted earlier). In all the debates of recent years that revolve around the inability of our society any longer to finance Social Security, or health care, or education, or adequate public housing, it is hardly ever mentioned that our "inability" to do so is not "economic" but political, a consequence of the ability of those at the top of our pyramids of income, wealth, and power to use their resources to make those pyramids always steeper—not least by having their taxes reduced and the bottom 90 percent's increased.[16] That particular process—and the tax structure accompanying it—is the key area for reform: *and* among the very most difficult.

Jobs and Incomes

The financial community, which has taken an increasingly dominant role in setting U.S. socioeconomic policy—cut the deficit, balance the budget, cut social expenditures, don't let unemployment get too low—has at its apex of control the Federal Reserve System, our central bank, fittingly called "the lender of last resort." Thus, when in 1987 Wall Street took a sharp dive—a 500-point drop in the Dow—and the whole world's financial system began to wobble and shake, it was the Fed's shoveling out of money as "loans" that plugged the dike just as it was preparing to break wide open. Without that lender of last resort, who knows what the economic world would have been like in the past decade?

Such an institution for providing the financial world and thus the economy with more stability than it otherwise would have is found in all nations now; the United States was the last among the leading countries to create it (in 1913). But we have yet to provide for workers an "employer of last resort." Again, and if and when we do that, we will by no means be the first country to do so, to guarantee that all those who seek work will be able to find it. As of now, however, we remain the nation that trusts most in the free market—or, to put it differently, the nation that allows the free market to do its damage with the least public constraints or assistance to workers (and increasingly, the environment).

That objective stance is definitely *not* taken when it is business that needs the help. As noted earlier, we have what has come to be called "corporate welfare" for big business and a Small Business Administration for those not at all big. We have long helped the businesses called farms, whether mostly small, as in the beginning, or mostly very big, as now. And weapons makers. And banks. And so on.

In 1996, after days and weeks and months of overt and concealed bargaining, the 104th Congress finally passed and the president signed a minimum wage increase. On that new minimum, one can work 8 hours a day, 5 days a week, 52 weeks a year, and end up with only $10,000–11,000 for the year. Presumably that wage is entry level for kids, and so we can say, "Well, they probably live at home, or get help from their parents, or . . . , something that will keep them from starving (or stealing)." But most of those jobs are being hunted down by men and women in their twenties and thirties, and there are (at least in New York City) ten to fourteen people seeking each such available job. Who's kidding whom?

To become both a just and a sane society regarding jobs and incomes we should start from a principle something like the following: (1) Everyone should have the opportunity through the normal educational process, and/or through vocational training programs, to become capable of doing more than unskilled work; (2) all such jobs should pay a livable (not a "minimum") wage, that is, a wage that will allow a normal family to live decently; (3) if such training and jobs are not available, the federal government (and/or state and local governments) should develop and/or participate in programs providing the appropriate training and programs to provide such work at such wages.

Objections: Can't be done. Will cause the deficit to rise, the budget to be out of balance. Would turn into "boondoggling" (make-work, and so on). Corruption. Laziness. Won't work. But it has worked, not only in other countries, but right here in the United States. It has worked on a large scale, for many years, with numerous positive effects for the country, as well as jobs for the workers. When? During the Depression, such a program was administered by agencies that came to be called "alphabet soup": PWA, WPA, CCC, NYA, TVA—respectively, Public Works Administration, Works Progress Administration, Civilian Conservation Corps, National Youth Administration, Tennessee Valley Authority. And there were others.[17]

What did they do? In order: PWA built bridges, roads, all kinds of buildings (e.g., hospitals, schools, libraries), airports, parks, swimming pools, athletic fields, you name it. Probably you've used many of those facilities hundreds of times and never knew they were financed by an "employer of last resort," the work done by otherwise jobless workers, presided over by profit-making private construction and other firms.

WPA? We can never know how many classes were taught, musicians were trained (and performed), artists painted (e.g., murals in public buildings), books written, actors performed, and so on, all made possible by WPA, together giving educational and cultural life in the United States a big boost.

CCC? Many thousands of young people were put to work in the forests and fields and valleys, making the earth safer, more beautiful, more useful, more accessible. Meanwhile, those young people were able to live healthily and do something useful and at least as interesting as a summer camp in the Poconos (or the streets in the city).

NYA? I was one of them, as a student at San Francisco Junior College (1936–1938), working with one of my professors, helping with research. It wasn't Ph.D. level, but it helped to pay the rent and I learned something.

And TVA. A different kind of effort, the Tennessee Valley Authority, which reclaimed an enormous river valley, preventing the occurrence of what had been frequent and disastrous floods while also providing cheap electricity and providing good construction jobs then, and many other good jobs since.

As I know from my NYA job, the wages paid were not high for the likes of me. They were often the minimum wage (established at that time); for construction and other jobs, much higher. As noted earlier, the New Deal didn't do as much as it should have, either to get us out of the Depression or to use the unused human and capital resources. But it was a much better accomplishment than anything going on right now. And we can do better than the New Deal, in part because we have it to study, in part because we're much richer now, in part because the social costs and risks of not doing so are much higher now than in the Depression.[18]

Health, Education, Housing, Social Security

Each of these, health, education, housing, Social Security, requires at least a book in itself, as does so much else discussed earlier. But the general principles that make sense can be stated (or restated) here, in the knowledge that anything more than that will, as it must, come out of much thought and discussion and political effort.

All of us need health, education, housing, Social Security, and it is also deeply necessary for the well-being of our society that such needs be met. Setting moral considerations aside, it is a continuing source of astonishment that so many people in our society can believe that the society can be well off while a large segment of the people are badly off. Moral considerations *are* set aside, of course, and their place is taken by "practical," usually meaning economic, considerations. And that too is astonishing. It is not difficult to come to the conclusion that our society's relative indifference to moral considerations plays a significant role in our irresolute efforts to resolve difficult social problems, which are often resolved only by default.

A program that would assure the health care, education, housing, and provisions for the old and infirm can be supported simply on the argument of its practicality. The financial and social costs of our status quo are already close to overwhelming, and the future will see both kinds of costs rise even further—as will the pains accompanying them.

The unmet needs in all these respects have already been detailed; suffice it here to say that those needs cannot be met adequately by the free market, or by the kind of unfree markets that exist for all of them. Just as there should be a national health insurance (single-payer) program for health care, so should there be for the other three areas—with, as always (as in European programs), additional (free market) opportunities for those well-off.

Whatever the seeming and real differences between the four areas, the similarities are more important: In all cases the starting point must be the needs (and possibilities) of those involved, the human and social benefits of meeting those needs, and the human and social costs of *not* meeting them. We are already well along the path to knowing the early costs of our failure; what we have yet to experience would be the great satisfaction of living in a society that *does* meet such needs.

Gaining that, what then would be lost? The rich would be constrained to stay only very well-off indeed; business would be constrained from some of its present freedoms (financial or environmental) but would function in a still profitable and much stabler society. Some of the rich and some in business would never "relax and enjoy it." There are already dozens of millions who never relax and enjoy. It would be a good trade. And in a genuine democracy the trade would be accomplished. Can we move toward that?

Democratic Politics

Because of the combination of need and possibility, there has probably never been a more likely period in our history to move in those directions; and it is not easy to point to a period in which so many people are angry, desperate, gloomy, pessimistic. We are a nation in which the word "problem" has become as common as the dirty air. But as has long been noted, the consciousness of social problems arises from a perception of a gap between what is and what could be; the sense of problem arises from a sense of the possibility of a better reality.

What *could* be, however, means that which is possible, not that which is probable. There is the possibility, but no present probability, in the United States that we will move in the directions suggested throughout this book. For possibility to become probability and then, in growing degree, reality depends upon what we as a people do or don't do politically. What we have been doing is quite a lot at the very top and practically nothing as one moves down through the middle and toward the bottom of the population.

What those at the top do is both motivated and thoroughly lubricated by their wealth and power. They pay or cajole to keep or get what they want, directly and indirectly—through lobbying, through campaign contributions ($1.5+ billion in the 1996 elections),[19] the media, and elsewhere. An entirely different political effort is required to democratize this society; it will be fueled, not by our money, but by our political work. And that's a fact, not a probability.

The time for the necessary political work to begin was many years ago. But today is the best time now available—and dreary and deceptive election-year displays won't divert us. It does help to be in between elections, however. In that connection, it is useful to remember that when FDR was elected in 1932, so was a conservative Congress, on both sides of the aisle. Two years later, amid rising discontent, both House and Senate shifted significantly away from conservative toward moderate or liberal members; and two years further on, in 1936, FDR ran as a genuine liberal (and was reelected then and twice more).

The period between now and 2000 can be used to put in place several foundation stones or, more accurately, to *continue* and to expand the work that is already under way: (1) The two major parties must become aware of a threatening reality that consists of a meaningful third party (or parties), not as a force that seeks a winning presidential candidate in the year 2000, but one that *can* affect local and state elections—including not only city and state governments but also members of the House and Senate. (2) Such political efforts, whether in the form of a third party or other contending institution, must make it clear to the major parties that the people of this country realize that competition and discord among and between themselves—in terms of color, or gender, or occupation, or anything—serves to harm their lives and help the already wealthy and powerful. (3) Such understanding must carry with it two implications—that we learn to work together much, much more than we ever have before and that we become accustomed to working more politically, being more politically involved, than ever before.[20]

In the mid-1970s, as the country was preparing to celebrate its two hundredth birthday, I wrote a book that, like this one, was a critical commentary on how far we as a people and a nation had drifted from what we had for so long seen as our dream. I called the book *The Twisted Dream*, and I closed it with an admonition written by the great Carl Sandburg in the 1930s: "America was promises."[21]

It still is, at least for a while. But now as always, when we do not actively seek to realize those promises, they become lies. Now still, as I wrote in that earlier book, "Decency, sanity, and safety require that those promises be redeemed; with effort, patience and impatience, and love, they can be." And if they are not?

Notes

Chapter One

1. Samuel Bowles, "What Markets Can—and Cannot—Do," *Challenge*, July-Aug. 1991.

2. From the 1996 Report of the Bank for International Settlements (BIS). The BIS expectation was that the daily amount would rise by 30 percent annually, which would make the daily total for 1997 over $3 trillion per day, twenty times that of the late 1980s. The executive vice president of the Bank of America responded to these figures by warning that all this "poses risks that are growing much faster than the capacity of the banking system to carry them" (*International Herald Tribune* [hereafter, *IHT*], Feb. 5, 1996).

3. Adam Smith, *Wealth of Nations* (New York: Modern Library, 1937), p. 250.

4. Thorstein Veblen, *The Instinct of Workmanship* (New York: Macmillan, 1914), p. 347.

5. These and connected matters will be more fully treated in Chapter 3.

6. Lawrence Mishel and Jared Bernstein, *The State of Working America, 1994–95* (Armonk, N.Y.: M. E. Sharpe, 1995), pp. 44–45. (Hereafter, this volume will be cited as M/B.)

7. A generic, although larger than usual, example early in 1995 was the news that AT&T's laying off 40,000 middle managers was "greeted favorably by the market"—preceded less than a year earlier by AT&T's announcement of $4.7 billion in profits.

8. John Maynard Keynes, *Laissez-Faire and Communism* (New York: New Republic, Inc., 1926), p. 131.

9. M/B, p. 41.

10. For a full treatment of Bentham's writings on economic matters, see W. Stark, ed., *Jeremy Bentham's Economic Writings* (London: Allen & Unwin, 1954), 3 vols. The quoted passage is taken from his essay in *Annals of Agriculture*, vol. 31, p. 283 n.

11. A detailed and documented discussion of these and related matters may be found in the definitive work of J. L. and B. Hammond, *The Rise of Modern Industry* (New York: Harcourt, Brace, 1926). Even greater detail is put forth in their monographs, *The Town Labourer, 1760–1832*, and *The Village Labourer, 1760–1832*, both in two volumes (London: Longmans, Green, 1911–1917, pub. for Guild Books). See also their *The Bleak Age* (London: Penguin Books, 1937). The conditions they report in these books, all concerned with what came to be called the "Industrial Revolution," have been reproduced in the previously (or still) colonized countries of Asia, Latin America, and Africa in recent decades, with some

remnants (or reproductions) in the established industrial nations, e.g., "sweat-shops."

12. It may be noted as an aside that the wildly diverse composition of the U.S. Right—ranging from those opposed to abortion and gun control to those opposed to taxes, among other such issues—a recent source of its main strengths, may well be the cause of a future political defeat.

13. That phrase is the title of chap. 3 of Garry Wills, *Nixon Agonistes: The Crisis of the Self-Made Man* (New York: Boston: Houghton Mifflin, 1969), wherein Wills pursued the development of that "politics" in a manner both illuminating and depressing.

14. For one of the best of several treatments of that process, see Mark Hertsgaard, *On Bended Knee: The Press and the Reagan Presidency* (New York: Farrar, Straus and Giroux, 1988).

15. Lest this characterization of behavior in the financial world seem a caricature, see Michael Lewis, *Liar's Poker* (New York: Norton, 1989). Lewis was a trader at one-time most solid of bond houses, Salomon Brothers, and has a regular column on financial matters in the *New York Times Sunday Magazine*. You will be amused at the "animal house" behavior of the (dominantly young) traders—that is, until you remember that the world economy and our domestic political economy are dominated more by those markets than by any other sector. Treating of the financial world on a broader and deeper, but no less terrifying, scale is R. T. Naylor, *Hot Money and the Politics of Debt* (New York: Simon and Schuster, 1987).

16. For a full presentation of Gilder's views, see his popular and influential book, *Wealth and Poverty* (New York: Basic Books, 1981).

17. The historical data and charts for income and wealth in M/B, esp. chaps. 1 and 5, show this change clearly and are reinforced by the movement toward regressivity in the tax structure shown in M/B, chap. 2. A more popular treatment of this and connected matters may be found in Donald L. Barlett and James B. Steele, *America: What Went Wrong?* (Kansas City: Andrews and McMeel, 1992). The authors are reporters for the *Philadelphia Inquirer*, their book an outcome of a long series of investigative reports. Of great interest on these income, wealth, and taxation trends are the recent books of Kevin Phillips, a Republican fearful that his party has gone too far and too fast. See *Boiling Point: Democrats, Republicans and the Decline of Middle Class Prosperity* (New York: Harper Perennial, 1993), written *before* the latest developments.

18. Economic theory has three subdivisions: micro, macro, and trade theory. Micro deals with functioning of commodity and labor markets, macro with the overall processes of economic expansion and contraction, and trade theory with international markets. As will be discussed later, John Maynard Keynes (1883–1946) was the principal shaper of macro theory. That theory guided monetary and fiscal policies to one important degree or another in the post–World War II years and to a much lesser extent during the 1930s, when the theory was formulated. Since the 1970s, "Keynesianism" has been very much shoved aside in favor of "monetarism," the pre-Keynesian macro theory—whose basic argument was to leave the economy alone (except for manipulations of the supply and cost of borrowed funds): Let the free market "decide," come hell or high water. Today that position means that the federal government should not engage in deficit financing to curb recessions or take us out of a depression.

19. A rich technical analysis on this point may be found in the substantial (55-page) essay of Herman Daly and Robert Goodland, "An Ecological-Economic Assessment

of Deregulation of International Commerce Under GATT," a "Discussion Draft" is-
suing from—of all places—the Environment Department of the World Bank, of
whose staff the authors were then (1992) and may still now be members. The ideas
they put forth were their own, not those of the bank. One can read a more popular
version of the same arguments—on the social and environmental consequences of free
trade with capital mobility—by Herman E. Daly, "From Adjustment to Sustainable
Development: The Obstacle of Free Trade," in the collection entitled *The Case
Against Free Trade: GATT, NAFTA, and the Globalization of Corporate Power* (San
Francisco: Earth Island Press, 1993). Other contributors include Ralph Nader, Wendell Berry, Thea Lee, and Jerry Mander. As will also be seen in Chapter 3, even when
capital *was* essentially immobile (that is, in the nineteenth century), the consequences
of global free trade in Ricardian terms were such as to assure that the then-leading
economic power (Great Britain) would remain just that; and to be the leading economic power was also to be the leading power in all other terms. Thus, for example,
neither Germany nor the United States was "Ricardian." And both became powerful.

Chapter Two

1. The data on wealth are found in Lawrence Mishel, Jared Bernstein, and John
Schmitt, *The State of Working America 1996–97* (Armonk, N.Y.: M. E. Sharpe, 1997),
p. 279, table 5.2. (Hereafter, this volume will be cited as M/B/S.) Those on income,
interest payments, and the like, along with much else (including an apt analysis of
Reagan's "triumphs"), were provided by Garry Wills, "It's His Party," *NYT Magazine*, Aug. 11, 1996. "His" means Reagan's. David Stockman's role as Reagan's first
budget director was also discussed in that piece; what Stockman said provided a fundamental insight into the nature of Reagan's administrations. While he was still
working in the White House and also after he left Washington for Wall Street (at
$400,000 annual starting salary), Stockman revealed that the tax reduction/military
expenditure increase was conscious and deliberate, simultaneously satisfying three
important aims of Reagan and his advisers: lower taxes for the well-off, an expanded
military, and an additional reason to curtail liberal programs. All this was made indis-
creetly clear in an interview Stockman had with journalist William Greider, published
in the *Atlantic Monthly* in 1981 (reprinted in Greider's *The Education of David
Stockman and Other Americans* [New York: New American Library, 1986]). You can
read about that and other essentially scandalous processes in Stockman's own book,
The Triumph of Politics (New York: Harper and Row, 1987). Stockman, in his early
thirties when appointed by Reagan, was deeply critical of virtually all of that: A
strong believer in balanced budgets *and* cutting social expenditures, he did not support increasing expenditures for the military while also cutting taxes, which un-
leashed the greatest increase in the national debt in U.S. history. Indeed the debt accumulated in Reagan's years exceeded the *total* for all our history (in 1990
dollars)—which included, of course, the Civil War, two world wars, plus Korea and
Vietnam. His record is likely to stand.

2. Robert Eisner, *The Misunderstood Economy: What Counts and How to Count
It* (Boston: Harvard Business School Press, 1994). Eisner, a former president of the
American Economics Association, wrote the book with the general public in mind. It
is as readable as it is useful. Because financial power and processes are behind so

much of this and other troubling developments, it may be useful here to note a recent book that does much to illuminate the use and misuse of that power and the dangers associated with those processes and also proposes numerous important reforms: Gary A. Dymski, Gerald Epstein, and Robert Pollin, eds., *Transforming the U.S. Financial System: Equity and Efficiency for the Twenty-First Century* (Armonk, N.Y.: M. E. Sharpe, 1993, for the Economic Policy Institute).

3. Some of these and other data are part of a fascinating essay by John Cassidy, "Ace in the Hole," *New Yorker*, June 10, 1996.

4. Von Hayek taught at the University of Chicago in the 1940s, then as now the center of free market economics. Before he came to the United States he was deeply involved in the conservative politics of his native Austria. His fame in this country was provided by his book *The Road to Serfdom* (Chicago: University of Chicago Press, 1944). Analytically, it was the direct precursor of Milton Friedman's basic offering, *Capitalism and Freedom*, published by the same press, 1962. The aim of both books was to eliminate the reforms of the New Deal—which led to "serfdom," as Hayek saw it and, at least as important to Friedman, inefficiency.

5. Quoted in Stephen Pizzo, Mary Fricker, and Paul Muolo, *Inside Job: The Looting of America's Savings and Loans* (New York: McGraw-Hill, 1989), p. 12.

6. The generalizations to follow in the text concerning jobs and milex will be supported and explored further in Chapters 4 and 9, respectively.

7. For these and related data, see Thomas Michl, "Debt, Deficits, and the Distribution of Income," *Journal of Post-Keynesian Economics* 13, no. 3, Spring 1991, pp. 351–365. For a broader analysis and survey of the tax situation, see Joseph A. Pechman, *Tax Reform, the Rich and the Poor* (Washington, D.C.: Brookings Institute, 1989). Pechman, who died recently, was probably the most widely respected of tax specialists.

8. For these and other data for the period, see George Soule's definitive study, *Prosperity Decade: From War to Depression, 1917–1929* (New York: Holt, Rinehart and Winston, 1947).

9. K. Phillips, *Boiling Point*, p. 107.

10. Jan. 11, 1996.

11. M/B/S, p. 44.

12. If a "flat tax" could be justified at all, it would be for Social Security deductions/taxes. Now everyone pays 7.65 percent up to about $60,000; over that, nothing. If those with incomes over $60,000 were to pay that same "flat" rate on the rest of their income, that would go far to take care of the presumed "crisis" of Social Security (see Chapter 6).

13. Louis Uchitelle, "Retirement's Worried Face," *New York Times* [hereafter, *NYT*], July 30, 1995. It needs saying that the privatization of "social security" means the return to a world in which, except for the well-off, there was *no* security regarding old age or disability.

14. On this matter, see Ben Bagdikian, *The Media Monopoly* (Boston: Beacon Press, 1983), and the substantial investigative report of the *Nation*, "The National Entertainment State," June 3, 1996. Bagdikian has been assistant managing editor of the *Washington Post* and dean of the Graduate School of Journalism at the University of California, Berkeley. His study is disturbing enough in its highlighting of the intense concentration of control in the media world. But his data were from the early 1980s. The *Nation* study, complete with a four-page foldout table, one page for each

of the four giants—General Electric, Time Warner, Disney/Cap Cities, and Westinghouse—makes the findings of Bagdikian seem almost quaint. Not only do these four control the four major networks (American Broadcasting Company [ABC], National Broadcasting Company [NBC], Columbia Broadcasting System [CBS], and Turner Broadcasting/Cable News Network [CNN]) and other elements of the media, but they also control a good share of the plastics, appliance, nuclear, and many other industries. It would be difficult to be "neutral" about political processes with such interests. For a critical study of how the media influence public opinion, see what is already becoming the classic study by Edward S. Herman and Noam Chomsky, *Manufacturing Consent: The Political Economy of the Mass Media* (New York: Pantheon, 1988).

Chapter Three

1. A reminder here also of Ricardo's assumption of capital immobility—in his day a valid assumption to make; however, his theory was valid only for Britain. A mainstream, comprehensive, and readable treatment of evolution of the world economy is William Ashworth, *A Short History of the International Economy Since 1850* (London: Longmans, 1964). A critical analysis of Britain's heyday by one of the most astute of economic historians is E. J. Hobsbawm, *Industry and Empire* (New York: Pantheon, 1968).

2. In Germany there was at least a contest—between "Smithismus" and the mercantilist principles of Friedrich List—won by List (who had visited the United States to study *our* mercantilist policies in the early nineteenth century). Elsewhere there was discussion, but in France, Italy, and Japan—among most others—there was never serious consideration of Ricardian principles of free trade. The leading "political economist" of France in the seventeenth century, Jean Baptiste Colbert (first minister of Louis XIV), who represented the vital center of "mercantilist" ideas, said: "Commerce is carried on by 20,000 vessels and that number cannot be increased. Each nation strives to have its fair share and to get ahead of the others. The Dutch now fight this war [of trade] with 15,000 to 16,000 vessels, the English with 3,000 to 4,000 and the French with 500 to 600. The last two countries can improve their commerce *only* by increasing the number of their vessels and can increase the number *only* by paring away from the 15,000 to 16,000 ships. ... It must be added that trade causes perpetual strife both in time of war and in time of peace between all the nations of Europe to decide which of them shall have the greatest share" (emphasis added). (Quoted in Eli Heckscher, *Mercantilism* [London: Allen and Unwin, 1935], vol. 2, pp. 26–27, the classic on that era.) Colbert is still influential in French political economic thought (De Gaulle was viewed as direct descendant of Colbert with respect to mercantilist ideas).

3. For a comprehensive and illuminating treatment of the colonizing (et cetera) process since the fifteenth century, see L. S. Stavrianos, *Global Rift: The Third World Comes of Age* (New York: William Morrow, 1981). Covering much of that same ground, along with much else of importance related to it, is Noam Chomsky, *Year 501: The Conquest Continues* (Boston: South End Press, 1993).

4. "Break Up the Monoculture," in *Nation*, July 15/22, 1996. Norberg-Hodge is director of the Society for Ecology and Culture and codirector of the International Forum on Globalization-Europe. That issue of *Nation*, under the rubric "It's the

Global Economy, Stupid: The Corporatization of the World," has seven substantial essays on the various dimensions of globalization, plus a resource guide to books, articles, and interested organizations.

5. Korten is the author of the recent *When Corporations Rule the World* (New York: Kumarian, 1995). The quotation is from his essay "The Limits of the Earth," *Nation*, July 15/22, 1996.

6. Incisive and indispensable for understanding both the growth and reasons for the subsequent decline of that world economy is Fred L. Block, *The Origins of International Economic Disorder* (Berkeley: University of California Press, 1977). A later study, covering some of the same ground, but with the advantage of a decade more of observation, is Joyce Kolko, *Restructuring the World Economy* (New York: Pantheon, 1988). Kolko probed deeply into the rise and functioning of the TNCs, their relationships with the state, and the tangled processes leading to stagflation and financialization.

7. The top ten among them are Shell, EXXON, International Business Machines (IBM), GM, Hatachi, Matsushita, Nestle, Ford, Aleatel Alsthorn, and General Electric (GE).

8. Richard Barnet and John Cavanagh, *Global Dreams: Imperial Corporations and the New World Order* (New York: Simon and Schuster, 1994), p. 15. For these and connected matters in the U.S. economy, see also Richard Barnet, "Lords of the Global Economy: Stateless Corporations," *Nation*, Dec. 19, 1994. The data on the TNCs accumulate at an accelerated rate, as their size and importance do. Thus Cavanagh (misspelled Kavanagh), along with Sarah Anderson, in a comment printed in the *IHT* (Oct. 10, 1996), added that (1) along with their 25 percent share of world production, the top 200 TNCs employ but three-quarters of 1 percent of the world's workers, (2) the top 5 of the auto TNCs have 60 percent of global sales, the top 5 in electronics have half, and the top 5 in airlines, aerospace, steel, oil, personal computers (PCs), chemicals, and the media have 30 percent or more, (3) the sales of the largest 200 TNCs are bigger than the *combined* economies of 191 countries, almost all minus the biggest 9, and (4) all this is growing at an accelerating rate.

9. Article by veteran foreign affairs journalist of the *Los Angeles Times*, William Pfaff, in *IHT,* March 16–17, 1966. Pfaff went on to say: "In short, it is perfectly possible that America's export successes and its big rise in corporate profits in the last decade would have happened without globalization. The country sold more abroad because the dollar was cheap, and the corporations that did the selling got rich. Corporate executives congratulated themselves on their brilliance and raised their own salaries." In 1996 the yen lost about half of *its* value against the dollar (and the deutsche mark also fell, but less so), developments unlikely to ease the downward pressures on jobs and wages here or in the other leading nations.

10. A quite simply extraordinary fact: "The world's billionaires have a combined net worth of $760 billion, equal to that of the bottom 45 percent of the world's population." Barnet, *Nation*, July 15/22, 1996.

11. Cited in the review of Soyinka, *The Open Sore of a Continent: A Personal Narrative of the Nigerian Crisis* (New York: Oxford University Press, 1996), by Robert D. Kaplan, *NYT Book Review*, Aug. 11, 1966, p. 9.

12. Normally, *corporate welfare* refers to congressional favors in the form of tax breaks and subsidies that artificially maintain and/or enrich various companies and industries. For a perusal of the favors done by the 104th, budget-balancing, Congress,

see the millions or billions granted to what Daniel Franklin called "Ten Not So Little Piggies: Some *Real* Budget Busters," in an article of that name, *Nation*, Nov. 27, 1995.

13. Reports show that many of those performing that very cheap labor—e.g., $2.00 per day in Indonesia, as the norm—are eager to have that "opportunity." At least two points are relevant in that connection: (1) In Indonesia, Honduras, and many other similar countries, the governments, which are or have been U.S. supported, engage in repressive politics in labor and other realms; (2) the TNCs involved are not bound by "economic laws" to pay such low wages. In textiles, for example, labor costs per unit of product are under 10 percent of total costs.

14. "Globalization and the American Dream," p. 2, a pamphlet put out by Global Exchange, 2017 Mission Street, Room 303, San Francisco, CA 94110. The data are derived from *Corporate Power and the American Dream* (New York: Labor Institute, 1996), p. 6. The Global Exchange pamphlet (8 pages) provides other useful data plus a compact analysis. NAFTA's three members are the United States, Mexico, and Canada. It has become a sort of merry-go-round on which U.S. jobs are being lost to Mexico, preceded and accompanied by Canadian jobs lost to the United States (since 1988, when the U.S.-Canada treaty was signed). "The results of these policies have been devastating for most Canadians. Several hundred thousand jobs and many hundreds of manufacturing companies have fled to lower-wage American states.... Like the United States we are creating a contingency work force of part-time, low-wage jobs with no security and few benefits" (Maude Barlow and Tony Clark, "Canada—The Broken Promise," *Nation*, July 15/22, 1966).

15. Amartya Sen, *Poverty and Famine: An Essay on Entitlement and Deprivation* (Oxford: Clarendon Press, 1981), p. 1. The data on malnutrition are provided annually by UNICEF, and the dire numbers continually rise.

16. For the history of this grim and quite unnecessary tragedy, see Cecil Woodham-Smith, *The Great Hunger: Ireland, 1845–1849* (New York: Harper and Row, 1962). A personal addendum: My great grandfather was one of those who emigrated, coming directly to pre–Gold Rush San Francisco in 1846. Of his four sons, one became a successful rancher and then merchant, another became the sheriff of San Francisco. The other two might, however, fit the stereotype of the shiftless Irish: one, my grand-uncle Cleophas, was first a Jesuit priest, then a murderer, later, having fled the area to Utah, a breeder of fast horses (Butch Cassidy and the Sundance Kid among his customers), and then was himself murdered by a rustler, in 1898; the last brother was a horse thief, caught at it, and hanged some miles south of San Francisco. Good genes, bad genes, who can say?

17. The analyses appropriate to the problem were put forth almost a half century ago by K. William Kapp, in *The Social Costs of Private Enterprise* (Cambridge: Harvard University Press, 1950). In that book and other writings Kapp pursued the notion of "external costs," developed in the nineteenth century, costs consequent upon production but paid by the society, not the producers—for example, the cost of cleaning up the air from a polluting factory (and the costs of *not* cleaning it up). As industrialization proceeded to raise those costs, the economics profession seemed to lose its interest in the analyses—except for the few who, like Kapp, became outsiders in the process of pursuing it. An excellent broad survey is John E. Ullmann, ed., *Social Costs in Modern Society* (Westport, Conn.: Quorum Books, 1983). And see the more recent collection in the economic realm by Martin O'Connor, ed., *Is Capitalism Sustainable? Political Economy and the Politics of Ecology* (New York: Guilford Press, 1994).

18. This "supply-side economics," pursued in the Reagan and Bush administrations and still advanced by the GOP, reverses the Keynesian analysis of savings and investment: Keynes saw savings as rising as income rises and the rate of interest as a deterrent to (a cost of) real investment. That is, he did *not* see savings as a response to rising interest rates, but rising interest rates as a response to rising expectations of profits by companies expecting (for a variety of reasons) rising demand for their goods, a reason to increase their productive capacities: real investment. Rising net savings from rising incomes—all of which belong to the top 10 percent of income receivers—means a lower percentage of disposable incomes going to consumer spending. In turn that signifies, not expanding, but contracting, markets for producers, and falling profit expectations: Thus, effective demand has to be boosted by government spending, financed by borrowing, paid for by a progressive tax system on the rising incomes accompanying economic expansion. All that worked in the 1960s, bringing rising real incomes (*after* taxes) for workers and owners alike—and, in the stagnating 1970s, a tax revolt.

19. The Herman E. Daly essay cited earlier ("From Adjustment to Sustainable Development") is relevant here again. Daly argued against growth as such as means or end and for "sustainable development"—where economic health becomes dependent upon qualitative rather than quantitative change. (Some of what that might mean will be put forth in Chapter 10.) For a broad critique of "the market," its economics, and what might be called its support system, see Edward S. Herman, *The Triumph of the Market: Essays on Economics, Politics, and the Media* (Boston: South End Press, 1995). Herman has long been on the faculty of the University of Pennsylvania's Wharton School of Finance and is a recognized authority on finance and on the structure and functioning corporate power. It may be added that the need for policy instruments creating qualitative, not just quantitative, change was very much at the center of Keynes's own position, found in book 6 of *The General Theory*, "Short Notes Suggested by The General Theory." There he wrote of the need for "social consumption and investment," the consequences of which would lead not only to economic expansion but also to a downward redistribution of real income (through the combination of social spending—on public housing, for example—and progressive tax policies). See also Lynn Turgeon, *Bastard Keynesianism: The Evolution of Economic Thinking and Policymaking Since World War II* (Westport, Conn.: Greenwood Press, 1996), for understanding both the nature and evolution and the contamination of Keynes's analysis and policy.

20. John Le Carré may not be a social scientist, but he is an astute observer of that reality, as evidenced in this comment he made in an interview with *Washington Post* reporter David Streitfeld (published Nov. 7, 1996): "The mere fact that communism didn't work doesn't mean that capitalism does. In many parts of the globe it's a wrecking, terrible force, displacing people, ruining lifestyles, traditions, ecologies and stable systems with the same ruthlessness as communism."

Chapter Four

1. And Smith's closely connected belief that eliminating all hindrances to completely free markets would render undesirable and unnecessary social interventions of *any* kind on behalf of economic problems, for in such a society there would *be*

none. If there were, it would do more harm than good to seek resolutions outside the free market.

2. A probing historical and philosophical analysis of alienation as it arises from conditions of work (among other sources and consequences) is Bertell Ollman, *Alienation* (Cambridge, UK: Cambridge University Press, 1971). It is worth noting that modern usage of the term *alienation* began with Hegel. Marx adapted the notion of alienation to powerlessness in the economic process. By the end of the nineteenth century specialists called "alienists" were what today we call psychiatrists and psychoanalysts. Ollman's book includes all these usages, with emphasis on socioeconomic processes.

3. For an engrossing survey of what "labor" usually means, see Studs Terkel, *Working: People Talk About What They Do All Day and How They Feel About What They Do* (New York: Pantheon, 1972). Studs Terkel's long-running radio talk shows were the source of his many books consisting of interviews with all kinds of people—on the Depression, on racism, on life in its many dimensions—*Working* includes farmers, copy editors, actors, hookers, chief executive officers (CEOs), lawyers, priests, and dentists. Many enjoy what they do for their incomes, most do not; most share the view of their job as stated in one of the several quotes introducing the book: "It sure grinds me down sometimes."

4. Harry Braverman, *Labor and Monopoly Capitalism: The Degradation of Work in the Twentieth Century* (New York: Monthly Review Press, 1974), chap. 1. For the seminal work on this area of life, see Veblen, *The Instinct of Workmanship*. Veblen saw that "instinct" as constituting the "constructive bent" of our species, acting in opposition to our strong predatory inclinations—demonstrated in much of business as well as in warfare. A recent book concerned with what we have lost in our work lives as we have "modernized" is Jerry Mander, *In the Absence of the Sacred: The Failure of Technology and the Survival of the Indian Nations* (San Francisco: Sierra Club Books, 1991). It may be necessary to add that none of the views presented in these books is opposed to industrial progress as such. They are critiques of the misdirection and misuse of that progress that causes it to be harmful to people and to the rest of nature.

5. Smith, *Wealth of Nations*, p. 15.

6. Ibid., pp. 734–735.

7. The basic text for today's guiding neoclassical economics was first published over a century ago: Alfred Marshall, *Principles of Economics* (London: Macmillan, 1890). Marshall analyzed the disutility of labor as arising from "bodily or mental fatigue, or from its being carried on in unhealthy surroundings, or with unwelcome associates, or from its occupying time that is wanted for recreation, or for social or intellectual pursuits. But whatever be the form of the discommodity, its intensity nearly always increases with the severity and the duration of the labour" (p. 117).

8. Both these generalizations might seem exaggerations. The fuller discussion that follows shortly will provide ample evidence for them. Suffice it to say here that official unemployment data are systematically skewed to understate levels of joblessness by a broad margin—most especially in regard to those hardest hit.

9. Consider these data on current debt and family bankruptcies: (1) Consumer credit outstanding as a percent of disposable income in 1996 was 21 percent (a record) and rising; (2) the number of families filing for bankruptcy in 1996, 1.1 million, was the high-

est in history (the earlier high, as the recession of 1990–1992 ended, was 900,000); and (3) the average amount owed at the time of filing (also a record) was more than $130,000 (compared to $90,000 in 1992). Startling figures, made all the more so because they occurred not during or as the result of a recession but in the midst of a five-year economic expansion. But surely the banks will rein in this dangerous spree of borrowing, given that their attendant losses are about $1 billion per year? It seems not: "The added expense is in fact a planned consequence of their efforts to win business in an increasingly crowded market by making higher-risk loans. The banks are allowing far higher credit limits than their customers' incomes would have warranted in the past. And they are giving new credit to people they previously would have shunned, including those in their first jobs, those with low incomes and even those who have just emerged from bankruptcy." Consumer credit is growing at 9 percent annually, now totaling $1.2 trillion, about a third of which is on credit cards. All this and more is found in a full-page report in the *NYT,* Aug. 25, 1996. This did not begin yesterday, of course: I remember being startled in the early 1970s on a college campus by the sight of several tables in a well-traveled area, each table with someone from a different bank or credit card company, and the invitation "Sign up now: no references necessary." And there were always some in line at each table. What was that personal ethic of old Ben Franklin—"A penny borrowed is a penny spent"? Something like that.

10. For Britain, see Alfred E. Kahn, *Great Britain in the World Economy* (New York: NYU Press, 1946); for the United States, see Soule, *Prosperity Decade.*

11. As is also true of, among others, census data. Almost all statistical data (including that which constitutes polling results) are, perforce, collected on the basis of "sampling"—that is, upon an analysis that decides which fractions of the appropriate population are representative. The "political" nature of the resulting procedures and methods is well illustrated in recent controversies over the underrepresentation of the urban core and, within that, of the poorest areas and their inhabitants—and its serious impact on state, local, and federal expenditures of various sorts. An enlightening study on these and connected matters is Norman Frumkin, *Tracking America's Economy* (Armonk, N.Y.: M. E. Sharpe, 1992). Among the explanations you will find there is that "all persons are counted equally [as employed] if they are paid for an hour or more of work per week" (p. 178).

12. The data for unemployment in Western Europe are considerably more reliable than in the United States or Japan. The explanation for the difference is the considerably greater degree of influence over governmental ways and means wielded by organized labor and social democratic political parties. Even so, the European rates also tend to be on the low side of reality. The London branch of American Express—one of the larger financial entities, with a practical interest in the state of economies—commissioned its own study of these rates in the leading countries of the world economy in early 1994. The findings include the following differences between official and probable, in that order: France, 12.0 vs. 13.7 percent; Britain 9.8 vs. 12.3 percent; Japan 2.7 vs. 9.6 percent; United States, 6.4 vs. 9.3 percent (*IHT,* Jan. 25, 1994). Shortly thereafter the International Labor Organization of the UN reported that "for the first time since the Great Depression of the 1930s the industrial countries, as well as developing states, are facing long-term, persistent unemployment"—which, at the time of the report, was estimated at the global level to be about 30 percent of the world's labor force (*IHT,* March 7, 1994).

13. Taking care of the children and the house is not counted in the official data, for it is "outside the market"—in the same category as criminals, professional gamblers, and other illegals.

14. Jeremy Rifkin, *The End of Work: The Decline of the Global Labor Force and the Dawn of the Post-Market Era* (New York: Putnam, 1995), p. 10. This book is the best available on the causes and consequences of current quantitative and qualitative tendencies in this area.

15. See the useful report "Job Stats: Too Good to Be True—The Real Un(der)employment Rate," by Mark Breslow, in *Dollars and Sense*, Sept./Oct. 1996. This bi-monthly periodical is an always-helpful source of the realities of ongoing economic conditions, written quite deliberately—and successfully—to be readable by those without economics training. Published by the Economic Affairs Bureau, Inc., One Summer Street, Somerville, MA 02143.

16. These are among the conclusions of the report, appearing on the first day, March 3, 1996. The report ran March 3–9, 1996. Subsequent days pursue the details. It soon came out as a book: *The Downsizing of America*, by the *New York Times* (New York: Times Books/Random House, 1996).

17. I have borrowed the phrase from the excellent book of Barbara Ehrenreich, *Fear of Falling: The Inner Life of the Middle Class* (New York: Harper Perennial, 1990)—a fear realized now on a much larger scale than seemed likely in 1990, when the book was published.

18. *IHT,* Oct. 23, 1995.

19. *NYT,* Jan. 5, 1995.

20. This information and further details, considerably more daunting than the brief comments in this text, may be found in David M. Gordon, *Fat and Mean: The Corporate Squeeze of Working Americans and the Myth of Managerial "Downsizing"* (New York: Free Press, 1996). Gordon—whom I knew when he was a child (I was his father's teaching assistant at Berkeley)—died in early 1996, at the age of fifty-one. His last published writing, also valuable for this chapter's concerns, was in the *Nation,* June 17, 1996: "Values That Work." Instead of scapegoating "corroding values" for our social problems, Gordon wrote there that he "would argue instead that the wage squeeze and the confrontational strategy underlying it account for many of the most notorious economic and social problems in the United States." As a writer and as a professor at the New School for Social Research, David Gordon was a much-liked and admired inspiration for many young economists in recent years.

21. *NYT,* Nov. 2, 1995.

22. M/B/S, pp. 224–226. U.S. CEOs earn double the average of the other thirteen countries, whose workers on average earn more than those here.

23. *NYT,* Nov. 29, 1995.

24. He was a deputy assistant secretary. Quoted in *NYT,* June 23, 1995.

25. *NYT,* July 9, 1996.

26. *NYT,* Aug. 23, 1996.

27. See the essays "The States Are Not Strong Enough," by Kathleen M. Sullivan, and "Big Government Is a Check," by Alan Brinkley, in the *NYT Magazine,* Aug. 18, 1966. The authors are (respectively) professors of law at Stanford University and of American history at Columbia University. Their essays are part of the forthcoming Twentieth Century Fund book of Richard C. Leone, ed., *New Federalist Papers,* con-

cerned with "what is probably the broadest challenge to the Constitution since its ratification in 1789." It was the "states' righters" of those days who prompted Madison's *Federalist Papers*—still the basic argument for a strong federal government.

28. Union membership (including jobs in both the private and governmental sectors) peaked at 34.7 percent of the U.S. workforce in 1954; in 1995 it was 14.9 percent—with, however, a seeming slow rise in progress.

29. The data to follow are all from the annual surveys of *Fortune*. Those concerning the Top 500 U.S. corporations are from the issue of Apr. 29, 1996, those for the Top 500 global corporations from the issue of August 5, 1996. *Fortune* produces these surveys every year, presenting an enormous amount of data concerning revenues, assets, profits, stockholders' equities, and employees, for all the companies, with numerous breakdowns by sector, and so on. What has now become a tradition began in the 1950s with "The Fortune 500," concerned solely with U.S. industrial corporations. Over time that was joined by the Top 50 utilities and other sectors. With advent of the TNCs, the Top 500 are no longer industrial, but *all* corporations, domestic and global.

30. *IHT,* Jan. 22, 1996.

31. Using more recent official (and understated) measures of poverty, about half the population was at or below the poverty level in the late 1920s: In the last year of that "prosperity" 51 percent had incomes of $3,000 (in 1962 dollars) or below, the official poverty level established in the Johnson administration (Herman P. Miller, *Rich Man, Poor Man* [New York: Thomas P. Crowell, 1964], p. 29). The details of and reasons for the bifurcation of the 1920s—called a "dual economy"—are provided in Soule, *Prosperity Decade.* Not least among the important similarities between then and now is the marked process of "financialization" of the economy—increasing speculation in securities and real estate and relatively stagnant real investment rates—from the mid-1920s up to the crash of 1929, from the 1970s to the present.

32. We have short memories. It may be understandable that the job and socioeconomic improvements of the New Deal are lost in the past; but more recent "governmental interventions," such as the GI Bill, which allowed millions of veterans (myself included) to gain an otherwise unobtainable university education, and the GI Home Loan project for subsidizing mortgages (through interest rates), taken together, did much to stimulate the economy in quantitative terms and to improve it—and the lives of the vets—in qualitative *and* quantitative terms. The New Deal's Works Progress and Public Works Administrations (WPA, PWA) and other lesser efforts in agriculture and colleges provided the same kinds of stimuli and social gains. Some of the details of those programs will be provided in Chapter 6; let it be said here only that without those programs thousands of schools, libraries, airports, would have remained unbuilt and musicians, writers, actors, teachers, unemployed. It took a war and its veterans to make it easy to get the GI Bill; is not the desperation of at least a fifth of our population sufficient to move sensibly—and decently—today?

33. *NYT,* Oct. 26, 1995.

34. An informative discussion and analysis of the deterioration of organized labor is Thomas Geoghegan, *Which Side Are You On: Trying to Be for Labor When It's Flat on Its Back* (New York: Penguin, 1992). Geoghegan became a "labor lawyer" almost by chance, became involved, and went on from there—much to his surprise and sorrow, and to his readers' benefit.

Chapter Five

1. The generalizations soon to follow will be based on various volumes of the *State of Working America* series, abbreviated as follows: Lawrence Mishel and David Frankel, *State of Working America, 1990–91* (Armonk, N.Y.: M. E. Sharpe, 1991): M/F; Mishel and Bernstein, *1994–95:* M/B; Mishel, Bernstein, and Schmitt, *1996–97:* M/B/S.

2. M/B, p. 1.

3. Data released by the Census Bureau at the end of September 1996 make necessary a partially qualified modification of that statement: The median household, for the first time since 1989, had an increase in its income of $898 (2.7 percent over the preceding year). However, the bureau also reported that as that was happening, "earnings for both male and female full-time workers declined, [and] that more people in a household are working or that more wage earners are working at more than one job" (*NYT*, Sept. 28, 1996).

4. M/B/S, p. 3.

5. M/B/S, pp. 51, 58.

6. M/B/S, p. 51.

7. M/B/S, pp. 48–49.

8. M/F, pp. 29, 31.

9. M/B/S, pp. 5, 10.

10. M/F, p. 21.

11. M/B/S, p. 51.

12. M/B, p. 41.

13. M/F, p. 24.

14. M/B/S, p. 273. The quoted statement serves as the introduction to their chap. 5, "Wealth: More for the Wealthy, Financial Decline and Insecurity for the Majority," which contains a broad variety of important data in this area. Their data in turn are largely derived from the important study of Edward N. Wolff, *Top Heavy: A Study of Increasing Inequality of Wealth in America* (New York: Twentieth Century Fund, 1995).

15. These data and many others are found in a substantial article in the *NYT*, "Gap in Wealth in U.S. Called Widest in West," Apr. 17, 1995. Much of the article depends upon the study by Wolff, *Top Heavy*.

16. Paul Krugman, "The Wealth Gap Is Real and It's Growing," *NYT* Op-Ed, Aug. 8, 1995.

17. M/F, p. 153.

18. M/B/S, pp. 291–292.

19. M/F, p. 161. By September 1996, delinquencies on credit card accounts had broken all records, rising to 3.66 percent of all accounts, the highest rate since the American Bankers Association began to collect such data (1974). One consequence is that "issuers are cutting back on riskier credit card lending programs, lowering credit limits, lengthening the time between automatic credit-limit increases." *NYT*, Sept. 8, 1996. This is the first such reversal of the decades-long policy of encouraging "poor risks" to have credit cards, noted in an earlier chapter; it cannot help but place downward pressure on consumer expenditures, and thus on the economy as a whole.

20. Kevin Phillips, *The Politics of Rich and Poor: Wealth and the American Electorate in the Reagan Aftermath* (New York: Harper Perennial, 1991), p. 130.

21. In 1987, for example, per capita tax revenues were just 30 percent of GDP in the United States. All other industrialized countries had higher rates, as high as 37.6 in Germany, 48.0 in the Netherlands, and 56.7 in Sweden. Similarly, the "index of progressivity" (denoting taxation based on ability to pay) was lowest here—that is, our system is the most regressive. These and other data are to be found in the excellent survey by Jay Mandle and Louis Ferleger, "Americans' Hostility to Taxes," *Challenge*, July-Aug. 1991. Such data are collected regularly in the annual *Statistical Abstract of the United States*.

22. Joseph Pechman, *Tax Reform* (Washington, D.C.: Brookings Institution, 1989), p. 27. It is worth noting that Pechman's data are derived from Internal Revenue Service (IRS) reports and include capital gains income—between which and the census data used for income distributions there is a substantial difference. Thus, census data for 1967 show the top 5 percent receiving 15.2 percent, whereas IRS data show 19.6 percent—an additional 25 percent. Pechman's data did not go beyond 1986; the share of the top 95 percent in 1989 shown as 17.2 percent in census data would be closer to 30 percent were capital gains included, given that in 1986 their share was 26.6 percent and subsequently rose. Pechman was also the source used by Mandle and Ferleger for the tax progressivity figures noted earlier.

23. "Soaking the Poor," *Dollars and Sense*, July/Aug. 1991, p. 9. In "Comparing Social Paychecks," an earlier study in the same periodical (Oct. 1989), it was shown that expenditures on social programs (health, job injuries, old-age insurance, family allowances, and public assistance) in the United States in 1983 amounted to 10 percent of GDP, one-third those of Sweden, half those of Germany, and those of Canada were 50 percent greater: those on the bottom in the United States pay a relatively high percentage of their incomes in taxes for a relatively low amount of social expenditures.

24. M/B/S, p. 105.

25. The rise in wages in 1996 has been noted, as was a qualification about its origin and meaning.

26. For these and related data and developments, see the excellent essay by John Cassidy, "Who Killed the Middle Class?" *New Yorker*, Oct. 16, 1995.

27. For a crisp and useful discussion of the similarities between Malthus and his current followers, see John Hess, "Malthus Then and Now," *Nation*, Apr. 18, 1987. The Malthus quote leads off that article.

28. But now, as with Malthus, we are warned that such a rise cannot continue, that population growth will exceed the ability of the earth to feed us all. Today's arguments are often Malthusian, jot and tittle; there are others, however, who make that argument of "not enough food in the future" on grounds of environmental damage, most especially the warming of the earth and desalinization. For a useful summary of the latter positions, see the review essay of Bill McKibben, "Some Versions of Pastoral," *New York Review of Books*, July 11, 1996. If, as is quite possible, these doomsayers are right, the solution is not to be found in letting the poor starve but in transforming our processes of production and taming our appetite for economic growth. Such matters will be discussed in Chapter 8.

29. For a convincing analysis that supports this position, see the work of the Brazilian scientist Josué de Castro, *The Geopolitics of Hunger* (New York: Monthly Review Press, 1977; first published in 1952 as *The Geography of Hunger*).

30. This point will be elaborated upon in Chapter 6 in the discussion of welfare. Careful studies have shown that there are already many more now needing than find-

ing entry-level jobs, and that those who do manage to get such jobs remain in poverty, even though working full-time. (The minimum wage in 1997 is $5.15/hr.; even $7.50/hr.@ 40 hrs. for 50 weeks = only $15,000/yr., just beneath the poverty level for one seeking to support a family.)

31. See the definitive work of Hobsbawm, *Industry and Empire.*

32. This unbelievable (and forgotten) process is recorded in the book by the much-respected sociologist Clair Wilcox, *Toward Social Welfare* (Homewood, Ill.: Irwin, 1969), pp. 26–27.

33. M/B/S, p. 297.

34. Some of the realities, especially those that can be traced with facts, are presented with stark clarity in a marvelously constructed and researched—and easily read—book, Randy Albelda, Nancy Folbre, and the Center for Popular Economics, *The War on the Poor: A Defense Manual* (New York: New Press, 1996). The authors are part of the same group that publishes the useful monthly *Dollars and Sense.* The structure of *The War on the Poor* is most helpful. On facing pages, one finds "Myth" and "Reality," as in this excerpt from pp. 48–49: "Myth: 'The current welfare system destroys families'—Rep. Bill Archer, R-Texas." "Reality: Divorce rates are increasing in most developed countries and are higher in the U.S. than in countries with far more extensive welfare programs." That is followed by a substantial chart showing relevant conditions in France, the UK, Sweden, and the U.S. for various years, and a quote from economist Lester Thurow: "The traditional family is being destroyed not by misguided social welfare programs coming from Washington . . . but by a modern economic system that is not congruent with 'family values.'" There is abundant documentation for all the "myths" and all the "realities." The book is at once the most efficient *and* entertaining education one could get on these matters. That book was preceded by another under the direction of Nancy Folbre, *The New Field Guide to the U.S. Economy: A Compact and Irreverent Guide to Economic Life in America* (New York: New Press, 1995), which presents illuminating (and debunking) data on all aspects of economic life, much enlivened by cartoons, as well as charts and tables.

35. That it can be done, and that to do so requires extraordinary endurance combined with luck, is wrenchingly shown in the fine book by Claude Brown, *Manchild in the Promised Land* (New York: Macmillan, 1965). Brown was arrested for dealing drugs many times as a juvenile, sent to reform school more than once, and at the age of thirteen was lucky enough to be taken in hand by a teacher at such a school. He became a lawyer (and a fine writer).

36. See Herbert J. Gans, *The War Against the Poor: The Underclass and Antipoverty Policy* (New York: Basic Books, 1995). Gans teaches at MIT.

37. These data (and much else that is relevant) are put forth in the excellent collection entitled *Economic Inequality and Poverty: International Perspectives*, edited by Lars Osberg (Armonk, N.Y.: M. E. Sharpe, 1991). See especially chap. 2, by Timothy Swerdling.

38. A book that explores these attitudes fully and scathingly is William Ryan, *Blaming the Victim* (New York: Vintage, 1971). Ryan showed that such attitudes themselves, because they are developed within the socializing framework of a powerful ideology, if not blameless, are explicable in ways going beyond character deficiencies on the part of those who hold them.

39. M/B/S, pp. 295–296.

40. M/B/S, pp. 296–297.

41. M/B/S, pp. 304–305.

42. M/B/S, pp. 331–333.

43. M/B/S, pp. 344–345. The Census Bureau data of September 1966, noted earlier, confirms that point: The reduction of the poverty rate and the increase in real wages were both opposed to the trends preceding 1996.

44. M/B/S, p. 314, table 6.13.

Chapter Six

1. I have headed this section with the title of a brief but profound inquiry by the social philosopher Michael Ignatieff, *The Needs of Strangers* (London: Chatto and Windus; Hogarth Press, 1984), whose ideas have been built upon in what follows.

2. Not only the United States, of course; nor did it begin here. Having taken hold first in Britain and spreading to our shores in the colonial period, the outlook has had a more limited existence in the other capitalist countries until recent decades.

3. Ignatieff, *The Needs of Strangers*, p. 50.

4. Those served by the present welfare system for other reasons (because of disability, for example), can be served amply by something *not* a welfare system—as we know it.

5. See Osberg, *Economic Inequality and Poverty*, chap. 7, for the foregoing and related data.

6. Frances Fox Piven and Richard Cloward, *Regulating the Poor: The Functions of Public Welfare* (New York: Vintage, 1971), pp. xiv–xvii. This pathbreaking study, prompted by the developments of the 1960s, was followed by what may be seen as a supplement by the same authors, *The New Class War: Reagan's Attack on the Welfare State and Its Consequences* (New York: Pantheon, 1982). See also the fine collection of essays by Fred Block, ed., *The Mean Season: The Attack on the Welfare State* (New York: Pantheon, 1987), and Michael B. Katz, *The Undeserving Poor: From the War on Poverty to the War on Welfare* (New York: Pantheon, 1989).

7. AFDC payments also provide for disabled children; OASI over time has been amended and expanded to become Old Age, Survivors, Disability, and Health Insurance (OASDHI)—payments for the aged, their survivors, Supplemental Security Income (SSI) for the aged, blind, and disabled, and health insurance (Medicare, begun in 1966). Medicaid, begun along with the federal Medicare program, has all states offering basic health services to certain very poor people: those pregnant, aged, disabled, or blind, and families with dependent children. The details and developments concerning both Medicare and Medicaid are taken up in Chapter 7; here we confine ourselves only to AFDC and OASI.

8. The possibility of receiving nothing will be discussed further on. It is worth remarking that the most generous pension *and* health care program in the United States is that for the military—with the possible exception of top business executives, members of Congress and state legislatures.

9. Jonathan Kozol, *Amazing Grace: The Lives of Children and the Conscience of a Nation* (New York: Crown, 1995), p. 6.

10. The next six items are taken from Albelda, Folbre, and the Center for Popular Economics, *The War on the Poor*, pp. 26–27. Their source for each item is noted.

11. Keith Bradsher, *NYT*, Aug. 14, 1995.

12. *The State of America's Children Yearbook 1995* (Washington, D.C.: Children's Defense Fund, 1995), p. 19.

13. Ibid., p. 20.

14. *Wasting America's Future: The Children's Defense Fund Report on the Costs of Child Poverty* (Boston: Beacon Press, 1994), p. 79.

15. *The State of America's Children*, p. 101.

16. Ibid., p. 18.

17. M/B/S, p. 313.

18. *NYT*, Aug. 23, 1996, using government data.

19. Edelman's comment was reported by Bob Herbert in his Op-Ed column of the *NYT*, May 27, 1996.

20. The UNESCO report was noted in *IHT*, Nov. 28, 1995.

21. The UNICEF report was in *IHT*, Nov. 31, 1993, on the editorial page.

22. Quoted by Bob Herbert in his essay "Welfare Hysteria," *NYT*, Aug. 5, 1996, Op-Ed page. Herbert added what is widely known and accepted: "No one believes that the mothers or grandmothers of all those children will find gainful employment."

23. As it was enough to cause the resignations of three senior officials from the Department of Health and Human Services—Mary Jo Bane, Peter Edelman, and Wendell E. Primus—all Clinton appointees concerned with welfare, after he signed the welfare reform bill in August 1996. While still in his job, Primus had argued that the bill would soon push 1 million children into poverty. *NYT*, Sept. 12, 1996.

24. This section has as head the title of a full-page of tables and charts in *NYT*, June 10, 1994, from which many of the data now to be noted have been taken (unless otherwise indicated).

25. William Julius Wilson, "When Work Disappears," *NYT Magazine*, Aug. 18, 1996 (adapted from his simultaneously published book: *When Work Disappears: The World of the New Urban Poor* [New York: Knopf, 1996]).

26. The general impression that most Americans are against welfare is an apt example of how polls create false impressions by the manner in which they ask their questions. A poll undertaken in fall 1995 (by the Center for the Study of Policy Attitudes) yielded the following results (among others): 84 percent thought "society has a moral obligation to alleviate poverty"; more people believed that "government has a responsibility to try to do away with poverty now than those polled in 1964: 80 percent to 70 percent"; 84 percent thought that poverty programs are a good idea, but badly carried out; 90 percent thought it would be wrong to cut off welfare benefits if there were no *guaranteed* job available. And there were many other questions with similar qualitative responses. Reported by Doug Henwood in his *Left Business Observer*, Sept. 1995.

27. Ten times or more. As Chapter 9 will show, what are classified as "defense expenditures" are understated by almost half. Other military expenditures are in other departments' budgets—on nuclear weapons and military-connected space, military aid abroad, the share of interest on the national debt due to past and present military activities, and so on. Moreover, the Pentagon's programs combine corruption with waste to a degree unmatchable in other programs. On September 24, 1996, the day that Congress passed and the president signed the 1997 Pentagon budget for $256.6 billion, Russell Baker called his *NYT* column "Except for the Pentagon" and commented: "It is people with no lobby who ought to shudder every time somebody happily declares, 'The era of big government is over,' neglecting to add, 'except for the Pentagon.'" Baker might have added that the amount signed on for by the presi-

dent, "most of it to buy weapons and research new ones" ("Clinton Signs Bill . . . ,"
NYT, same day), was $11+ billion more than he had asked for, and—"in an election-
year nod to the popularity of military programs"—an increase over the 1996 military
budget. Chapter 9 discusses and documents such matters in some detail.

28. See the *NYT* Op-Ed essay, "What Inner-City Jobs for Welfare Moms?" by
Katherine S. Newman, who directed the study. New York City might not seem to be
representative, given the widespread notion that it is undisciplined, or worse. But the
percent of those on welfare there—13.1—is notably lower than that for Detroit,
Cleveland, Miami, Milwaukee, and Philadelphia, and not much higher than Boston,
Los Angeles, and San Francisco (*NYT,* Aug. 25, 1996). Newman (a professor of an-
thropology, Columbia University), in her book *Declining Fortunes: The Waning of
the American Dream* (New York: Basic Books, 1993), provided the framework for
understanding what she called "downward mobility and the politics of resentment"—and the growth of poverty and the policies of meanness that accompany it.

29. Consequent upon a bill signed by President Kennedy in the last month of his
life, the Mental Retardation Facilities and Community Health Center Act of 1963.

30. The text of Senator Moynihan's speech to the Senate of December 12, 1995,
covering this and related points, was reproduced in the *New York Review of Books,*
Jan. 11, 1996, as "Congress Builds a Coffin." Therein he told of the background and
signing of the relevant legislation, in which he participated—and from which he
learned and now regretted.

31. *San Francisco Chronicle,* Apr. 7, 1995.

32. The summary that follows is taken from Robert Pear, "Overhauling Welfare: A
Look at the Year Ahead," *NYT,* Aug. 7, 1996.

33. That language is found in the article "Drive for Block Grants Pitting State
Against State," *NYT,* June 28, 1995, which discusses this and related questions. A major issue involved in block grants arises from the fact that Congress allocates a sum to
be divided between the states, on terms that are usually in flux: Thus, as the article put
it, "Giving the Sun Belt states more would mean giving the Northern states less."

34. *NYT,* Sept. 15, 1996.

35. This section is headed by the beginning of the last line of *King Lear* (V, iii).
Here a personal note, in the nature of a disclaimer. As 1996 ended, my seventy-eighth
year began, so it could be thought that what follows in the text is the special pleading
of an old geezer. It is not. I live in substantial material comfort, am in fine health, and
continue to work as a teacher and writer—spending half of each year in San Francisco and the other half in Bologna, Italy, in a lovely marriage. Fortunately, however,
and unlike most others, my wife and I are not solely dependent upon my OASI benefits, which amount to less than $16,000 annually. That low amount is, however,
among the highest—although I began my contributions in the first year of OASI and
(except for the war years) contributed until my retirement in the 1990s, having
earned in forty years of that period a professor's income, which placed me in the
highest quintile. My comfort depends largely on the retirement income from my university employers over the decades. Though many retired workers have such pensions—especially those who were in strong unions—the majority do not. Moreover,
retirement incomes from other than OASI have been in decline in recent years for a
variety of reasons, as will be seen, not least of which has been the decline of union
strength. Nor should it be forgotten that many people who have worked all their
lives have only part of that time, or none of it, been covered; and they are those

whose incomes all along have been and still are among the lowest: farm workers, domestic servants, and the like.

36. Throughout, I use the word *old* instead of *senior* or *elder* or *aging* or other euphemisms now current, only partly because those tortured usages seem to be designed for the users', not the old's, purposes.

37. But see below, where it is pointed out that at least half of the employer contribution is paid by the employee.

38. It may be remarked that the Scandinavian nations (Denmark, Finland, Norway, and Sweden) and Germany (along with Austria) still provide the most comprehensive and generous of social programs of the industrialized countries. See Osberg, *Economic Inequality and Poverty.*

39. Broadus Mitchell, *Depression Decade: From New Era Through New Deal, 1929–1941* (New York: Rinehart, 1947), p. 308.

40. Phillips, *Boiling Point*, p. 107.

41. This quotation and the one following it are from William Greider, *Who Will Tell the People: The Betrayal of American Democracy* (New York: Simon and Schuster, 1992), pp. 92 and 80, respectively. Greider was using the rates and limits of 1990 for his comparison.

42. The misuse of which, in order to conceal the true magnitude of the federal deficit, was noted in Chapter 2.

43. As asked by Robert Kuttner in a succinct and knowledgeable essay, "Plans for Social Security's Future," *Washington Post*, March 9, 1996, wherein other pointed questions were also raised.

44. For the larger picture and its details, see David Cay Johnston, "From Washington, The Fading Pension," *NYT*, May 4, 1995.

45. Uchitelle, "Retirement's Worried Face."

46. U.S. Bureau of the Census, 1994.

47. As economist Richard B. DuBoff pointed out, "actuarial balance [for Social Security] might be achieved by removing the income ceiling on the payroll tax . . . and levying it on all incomes without upper limit." "Thurow on Social Security: The 'Left' Strikes Again," *Monthly Review*, Oct. 1996, p. 7. This is a generally useful article on both this and connected fiscal matters.

48. John A. Brittain, *The Payroll Tax for Social Security* (Washington, D.C.: Brookings Institution, 1972), pp. 1–2, an exhaustive analytical and empirical study—but also readable. The author, a leading statistician, went on to show that a good half of the employers' contributions are in fact paid by employees (he noted [p. 22] that Milton Friedman concurs with this judgment) and that the employees' real rate was at about 10 percent (as against a nominal rate of about half that). At today's nominal rate of 7.65 percent, the effective rate for the poor worker would be closer to 15 than to 10 percent. Brittain proposed that a progressive income tax combined with exemptions take the place of the present system.

Chapter Seven

1. R. H. Tawney, *The Acquisitive Society* (New York: Harcourt Brace Jovanovitch, 1920), p. 180.

2. Those deep traditions also had many negative and cruel elements to them; we are not listing here all the negative and cruel elements of today's social processes either.

3. But not what his original mentor, Adam Smith, could have accepted. Quite apart from all else, one can only imagine the turbulence in the good Scot's grave were he to hear of "for-profit hospitals," "for-profit armies," "for-profit prisons," "for-profit everything," not to mention having TV in the classroom dishing up ads for this or that commodity to little minds already getting too many hours of that at home. Whatever was wrong with prisons and hospitals and schools in his day, they were not operating for profit even when they were private. Today's free market devotees would observe, "And that, of course, is what was wrong with them."

4. The very need to clarify that distinction is very "American." Unions in Europe have virtually always been socialist (or social Catholic) unions, with a program that goes well beyond wages and working conditions, including the creation of a different—noncapitalist—society. In this country, where unions have normally been called—without irony—"business unions," their principal function has been to gain the right to collective bargaining, union recognition, and improved wages and working conditions. Not until after World War II did their program include "benefits": health care and pension programs (partially or entirely paid for by employers) and paid vacations. (It may be added that in the United States, at their most generous, paid vacations have been for two weeks; in Western Europe the average is closer to a month.)

5. When, in the 1890s, a sizable group within the American Federation of Labor (AFL) sought to have socialism designated as the AFL's ultimate goal, it was soundly defeated. Despite the rise of the more militant and left-leaning Congress of Industrial Organizations (CIO) and a noticeable and active number of Communists in the CIO (and its subsequent merger with the AFL), that defeat has remained unchanged. The only significant exception to these generalizations was the Industrial Workers of the World (IWW, called "Wobblies," founded in 1905). They were essentially an anarchist group, believing in worker-owned and -controlled industries—a kind of "guild socialism"—and a highly decentralized power structure in the economy and state. They opposed World War I, many were imprisoned (and many lynched, often by unionists), and—though presumably dissolved in 1925—the movement lasted through the years until, after World War II, it dwindled into insignificance.

6. The monthly *Dollars and Sense* devoted a special issue (May 1993) to "The Health Care Emergency: Who's Paying; What's Wrong?" It was an apt summary and analysis of health care in the United States. What follows is in part derived from various of its essays—including that by Edie Rasell, "A Bad Bargain: Why U.S. Health Care Costs So Much and Covers So Few," which provides much data comparing the United States and other OECD countries. Rasell is a physician-researcher with the Economic Policy Institute.

7. Joseph White, *Competing Solutions: American Health Care Proposals and International Experience* (Washington, D.C.: Brookings Institution, 1995), pp. 149–155. The comparisons are with Canada, Germany, Australia, France, Japan, and Britain. It is among the most technical, analytical, and comprehensive of such studies, carried out in the best of economic thoroughness. None of the other countries had an uninsured population of even 1 percent, as compared with our 15+ percent. The headings in the areas noted are White's. The 1.2 percent of GDP referred to in the final item is almost exactly equal to the total annual cost of the federal welfare budget—before reform.

8. White, *Competing Solutions*, pp. 291–292.

9. Some qualifications to the foregoing can be made, for better and for worse: On the better side, in some cities (such as San Francisco, my own) the "county hospi-

tal"—associated with the University of California medical school—provided more than emergency room services for the indigent: surgery, hospital stays for tuberculosis and other grave conditions, services simply unavailable for most in the nation. "The worse" was the case in much of the rural South up into the 1960s, where and when *no* medical or dental care was available for rural blacks. Having worked as an orderly in surgery at San Francisco County (now General) Hospital in the years just before World War II, I can testify that the care received in that hospital—notably in surgery—would be defined as something other than "care" by reasonable medical standards: The poor were often seen—and so it was put, in those days—as "guinea pigs." (I can also testify that there has been a marked change for the better in recent years.)

10. Though the coal mines were elsewhere, the hospital for the injured miners was in the Bay Area. Kaiser Shipbuilding was developed and run by Henry J. Kaiser, one of the last of the bustling independent business giants. He went from cement to ships to health care and, among other ventures, to his first major failure, autos—producing a tiny car that made a lot of urban/ecological sense, but at a time when Americans were desperate to have a very long Cadillac with fins.

11. See Rasell, "A Bad Bargain," for these and other details.

12. HMOs—health maintenance organizations—were first given their name in the Nixon administration. They didn't begin to evolve in their present and ubiquitous form until much later.

13. When it is said that 40 million or more Americans are without coverage, left unsaid is that the coverage of at least twice that number is dangerously (to their health and solvency) inadequate—whether as measured by what is *not* covered at all, or covered only after high deductibles are paid, or covered only within a frighteningly brief time or amount limit. Thus, if by "coverage" one were to mean that the covered person need not have financial fears in the event of a particular, or a particularly serious, illness (a child with Down's Syndrome, an adult with testicular cancer or a difficult pregnancy, and many et ceteras), then the estimate could be hazarded that at least half of the American people—several times 40 million—lack adequate coverage. Even those like me, with Medicare and one of the most generous private programs (from a university career), and in good health, can find himself paying a few thousand dollars a year of uncovered health care bills—to doctors, a pharmacy, a hospital, an optometrist, etc. An excellent monograph on the "crisis" as one of health more than costs is Colin Gordon, *Dead on Arrival: The Clinton Health Care Plan; Why It Failed and What it Means* (Westfield, N.J.: Open Magazine Pamphlet Series, 1995) (P.O. Box 2726, Westfield, NJ, 07091; Fax [908] 654-3829). I depended on this pamphlet for much information.

14. Rasell, "A Bad Bargain."

15. An excellent critique of the functioning of that system as it stood by the opening of the 1970s is Barbara and John Ehrenreich, *The American Health Empire* (New York: Random House/Vintage, 1971). They follow the money path from doctors, hospitals, equipment manufacturers, pharmaceutical companies, and health insurance companies all the way to the result, always higher costs—and profits. The contemporary version of the same set of processes and structures, to which reference will soon be made, is the 25-page essay by Robert Sherrill in the *Nation*, Jan. 9/16, 1995, "The Madness of the Market: Dangerous to Your Health." It carries with it a useful listing of relevant books and reports on which its author depended.

16. Sherrill, "The Madness of the Market." It may be added that Medicare's administrative costs are higher than they would be were they the "single payer." For any one treatment, as many know, when there is coverage additional to Medicare (e.g., Blue Shield), one receives at least two (often as many as half a dozen) separate letters having to do with accounting matters. (Those least unwelcome have printed on them: "This is not a bill." One is left to wonder what it *is*.) Having had an aged mother and an aged aunt's medical correspondence to work through in the past, I know that neither of them—and neither was stupid—could make head or tail of what was being received. And it was bad for their health to worry about it.

17. Ibid. But physicians must still feel underpaid when they learn of the incomes of CEOs in HMOs and hospitals: In 1994 the average cash compensation was $255,000; for the top nine CEOs, cash plus stock options averaged $7 million (ranging from $2.8 to $15.5 million). *NYT*, July 9, 1995.

18. In a feature story on Medicare in the *NYT*, July 25, 1995, a conversation between Larry O'Brien (LBJ's chief adviser) and the president was reported as follows: "Larry O'Brien said, 'Mr. President, we can't get Medicare out of Ways and Means unless we give the doctors and hospitals the reimbursement system they want.' Mr. Johnson replied, 'Get it out.'" The source was Joseph Califano, subsequently secretary of Health, Education, and Welfare. The quote in the text is from Sherrill, "The Madness of the Market," p. 56, who took his main points from Howard Wolinsky's *The Serpent on the Staff: The Unhealthy Politics of the American Medical Association* (New York: Tarcher/Putnam, 1994). The reference to the increase in number of patients is reminiscent of what happened when National Health Service was introduced in Britain after World War II. Those opposed to the program argued that hypochondriacs and people with time on their hands would flood doctors' offices; indeed the offices *were* crowded, most of all, dentists' offices. After a period of "I told you so's," the practical realization dawned that there were not enough masochists to be responsible for that flood; the cause, rather—and Britain had been known for this for years—was the generally deplorable condition of the teeth of the British, most of whom earlier had never *been* to, never able to afford, a dentist.

19. Less than half the visits of Germany and Japan, 10–15 percent less than those in Canada or France; and about the same difference for days in hospital. Rasell, "A Bad Bargain."

20. See *NYT*, July 9, 1995, "HMOs Refusing Emergency Claims," and Aug. 20, 1995, "Public Hospitals Around Country Cut Basic Service."

21. One of them concerns me. A few years ago I had an operation involving the removal of a cyst. It was deemed that I could be taken home two to three hours from its conclusion, so my wife waited outside the recovery room. After two hours, wondering what was happening, she came into the recovery room where she found me lying unattended in a substantial pool of blood. I had been hemorrhaging for nobody knew how long. That happened in what is normally seen as the best hospital in San Francisco.

22. Sherrill, "The Madness of the Market," quoting George C. Halverson, *Strong Medicine* (New York: Random House, 1993). Sherrill extrapolated the 7,000 figure for the nation and estimated a conservative 80,000 "iatrogenically" killed patients a year. His essay also pointed to the fact that at "an Atlanta hospital half the drugs on a recovery room crash cart were expired, as were drugs in the emergency room and

other dispensing areas." At least there was an emergency room. "Iatrogenic" is a word coming into always more common use: It means that the genesis of the injury or death is the patient's medical care.

23. *NYT*, Aug. 5, 1993, "Study Links Paperwork to 25 percent of Hospital Costs." The study, authored by Steffie Woolhandler and David U. Himmelstein (both of Harvard Medical School), appeared in the *New England Journal of Medicine*.

24. *NYT*, Apr. 14, 1996.

25. See Sherrill, "The Madness of the Market," p. 59.

26. Paul Starr, *The Social Transformation of American Medicine: The Rise of a Sovereign Profession and the Making of a Vast Industry* (New York: Basic Books, 1982), quoted in Sherrill, "The Madness of the Market." Starr is a professor of sociology at Princeton and was one of those who worked on the development of the CHP.

27. Sherrill, "The Madness of the Market," p. 48.

28. And in part for one reason we can only hope Clinton might learn from: It appears that Gingrich lost his charisma and came to be seen as a danger when substantial percentages of the population (according to polls) saw their Medicare/Medicaid benefits imperiled. Also: FDR began as the moderate—not liberal—Clinton has chosen to be. But there is no doubt whatsoever that FDR's enormous and undying popularity stems from the socioeconomic liberal policies that are now being undone, and that gave him an unprecedented (and now constitutionally prohibited) third and fourth term.

29. Gordon, *Dead on Arrival*, p. 2.

30. In its Sunday issue of June 12, 1994, the *New York Times* devoted a 16-page special section to health care reform in which it examined the leading problems and data of health care, the nature of and an assessment of each of the four choices (whose labeling we are using here), and many essays raising other issues and "taking sides."

31. Ibid., article by Graetz and Tobin, "Players and Payers."

32. Compare the $30+ million (in current dollars) the AMA spent to stop Truman's national health insurance plan, 1949–1952, when he was giving it a second try. The AMA also gave almost $14 million to congressional candidates, 1983–1994. These data and those in the text are from Sherrill, "The Madness of the Market," p. 56.

33. For a systematic critique of the CHP while it was still being discussed in congressional committees and in public, see the essay by Steffie Woolhandler and David U. Himmelstein, "Universal Care? Not from Clinton," in the *NYT* special issue, June 12, 1994, which also makes a brief case for an NHI program.

34. Those data were presented in a story in the *IHT*, Nov. 9, 1995, "Medicaid Cuts to Hurt Children," quoting from an article in *Journal of the American Medical Association*—which, opposing proposed cuts in Medicaid, otherwise supported the larger legislation of which it was a part.

35. *NYT*, June 12, 1994.

36. I wish not to be at all "cute" in this; in all truth I was not conscious of Erikson's comment on sin when I compiled my own list to make the seven into eight. The quote from Erikson was used as the epigraph in Jonathan Kozol's first book, *Death at an Early Age* (Boston: Houghton Mifflin, 1967). Kozol's career as a writer began when he lost his job as a teacher, the reasons for which echo the words opening this section on education: Kozol was in his first teaching assignment, in a segregated ghetto school in Boston, and was let go because he would not yield when told that

his reading from the poems of Robert Frost, Langston Hughes, W. B. Yeats, and the like to eight-to-ten-year-old children could not be tolerated.

37. Jonathan Kozol, *Savage Inequalities: Children in America's Public Schools* (New York: Crown Publishers, 1991), p. 4.

38. Harry Truman used the term frequently during the 1950s, most especially to refer to Democratic presidential candidate Adlai Stevenson (who twice opposed and lost to Dwight D. Eisenhower). Stevenson had mild reservations about the cold war, a generally "educated" manner, and a skeptic's sense of humor.

39. *NYT*, Aug. 25, 1996. "Dilapidated Schools Are Bursting. . . . "

40. Those figures are misleading in one important respect. When the cost of providing special services—required for public but not for private schools—are excluded, "the cost of public school education has stayed almost steady in real terms since 1970. . . . [It] is that lower figure . . . which should be used when comparing the cost of public and private schools." Mano Singham, "The War Against Public Schools," *Z Magazine*, Oct. 1995. The author, a physicist, is "scientist-educator" for Project Discovery.

41. Folbre, *The New Field Guide*, pp. 6.13–6.14; and see Kozol, *Savage Inequalities*, for an extended discussion of such ratios and connected matters.

42. All the data in this paragraph are found in Singham, "The War Against Public Schools."

43. The data and quote on the first point are from the Special Educational Edition of the *IHT*, Oct. 19–20, 1996, for the second from Folbre, *The New Field Guide*, p. 6.16.

44. Because it is not entirely easy to see the historically trod upon in that fashion, when I was teaching about the distribution of income and wealth in Introductory Economics, I began with this question: I was born male, white, in 1919, in San Francisco, in a middle class family. Do you think that I would be standing here in front of you, with the comforts and powers of my position, if I had been born female, black, in 1919, in rural Mississippi, in a sharecropper's family? It still seems a useful question to ask. And to answer.

45. Among people just above being poor, and some below, it was customary to save very small amounts each month—as little as a dollar or two—which constituted the main supply of funds for small homeowners. The thrifts were typically, perhaps always, neighborhood banks—until the 1980s.

46. Pizzo, Fricker, and Muolo, *Inside Job*, p. 23. This book provides a useful brief history of the thrifts; its main concern, however, is with the S and L debacle of the 1980s, for which it is an indispensable source.

47. It should be understood that though subsidization or payment for all these varieties of housing programs and loans was provided by the government, the lenders, builders, and workers were all in the private sector. It remains a mystery why the private sector understands that so well for military spending and road construction, but usually balks at so much else. In 1965 the Department of Housing and Urban Development (HUD) was created to oversee all the programs we are noting. That much of what they have overseen has been stained by corruption does not, however, set it off from—for example—the Defense Department (as will be seen).

48. The estimate of one-third (30 million families) was given by Michael Stone, housing expert at the University of Massachusetts, Boston, quoted in Mark Breslow, "Profits from Poverty: Must Affordable Housing Mean Corporate Tax Breaks?" *Dollars and Sense*, July/Aug. 1994.

49. See Gary Knox, "Slums and Poverty," chap. 9 of John E. Ullmann, ed., *Social Costs in Modern Society* (Westport, Conn.: Quorum Books, 1983). In that same year an assessment of and program for housing was put forth by housing specialist Chester Hartman, *America's Housing Crisis: What Is to Be Done?* (London: Methuen, 1983). (There is no conflict between the 50 million individuals cited here and the 30 million families noted immediately before: A family is seen as having more than three members.)

50. "Section 8" refers to a program begun in the Nixon administration that has often served "as a linchpin for private developers or community organizations building low-income housing, because it guarantees a certain number of tenants at a predetermined rent." The tenants are subsidized for the amount of rent that is beyond 30 percent of their income. This has meant good incomes for developers, attorneys, and others not poor. In addition to making decent housing affordable for the tenant beneficiaries, it has provided a mix of population in any given development. One of the defects of public housing in the past was that many projects were *only* for the very poor, those not having jobs. And all hell broke loose, much of the time.

51. The quotations in this and the preceding paragraph are from Folbre, *The New Field Guide*, p. 6.12.

52. "G.O.P. Fights More Housing Aided by U.S.," *NYT*, March 3, 1996. The article points out that only "20–30 percent of those who qualify for Federal rental assistance actually receive it," and that the welfare reforms then probable (since enacted) "would take entitlement status away from Medicaid and welfare programs, too."

53. Nicholas Lemann, "The Public Housing That Succeeds," *NYT*, Op-Ed, May 5, 1996. Lemann, a serious student of ghetto life, is currently the national correspondent for the *Atlantic Monthly*.

Chapter Eight

1. Carson's *Silent Spring* (Greenwich, Conn.: Fawcett Publications, 1962) is still in print and still worth reading. The quote from her is from an essay she wrote about the same time, "Of Men and the Stream of Time," *Scripps College Bulletin*, July 1962, quoted in H. Patricia Hynes, *The Recurring Silent Spring* (New York: Pergamon Press, 1989), p. 7. Hynes's book is a comprehensive discussion of Carson's life and work and the environmental crisis. It is also a critical analysis of the difficulties faced by women in the world of science.

2. E. F. Schumacher, *Small Is Beautiful* (London: Abacus, 1974), p. 12 (still in print). By "small," Schumacher—an economist and engineer—meant "an appropriate technology," satisfying a combination of economic, social, human, and ecological standards.

3. De Castro's *Geography of Hunger* soon went out of print; it was republished as *The Geopolitics of Hunger*. Brazilian himself, the author made intensive studies in the poor countries, notably India. Affirming the same position, as well as finding the main causes for environmental deterioration in the rich countries, was a full-page ad in the *NYT*, Apr. 4, 1994, responding to the notion that "many people think it [population growth] is the biggest problem humanity now faces." Among a dozen or so points, the ad showed (1) that 95 percent of future population growth is expected to occur among the poorest 20 percent of the world's people; (2) that the most affluent

20 percent consume 75 percent of the world's energy and 85 percent of its forest products and account for 75 percent of all solid and toxic waste; (3) that Americans alone consume 250 times more nonrenewable energy per capita than those in the poor countries. The ad was sponsored by the Pew Global Stewardship Initiative— "designed to restore the United States to a position of leadership on problems related to rapid population growth and the unsustainable consumption of resources." A pleasant surprise, considering that the Pew Charitable Trusts derived their wealth from a major oil company.

4. In recent decades the agricultural technology of "the green revolution" has been much touted as resolving the economic problem of the poor areas. If anything, in bringing in large-scale capital, turning agriculture to exports, and pushing people off the land, it has ruined more than helped. See the essays in Bernhard Glaeser, ed., *The Green Revolution Revisited: Critiques and Alternatives* (London: Allen and Unwin, 1987). "Green," of course, is the color of ecological political economy, virtually all of whose representatives oppose "the green revolution" in agriculture as being the opposite of what is needed.

5. Murray Bookchin, "Toward an Ecological Solution," *Ramparts*, May 1970. His overall viewpoint is expressed in the *Green Reader: Essays Toward a Sustainable Society*, ed. Andrew Dobson (San Francisco: Mercury House), pp. 59–63. The book's excerpts from more than sixty essays provide a comprehensive overview of a large number of those (including Rachel Carson and E. F. Schumacher) who have contributed to the emergence of an "ecological consciousness."

6. A recent book emphasized problems previously unnoticed by scientists: Theo Colburn, J. P. Myers, and Dianne Dumanoski, *Our Stolen Future: Are We Threatening Our Fertility, Intelligence, and Survival?* (New York: Dutton, 1996). Colburn and Myers are biologists. In his foreword to the book, Vice President Al Gore viewed the book as a sequel to Carson's *Silent Spring*. The coauthors argued that certain "endocrine disrupters" (man-made chemicals), were severely upsetting the reproductive health of wildlife and humans over the globe. The chemicals behave like hormones (turning on and off chemical processes in the cells)—most important, estrogen, testosterone, and progesterone.

7. What follows is taken (most of it in direct quotation) from Matthew L. Wald, "Sealing of Nuclear Waste in Canisters Marks End of an Atomic Age Dream," *NYT*, July 9, 1996. The tone of Wald's report and its final paragraphs lead one to cross fingers and hope for the best. And to avoid Yucca Mountain.

8. As will be seen in Chapter 9, this is the same kind of win-win process used in Pentagon contracting: When a company (say, Westinghouse) makes mistakes on a contract, it then re-does and re-charges (on a cost-plus basis) for the re-doing.

9. The first quotation is from the UN weather agency, the second from the World Meteorological Organization, both reported in *IHT*, Oct. 5–6, 1996. On Aug. 4, 1996, the *NYT* reported that "NASA's Nimbus-7 satellite found that the annual average amount of UV-B, the portion of the ultraviolet spectrum that causes the most damage, had increased at a rate of 9.9 percent a decade at the southernmost parts of Argentina and Chile . . . , 4 percent for [North America], and 6.8 percent for Britain, Germany, Russia and Scandinavia. . . . Scientists consider the risks of further increases in ultraviolet radiation to be serious. Long-term exposure to UV-B from the sun is associated with two kinds of cancer—basal cell and squamous cell carcinomas—and is responsi-

ble for other harmful effects in humans, to the skin, the eyes and the immune system. It also harms some crops and interferes with marine life." (Whatever is being added to at an annual rate of 8 percent is doubled in twenty years.)

10. Kenneth Neill Cameron, *Atmospheric Destruction and Human Survival*, CES/CNS Pamphlet 3, p. 11 (available through P.O. Box 8467, Santa Cruz, CA 95061). In the United States, according to the EPA, over 28 percent of CFCs are released into the air from the 60 million automobile air conditioners—constructed so as "to be guaranteed to leak, according to one expert" (ibid.).

11. The reports were in the *IHT*, Feb. 8, 1996, and Oct. 5–6, 1996, respectively.

12. The scientists quoted are Richard A. Houghton and George M. Woodwell of the Woods Hole Research Center, as noted in the excellent monograph by Cameron, *Atmospheric Destruction and Human Survival*, p. 1. Cameron also summarized the earlier work of James E. Hansen (of NASA's Goddard Institute for Space Studies), who reported in 1988 that "the six hottest years on record were between 1980 and 1988." "The Reagan Administration, concerned that 'their own' scientist was now supporting the greenhouse theory, made unsuccessful efforts to alter these findings—which caused a minor front page scandal" in, among other elements of the media, the *New York Times*. Subsequently, 1990 and 1991 were added to the "hottest" list.

13. *Global Accord: Environmental Challenges and International Responses*, ed. Nazli Choucri (Cambridge: MIT Press, 1993), p. 295, in chap. 8, by Garry D. Brewer.

14. "Hurricane Angst Haunts Insurers," *San Francisco Examiner*, Sept. 15, 1996.

15. The reader is referred once more to the essays by Daly, "From Adjustment to Sustainable Development," and by Daly and Goodland, "An Ecological-Economic Assessment of Deregulation of International Commerce Under GATT," discussed in Chapters 1 and 3.

16. Richard Ives, in his book *Of Tigers and Men: Entering the Age of Extinction* (New York: Doubleday, 1996).

17. Much of the analysis and data concerning both general and destructive wastes are borrowed from my earlier *The Waste of Nations: Dysfunction in the World Economy* (Boulder, Colo.: Westview Press, 1989). A very useful analysis with specific data on both broad and narrow questions of efficiency and waste is found in S. Bowles, D. M. Gordon, and T. E. Weisskopf, "The Waste Economy," chapter 9 of *The Capitalist System*, ed. Richard C. Edwards, Michael Reich, and Thomas E. Weisskopf (Englewood Cliffs, N.J.: Prentice-Hall, 1986). (I took the figures on waste and GNP used later from that chapter.) The book is an excellent introduction to the political economy of contemporary capitalism.

18. See the definitive economic history of the 1920s, Soule, *Prosperity Decade*, chaps. 13–14.

19. Bowles, Gordon, and Weisskopf, "The Waste Economy."

20. This point may be seen as standing at the center of his penetrating essay, "Theses on Advertising," in Paul A. Baran, *The Longer View: Essays Toward a Critique of Political Economy*, ed. John O'Neill (New York: Monthly Review Press, 1969).

21. For example, the cost of building a mile of urban highway in 1991 was $100 million (a mile!); the cost for a mile of light-rail mass transit was $15 million. And keep in mind the great difference in air quality between the two.

22. The basic research on the shameful dismantling of the U.S. public transportation system by the triad of auto, tire, and oil companies was done by Bradford Snell.

He presented his findings before the U.S. Senate Subcommittee on Antitrust and Monopoly, 93rd Congress, 2nd Session. Published by the U.S. Government Printing Office as Bradford Snell, *American Ground Transport: A Proposal for Restructuring the Automobile, Truck, Bus, and Rail Industries*, U.S. Senate Document, 1972. It's a stunner, and perhaps still available from the USGPO.

Chapter Nine

1. For a thoroughgoing study of such waste (among other matters), see Walter Adams and James W. Brock, *The Bigness Complex: Industry, Labor, and Government in the American Economy* (New York: Pantheon, 1986). The authors are perhaps unique in being supporters of market competition as the ruling force in the economy while also being astute critics of the manifold ways in which business—especially big business—interferes with the free market, in their minds, more so than government, whose own interferences are frequently at the behest of business.

2. Those specific data were noted in *NYT*, July 3 and July 11, 1996. With the end of the cold war, rather than seek means of converting military to peacetime production, both the largest weapons contractors and the government have turned their energies and governmental expenditures toward maintaining the status quo ante. Although the maintenance of jobs has been invoked, in fact, as milex jobs decline in number in this country, they are outsourced and increase (for the same companies) in others, those who are the arms customers. There have been several recent studies of these and connected developments, the most accessible of which are Charles M. Sennott, "Armed for Profit: The Selling of U.S. Weapons," *Boston Globe*, Feb. 11, 1996 (12 pages), and William D. Hartung, "Warfare for Weapons Dealers: The Hidden Costs of the Arms Trade," 1996 ed., Arms Trade Resource Center of the World Policy Institute (67 pages). Both reports, evidently developed independently of each other, contain data and quotations from previous cold war stalwarts that are dismaying, to say the least. For example, from the *Boston Globe*: (1) "It has become . . . an absurd spiral in which we export arms only to develop more sophisticated ones to counter those spread out all over the world [by ourselves]" (Lawrence Korb, assistant secretary of defense under Reagan); (2) "The American military now defines its role as being able to protect US interests in two simultaneous regional conflicts. It seems absurd to be spending $250 billion a year to accomplish that goal while selling billions of dollars in exports to areas where those conflicts are likely to break out. We end up fueling the conflicts we seek to contain" (Randall Forsberg, director, Institute for Defense and Disarmament Studies).

3. Melman's first book in this area was *Our Depleted Society* (New York: Holt, Rinehart and Winston, 1965). His later books include *Pentagon Capitalism* (New York: McGraw-Hill, 1970), *The Permanent War Economy* (New York: Simon and Schuster, 1974), and, among more recent works, *The Demilitarized Society: Disarmament and Conversion* (Nottingham: Spokesman, 1988). Among his many articles, one of his most pertinent, where he compares the cost of milex to the United States and to the Soviet Union, is "The U.S.–Russian Conversion Crisis," *In These Times*, July 11, 1995. That biweekly journal frequently contains essays that analyze and offer alternatives to milex.

4. From *Statistical Abstract of the United States, 1994*, unless otherwise indicated.

5. Both the data and the reasoning of this and subsequent paragraphs may be found in the extraordinary book of Joel Andreas, *Addicted to War: Why the U.S. Can't Kick Militarism—An Illustrated Exposé* (New Society Publishers [4527 Springfield Avenue, Philadelphia, PA 19143], 1993). It is "extraordinary" not only in that it *is* illustrated (in cartoon style), but that it is both very funny and very shocking in what it shows—all of which is meticulously documented. A fine collection of essays bearing on the various dimensions of the military-industrial complex and its behavior is Robert Higgs, ed., *Arms, Politics and the Economy* (New York: Holmes and Meier, 1980). In the preface to the latter book you may find the figures concerning the $750 toilet seat and the like.

6. *NYT*, June 28, 1996.

7. As documents are released through the Freedom of Information Act, the list of such schools lengthens, and the crimes committed by their "students" slowly come to light. According to a *New York Times* editorial about one such school, the School of the Americas, "among its roughly 60,000 graduates, the school produced several of Latin America's most notorious strongmen of the 1970s and 1980s, including Panama's drug-dealing dictator, Manuel Noriega, and Roberto D'Aubuisson, who organized many of El Salvador's death squads" ("Shut the School Down," *NYT*, Oct. 1, 1996). The school is still operating—and adding to the budget deficit.

8. *NYT*, July 11, 1995.

9. See James Cypher, "The War Dividend," *Dollars and Sense*, May 1991. Although Cypher was prompted by the Gulf war to write that essay, it contains much that is generally useful concerning milex—as well it might, for Cypher is a prolific writer and authority on what has come to be called "military Keynesianism."

10. *NYT*, July 14, 1996.

11. *NYT*, July 10, 1995.

12. *Nation*, June 24 and July 8, 1996.

13. *NYT*, Feb. 7, 1995.

14. *Nation*, June 26, 1996 (emphasis in original).

15. The best-known of the hot wars in the cold war era are those in Korea and in Vietnam, of course. But what is known about those two wars—their origins and their costs, for example—is very slight. It need not be, for there is a substantial literature in existence, and it grows rapidly now that the cold war and its secrecy is fading. On Korea, for example, see the definitive work of Bruce Cumings, *The Origins of the Korean War* (Princeton: Princeton University Press, 1981), a more accessible version of which is Jon Halliday and Bruce Cumings, *Korea: The Unknown War* (New York: Pantheon, 1988)—a study that renders very problematic the official version of how and why the war began and continued. Moreover, although it is generally known that about 54,000 U.S. troops died in that war, Halliday and Cumings pointed out that more than 3 million Korean and at least 1 million Chinese were also killed (pp. 200–201). Similarly, the official version of the origins and nature—even the dating—of the war in Vietnam (and Laos and Cambodia) is murky at best when placed against the work of the diplomatic historian Marilyn Young, *The Vietnam Wars, 1945–1990* (New York: HarperCollins, 1991)—where, once again, the tragedy of almost 60,000 U.S. troop deaths (and some multiple of that in physical and psychological wounds: "The Federal Government has estimated that 150,000 to 250,000 veterans are home-

less on any given night" [*NYT*, Nov. 11, 1991]) is noted, but few indeed know of the estimated 3 million Vietnamese who lost their lives. And then there is Cambodia. Although it is widely understood that over a million lost their lives there, few indeed understand that the tragedy had its roots in the White House, its opposition to the neutralism of Cambodia's leader, Prince Sihanouk, and consequent support of the Khmer Rouge. All that was shown clearly in William Shawcross, *Sideshow: Kissinger, Nixon and the Destruction of Cambodia* (New York: Pocket Books, 1979).

16. For the most inclusive of such studies see Ann Markusen and Joel Yidken, *Dismantling the Cold War Economy* (New York: Basic Books, 1992). The excellent book by two economists is detailed (but readable) on both the growth and the potentials for conversion of the military-industrial complex. (It is available in paperback.)

17. *NYT*, May 12, 1990.

18. See the works of Melman and of Markusen and Yidken cited earlier.

19. Sennott, "Armed for Profit," p. B12. The companies are General Dynamics, Loral Corp., McDonnell Douglas, Raytheon, Lockheed Martin, and Northrop Grumman. General Dynamics does only military work and owns Electric Boat. The latter has for some time been building a $2.4 billion submarine (the "Seawolf")—an embodiment of one of the follies of milex: It will soon—probably before it is completed—be outdated by "the more versatile New Attack Submarine" (ibid.).

20. *NYT*, Sept. 14, 1995.

21. *San Francisco Chronicle*, July 1, 1996.

22. *U.S. News and World Report*, May 20, 1996.

23. An excellent and succinct summary of crimex is found in Patricia Horn, "Caging America—the U.S. Imprisonment Binge," *Dollars and Sense*, Sept. 1991. Probably the most useful ongoing source of scholarly information on crime and crimex is the National Council on Crime and Delinquency (NCCD). It has a monthly journal—*Focus*—and also publishes occasional monographs. I have used the Dec. 1990 issue, "America's Growing Correctional-Industrial Complex," by James Austin. For my overall framework on this crimex analysis, I have depended upon the excellent monograph by Austin and John Irwin, *Who Goes to Prison?* As the NCCD is not well known, I provide the address of its national headquarters: 685 Market Street, Room 620, San Francisco, CA 94105, for those who wish to obtain its literature.

24. *NYT*, Feb. 14, 1996.

25. *San Francisco Chronicle*, July 1, 1996.

26. July 16, 1995.

27. *Dollars and Sense*, Sept. 1991.

28. *NYT*, Op-Ed, June 26, 1995.

Chapter Ten

1. The "freer hand" for business was the National Industrial Recovery Act (1933). The heart of the act was to allow "self-government in business," inspired by the work of Gerard Swope, head of General Electric in the 1920s. "Self-government" meant government by the 835 "industrial codes," almost all written by their respective trade associations, and dominated by the largest companies. In the name of establishing "fair competition," the code authorities set prices (to which all companies had to adhere) below which no member could sell legally, and also set output quotas

for each company and geographic region: in effect, suspension of the antitrust laws. It is noteworthy that in 1934 an economic delegation from Nazi Germany came to study the workings of the program. The NIRA was declared unconstitutional in 1935; it was that more than any other decision that led FDR to try to force several justices off the Supreme Court—calling them "nine old men." The NIRA also gave labor the right to organize and bargain collectively but provided no means of enforcement to make those rights meaningful. That was done through the National Labor Relations Act (Wagner Act) of 1935. See Mitchell, *Depression Decade*, chap. 7.

2. I discussed all these developments (and those of the 1960s) in some detail, in my recent book *Blues for America: A Critique, A Lament, and Some Memories, 1919–1997* (New York: Monthly Review Press, 1997), chaps. 2 and 4.

3. For present purposes, the meaning of this is that the member nations of the EU will harmonize their monetary and fiscal policies by pursuing anti-inflationary policies, deficit reduction, budget balancing and, to accomplish that, the reduction of social spending. The pressures within these countries for that process are widely understood to be from their central banks and the financial sector (and allied politicians), with the resistance coming from workers and their unions and political parties. In 1996 and 1997 workers' political efforts have reemerged, after the long snooze to be noted in the text. Canada is not part of the EU, of course, but of NAFTA, so it is going through the same processes. In the article headlined "Angry Thousands in Ontario Protest Slashes in Canada's 'Caring Society,'" it is noted that "Mike Harris . . . has become a darling of Wall Street by slashing almost $1 billion from Ontario's budget, dropping more than 100,000 people from welfare rolls and proposing other spending cuts expected to reach nearly $6 billion, [which] will mean closing hospitals, raising university tuition and laying off civil servants, among other measures" (*NYT*, Oct. 28, 1996). Harris was the new leader of Ontario. Because all of Canada, with only 22 million inhabitants, is smaller than California, $6 billion in spending cuts is proportionately greater for one province (like our states) than anything happening in, say, New York or California.

4. The main exception to that generalization has to do with the growth of "Green parties" and their supporters. They are mostly *not* from the working class, and often there has been political competition between "red" and "green." More recently that has been seen as mutually self-defeating, and there is a noticeable tendency toward coalition and cooperation—a tendency that has considerable distance to cover before it will be able to reverse current negative tendencies.

5. Thus, and by way of example, at present the average rate of unemployment in the EU—as noted earlier—is over 11 percent (and the 1996 rate for Sweden, most thoroughgoing of the welfare states, is 14 percent). If present structures of production and adherence to world economic policies are maintained, it is very hard to see how EU unemployment rates can be reduced or social welfare policies be maintained. As will soon be argued, the broad base, size, and resource strengths of our economy give us much more leeway for change—in the direction the Europeans are now being forced to abandon.

6. "Boom in Corporate Earnings Is Fading," *NYT*, Nov. 2, 1996.

7. "Restructuring" has of course been going on for the past two decades or so; negative restructuring—"outsourcing" and the like, as detailed in Kolko's *Restructuring the World Economy*, discussed in Chapter 3.

8. The restructuring of economic sectors within and outside the United States was very much nourished by the new technologies in electronics, synthetics, and trans-

portation (jet planes and container ships)—all, it should be noted, outcomes of the years surrounding World War II.

9. That resource/market desperation was among the most important of the pressures toward the imperialism of the late nineteenth century. The United States, from its colonial days on, was of course an imperializing force in North America; our superabundant resource base was acquired so easily and "naturally" as to blur the fact that our "Westward expansion" was at the expense of others. One interesting consequence of this difference between us and Europeans is that the initially colonized United States has throughout its history been an anticolonial but not an anti-imperialist power. See William Appleman Williams, *The Roots of the Modern American Empire* (New York: Random House, 1969) and *The Contours of American History* (Chicago: Quadrangle, 1966), for a trenchant analysis of that particular point and a broader analysis of our history.

10. For example, the Depression of the 1930s, which caused immense suffering here, brought deeper and broader damage and pains elsewhere. Thus, although Germany and the United States both suffered a 50 percent decline in industrial production, the descent was from a higher level of per capita income here and did not plunge so deeply; the world wars left many millions dead in Europe (10 million from World War I, 60 million from World War II), compared with hundreds of thousands in each war for us. The major exception to this generalization was the devastation to the South during and after the Civil War; but the South is also the U.S. region that—until, perhaps, very recently—has been relatively conscious of the darker side of our history. For an illuminating treatment of the differences between the South and the rest of the United States, see C. Vann Woodward, *The Burden of Southern History* (New York: Random House/Vintage, 1961).

11. Longfellow, and before him Dryden, and before them Boswell, who commented on the oft-repeated saying in *The Life of Samuel Johnson*. Publilius Syrus (1st c. B.C.E.) had written, "Whom Fortune wishes to destroy she first makes mad," his version of an ancient Greek aphorism. They had something there.

12. Much more than a good start may be had by consulting R. H. Tawney, *Equality* (New York: Capricorn, 1961; originally published 1929). Though the book was written long ago, Tawney's wisdom and eloquence remain mind opening and relevant.

13. The first mainstream and path-breaking study of separation of ownership from management and control was by A. A. Berle and Gardner Means, *The Modern Corporation and Private Property* (New York: Macmillan, 1932). Berle returned to the same theme a generation later with *Power Without Property* (New York: Harcourt Brace Jovanovich, 1959), wherein, as is not uncommon in the mainstream, an explosive issue is brought up, examined, and put down again as though it were not explosive at all. A decade before Berle and Means, however, the same developments had been raised for examination, but outside the mainstream: Thorstein Veblen, *Absentee Ownership and Business Enterprise in Recent Times* (New York: B. W. Huebsch, 1923). In that book Veblen focused on the meaning of "physics and chemistry" for the economic process and emphasized (among other criticisms) the extraordinary wastefulness of the economy—in both its production and marketing.

14. Those wishing to pursue the matter of wealth in general would be both enlightened and amused by Lewis Lapham, *Money and Class in America* (New York: Weidenfeld and Nichols, 1987); or a broader analysis focused on recent years,

Phillips, *The Politics of Rich and Poor*. Both provide abundant references to other useful works. Lapham, himself from a wealthy San Francisco family, has been editor of *Harper's* monthly.

15. As most will know, a progressive income tax has the amount paid rising not only absolutely but relatively as income rises. Thus one with an income of $50,000 with a rate of 10 percent would pay $5,000 in taxes; one with an income of $100,000 would have a higher rate on that higher income—say 15 percent—and thus instead of paying $10,000, would pay $15,000. A "flat" or proportionate rate would be 10 percent irrespective of incomes. A sales (or Social Security) tax is retrogressive in that the rate is unchanged by income level: As was pointed out regarding Social Security, one with an income of $3 million pays the same amount as one with $50,000. Our federal income tax structure was quite progressive in the 1950s and 1960s; since then it has moved toward flatness (varying between 28 and 32 percent). A "steeply" progressive income tax—which will be proposed here—would have relatively high rates at the top income (say $200,000), rising steeply for amounts in excess of that (a "surtax").

16. This is the phenomenon of "tax expenditures" discussed in Chapter 2: The tax exemptions of those at the top (individuals or companies), given the level of governmental spending, quite simply require an increase of the taxes of everyone else—as income taxes, Social Security taxes, and so forth.

17. Once again, for those years and programs, see the excellent Mitchell, *Depression Decade*, chaps. 9 and 10 for details on these matters.

18. For a brief and eloquent appeal for this kind of program—one emphasizing education and ending the unnecessary tragedies of ghetto existence—see Wilson, "When Work Disappears."

19. That figure refers only to the presidential and congressional races. Some of that money was *not* from the wealthy and powerful, of course; but it is interesting to note that when the GOP accused the AFL-CIO of trying to buy the election, the expenditure was noted as under $40 million.

20. There is much good work going on, and mounting numbers of books providing useful analyses and programs. A good source of literature and ideas is the Open Magazine Pamphlet Series, cited in notes to Chapter 7. A broad program is put forth in that series by Juliet Schor, *A Sustainable Economy*, Pamphlet #31, Apr. 1995. In the last chapter of my *Blues for America*, there are various reading suggestions. There is also a remarkable new book, Wade Hudson, *Economic Security for All: How to End Poverty in the United States* (available through the Economic Security Project, 625 Leavenworth Street, San Francisco, CA 94107, Fax [415] 776-0251).

21. His massive biography of Abraham Lincoln is still considered both instructive and moving; and he is among those—along with Walt Whitman, Emily Dickinson, Langston Hughes, and Robert Frost—who have been seen as the quintessentially "American" poets. The quoted words are from his book-length poem, *The People, Yes*.

About the Book and Author

For the past twenty-five years, the United States has undergone a retrogression in its socioeconomic policies—facilitated and supported by most economists—thanks to the steady drumbeat of arguments by entrepreneurs and politicians who celebrate the free market for anything and everything and who advocate, among other follies, balanced budgets and reduced social expenditures. The consequences of these developments have already harmed millions of Americans; but in the present climate of opinion and politics, the policy direction is unlikely to be reversed.

Against the Conventional Wisdom is a rallying cry against this stampede. It seeks to provide an analytical counterattack, showing that what has become "common sense" is not good sense economically or socially; is neither necessary nor desirable; and will deepen existing troubles, not resolve them. We cannot afford to continue to relive the 1920s—when the same arguments (and lack of disagreement) prevailed, when budgets were balanced, when finance capitalism and speculation took center stage. At that time a large proportion of the workforce found itself pushed aside by the 1920s version of downsizing and outsourcing, and the rich became much richer.

In the opening chapters of the book, Douglas Dowd explores the reasoning and the realities of the free market ideology, in its original and present forms. Succeeding chapters treat in detail the human, social, and natural consequences of "rule by the market" over time and the dangers of allowing the market to rule today and tomorrow. The book concludes with suggested alternatives to current tendencies—alternatives that are simultaneously desirable, necessary, and realistic.

Douglas Dowd is a distinguished economist who has taught at Cornell, campuses of the University of California, and at the Bologna Center, Johns Hopkins University, Italy.

Index